RE_CYCLICAL URBANISM

VISIONS, PARADIGMS AND PROJECTS FOR THE CIRCULAR METAMORPHOSIS

Maurizio Carta
Barbara Lino
Daniele Ronsivalle

Editors

INDEX

1 RE-CYCLICAL URBANISM — 4

Re-cyclical urbanism — 6
A planning agenda for circular metamorphosis
Maurizio Carta

Cultural Commons — 32
Participatory governance of cultural heritage
Angela Alessandra Badami

**Metropolitan perspectives
and new lifecycles for the outskirts** — 44
Barbara Lino

Breaking the siege — 54
From the paleo- to the neo-anthropocene
Daniele Ronsivalle

The Cityforming© protocol — 60
Incremental and adaptive strategies
Maurizio Carta

2 SMART CIRCULAR PLANNING — 68

Hyper-metropolitan Palermo — 70
Unconventional strategies and mapping for circular metropolitan scenarios
Maurizio Carta

Innovation, circularity and local development — 92
Maurizio Carta

A smart land to reactivate territorial wealth — 104
Marilena Orlando

No externalities for closed-cycle cities — 114
Strategic environmental assessment and planning
Daniele Ronsivalle

3 PALERMO LIVING LAB — 122

The future of cities: between mending, grafting, and recycling — 124
Renato Bocchi

Circular metabolism — 128
Palermo south coast
Maurizio Carta

**The new metropolitan city and the southern suburbs.
Xl reverse Palermo** — 140
Barbara Lino

The south coast of Palermo   154
Planning the resilient city
Daniele Ronsivalle

Form which is transformed   158
Vincenzo Melluso

4 NOT CONVENTIONAL MAPS   166

From FabLab to FabCity: 168
The Palermo map of talents
Maurizio Carta

Adaptive cities, communities and technology   176
Maurizio Carta, Daniele Ronsivalle, Claudio Schifani, Carla Tumminello,
Carmelo Galati Tardanico, Simone Lucido, Maurizio Giambalvo

Palermo Living Lab on the road   188
Annalisa Contato

Re-postcards   214

5 RE-FORMING ROME   230

Roma 20-25. New life cycles for the metropolis   232
Maurizio Carta

Impact Regenerative Design: Paradigms, Strategies and Mapping   236
Enabling technologies for the city-laboratory in the metropolitan
city of Reggio Calabria
Consuelo Nava

The Research "Macro"   248

Rome Agri-Fab City   258
A productive landscape for a self-sufficient metropolis
Manuel Gausa Navarro, Silvia Brandi, Marco Ingrassia

Re-forming Rome   266
The Agri/Fab Metropolis
Maurizio Carta

Open source&shared urban design platform   272
Barbara Lino

Cityforming Rome: ideas and projects   276
Angelica Agnello and Mariateresa Caeti, Madalina Culcasi,
Francesca Montagna, Milena Lauretta

Re-forming Rome exhibition: a pedagogical machine   296
Annalisa Contato and Jessica Smeralda Oliva

RE-CYCLICAL URBANISM

1.1	**RE-CYCLICAL URBANISM** A PLANNING AGENDA FOR CIRCULAR METAMORPHOSIS Maurizio Carta	
1.2	**CULTURAL COMMONS** PARTICIPATORY GOVERNANCE OF CULTURAL HERITAGE Angela Alessandra Badami	
1.3	**METROPOLITAN PERSPECTIVES AND NEW LIFECYCLES FOR THE OUTSKIRTS** Barbara Lino	
1.4	**BREAKING THE SIEGE** FROM THE PALEO- TO THE NEO-ANTHROPOCENE Daniele Ronsivalle	
1.5	**THE CITYFORMING© PROTOCOL** INCREMENTAL AND ADAPTIVE STRATEGIES Maurizio Carta	

RE-CYCLICAL URBANISM

A PLANNING AGENDA FOR CIRCULAR METAMORPHOSIS

MAURIZIO CARTA

"There is one thing stronger than all the armies in the world, and that is an idea whose time has come"
Victor Hugo

Circular metamorphosis

When Eugene Stoermer introduced the term "Anthropocene" to denote the consequences to the planet of the industrial revolution due to humankind's acceleration of territorial, structural and climate changes[1], he could not have imagined that, over the last twenty years, a pervasive "anthropo-development" would have produced such anabolic effects as to make the human footprint on the planet so enormous. This footprint has been mistaken for that of a deity — a seductive demon — and has been the object of a permeating idolatry of endless growth. The aporias of this worship have given us comfort, leading to a steady erosion of territorial resources — land being the most evident and alarming synecdoche. Together with the land, the identity structures of the cultural palimpsests and the vegetation patterns of cities have been depleted; vital metabolisms have been anesthetized, water and wastecycles disrupted and mobility cycles have become inflexible, making them useless. The ability of urban settlements to maintain the necessary relations with their rural components has worn away. The productive and generative capacity of local factories has been suppressed by anesthetizing endogenous development factors. The regenerative value of maintainingbuildings and of caring for places has been forgotten and natural circular territorial processes have been cut off or rerouted.

Following the planet's numerous shudders that have gone unheard, after having many times exceeded the limits of development, often with dramatic consequences, the economic crisis of the last decade — whose virulence has infected the productive, social, cultural, and even political structures — has exposed the fallacy even to the firmest believers in the magnificent and progressive destiny. It has produced, on one hand, evangelists of the happy degrowth and vegans of development, "driving urban planners to disengagement or to a paralyzing sense of guilt" (Sijmons, 2014a). On the other hand, it has spawned the militant urban planners of an effective sustainable development. Visionary and pragmatic at the same time, they are convinced that we need to accept the challenge of living in a "good Anthropocene"[2], designing the transition and reactivating the traditional alliance between human and natural components as co-acting forces[3], guided by the ethics of a project to integrate people and nature, the city and the environment, as collective responsibility towards *Global Change* beginning with cities[4]. The neo-Anthropocene — for all purposes an "urban Anthropocene" (Swilling, Hajer, 2016) — we wish to enter, as a challenge in our commitment as researchers, teachers, and designers, requires a responsible and militant approach. It also requires the courage to face a metamorphosis that will not only reduce the ecological footprint of human activities on the planet, but also make use of collective intelligence — the noosphere — which arises from new ideas and sensitivity towards the environment, the landscape and cultural heritage, disseminating them globally in a renewed integral ecology that is converted into planning protocols, urban devices, and new lifecycles. We need to play a leading role in a structural change in which cities — in their metropolitan, reticular and rur-urban forms — are called upon to reactivate their territorial wealth, guided by urban planning that is able to guarantee new ways of converging cultural, economic, environmental and social sustainability. Not just by adopting renewed visions of the future or using new paradigms, but above all, by means of effective decisions, quality projects, and efficient processes. More advanced urban planning, which is more sensitive to identities and more geared towards innovation, is prompted to take on the responsibility of renewing the conditions of its existence, role, and involvement. As well as to reconsider its own epistemological core in relation to new sources and forms of knowledge and to consequently review its toolbox, replacing some worn-out regulatory instruments with more effective planning tools capable of acting jointly with the i creasing number of non-institutional urban planning practices. The European Commission has clearly stated that more intelligent, sustainable and competitive development requires a paradigm shift in which the territory is construed as a primary resource, considered the holder of "development cells", which are too often underused or mystified with regard to their real potential for use (EC, Directorate-General for Research and Innovation, 2012). Cities designed and built on land rent — on which Italy set a benchmark — need to be replaced with cities of social and cultural profitability, value creation and the production of jobs. Cities that recycle already-used land to avoid energy waste, smarter cities — not just technologically, but also wiser and more sentient ones, capable of activating collective intelligence —, and cities that are more dialogic and shared, and therefore more responsible. The European strategy contained in Horizon 2020 clearly states the need to use the potential of "urban mines" (abandoned areas, infrastructure and buildings), adapting new urban policies to the lifecycle approach (*Life Cycle Assessment*): from the procurement of raw materials (vacant land and abandoned buildings) to the end of the cycle (new uses and functions), using as little energy and resources as possible and, instead, reactivating latent energy.

Cities will have to act within a new evolutionary model, the result of innovation produced by the third industrial revolution and by start-ups, the actions of *makers*, and energy generated by creativity and by the metamorphosis of the *circular economy*. An urban model that is more responsible and capable of reshaping the objectives of tangible and intangible asset production, of revising energy and mobility protocols, and above all, of rethinking the settlement model: a new holistic way of thinking that elicits reuse, recycling and creative evolution within next-generation capitalism — "Capitalism 4.0", about which Kaletsky (2010) writes — which generates an economy — the *Next Economy* proposed and elaborated by Brugmans, van Dinteren and Hater (2016) — created from the integration of renewable energies and circular economy, able to produce new value from the re-cyclical processes of the new urban metabolism. The economic model supporting cities in the circular society must be able to generate local value, rather than an extractive economy that creates dependence on the exogenous strategies of large companies. We need to return to an urban economy that is sustainable in terms of facilitating territorial and human capital, dynamic and propulsive for the labor market, and which offers valid alternatives to the growth of inequality. In short, an urban economy guided by a social agenda. We thus need a new urban dimension that combines business with citizenship and facilitates interaction between education and work, and between housing and public space.

The task of administrators, urban planners, architects, citizens, and enterprises is to work on urban settlements characterized by cycle flows — some still vital, others produced by surplus and by the overproduction of changing urban complexes. It is also to work on the rhythms of the discontinued urban fabric and transforming infrastructure networks, which need to be addressed through their modification, removal or reinvention, thanks to which the components are recreated, without destroying them, by changing their functions in pursuit of a generative view and increasing their creative resilience. The beat of recycling and change will be the musical score that guides cities more and more constantly fluctuating between conservation and tranformation, identity and innovation (Mehrotra, Vera, Mayoral, 2016) in an accelerated metabolism of lifecycles. Recycling is not only one of the main keywords of the action of urban planning, architecture and design (Ciorra, Marini, 2011; Marini, Rosselli, 2014), but is also one of the most powerful guiding thoughts in the transformation from a wasteful linear economy to a regenerative circular one for cities and territories that wish to pursue sustainability, qual ity and creat ivit y (Car ta, Ronsivalle, 2015). In a circular economy, there are two types of material flows: organic ones, capable of being replenished in the biosphere, and technical ones, destined to increase in value in a system in which all activities, starting from mining and manufacturing, are organized so that the waste of one phase becomes a resource for the following phase. According to the principles of the circular economy, nothing is waste and everything that is discarded from one production process is the raw material for another production process. Moreover, the very design of a product is based on the possibility of dismantling its parts and reusing them in subsequent production cycles, based on supply chain cooperation and new production networks: a more creative "planned recycling" instead of consumerist planned obsolescence[5]. A more open and collaborative circular society based on sustainability and sharing is the catalyst that allows the economy to transfer its effects to the territory and lifecycles of the communities, activating and extending the dividend (Bonomi, Masiero, Della Puppa, 2016). A circular society demands new political responsibility — and responsibility for urban planning — so that cities may once again be welcoming to people, attractive of ideas, generative for businesses, and supportive to the community archipelagos. It requires the implementation of concrete actions to guarantee a new balance between rural, urban and developable, between landscaping weft and infrastructural warp, not just placing limits on the indiscriminate use of land, but above all, stimulating, encouraging and rewarding the reuse of already urbanized areas and the densification of functions. Planning cities in the era of the neo-Anthropocene and of the circular metabolism means rejecting the consolation of a molecular approach and accepting the challenge of an organic ecosystem approach, allowing ourselves to be guided by a new long-sighted vision to look towards the innovation horizon, but also to look back and retrieve wisdom, rituals and structurally self-sufficient circular practices not yet seduced by the demon of anthropic development. We also need effective paradigms and concrete projects, or commitments, to serve a discipline of urban planning that knows how to influence the urban metabolism, recombining the genetic code contained in the areas and flows to be put back into circulation. Although often fragmented or weakened, these flows are still able to generate new fabric if reactivated by the vital energy produced by the cycles of water, food, energy, nature, waste, people and goods. Flows which have an impact on the daily life of cities and which inevitably act on a large scale, contributing to the reticular connection of settlements. Reconnecting them with a holistic view of the metabolism is one of the greatest challenges to urban planners, designers, administrators and citizens who aim to give new impetus to the circular neo-Anthropocene, connecting its technical components with its social and moral dimensions (Sijmons, 2014b). Finally, we need new types of urban and regional planning with localizing strategies rather than comprehensive planning, plans that work with simple and adaptive rules rather than masterplans, and generative settlement actions alongside regulatory plans (Carta, 2015).

Re-cyclical Urbanism: paradigms, tools, and practices

I believe that we are witnessing the birth of the first forms of a *Re-cyclical Urbanism*[6], based on the recycling of areas, infrastructure, and landscapes and driven by adaptive and incremental circular processes. It is essential to investigate evidence of these processes and practices already underway to identify their parentage, recognize their epistemology, define protocols, but above all, shape the design devices needed to reimagine urbanism in the era of circular transition. Supported by a sufficiently robust theory, many theoretical and empirical studies are attempting to re-adjectivise urban planning (from *Open Source Urbanism* by Sassen, or *Landscape Urbanism* by Waldheim, to *Ecological Urbanism* by Mostafavi, among others) as a critique and antidote to urban planning models of the recent past. We need a new urban planning approach that is able to respond to the metamorphosis of the traditional European city model based on the density, centrality and identity of the urban form into ways of living and working in environments that are more rur-urban than urban, feature more vegetation than stone, are more reticular than confined, and more productive than consuming (Bergevoet, van Tuijl, 2016). *Recyclical Urbanism*, therefore, not only works on the tangible potential (areas, volumetric dimensions, infrastructure, landscapes), but also on the potential related to the memories and identities contained in the areas to be put back into circulation.

It is from these areas that 21st-century cities will have to produce new urban intelligence, firstly by rewriting abandoned "lines of code" (functions), reactivating unused "memory banks" (areas), and reclaiming inefficient urban "routines" (infrastructure). These are all urban materials still containing traces of vitality, which in many practices today provide resources for ecological planning and urban agriculture, infrastructure for sustainable mobility and selfsufficient production, crowdsourcing tasks, and places for sharing and social innovation.

Making the city re-cyclical thus means abandoning the traditional erosive linear logic to adopt a new "development operating system" — no longer closed and preset, but open source — which is not only enriched by the contribution of the various users but learns from experiences, adapting to spatial, social and economic contexts instead of stiffening them within predefined standards and rules. An operating system — urban planning intelligence — capable of generating a more sustainable, more responsible and also more creative city, and capable of rethinking urban community models to reinvent settlement forms, firstly by reactivating urban assets that have fallen into disuse, are undergoing change, or are in crisis. An intelligent city capable of reshaping the way we move, weaving new creative relationships with the environment and the landscape, and fuelling the production of urban settlement cultures, which can reactivate the vital organs of the city

SEVEN PARADIGMS OF RE_CYCLICAL URBANISM
CONCEPTUAL MAP

RE-NOWN
RE-TICULAR
RE-THINK
RE-SILIENCE
RE-SPONSIBLE
RE-MOTE
RE-MAKE

The Re-cyclical Urbanism concept map is a flow diagram representing the ramifications and evidence of each of the seven main paradigmatic branches: identity, polycentrism, knowledge, resilience, democracy, sharing, and regeneration. For each of the paradigms, concrete actions are defined that intercept the demand for recycling at the various levels of the landscape and peri-urban areas (landscape), the city and urban systems (city), infrastructure and networks (infrastructure), neighborhoods, buildings and public spaces (districts), social innovation (social innovation), and digital craftsmen (makers), identifying the ramifications, origins and offspring in order to trace a map that can give us our bearings and guide subsequent experimentation.

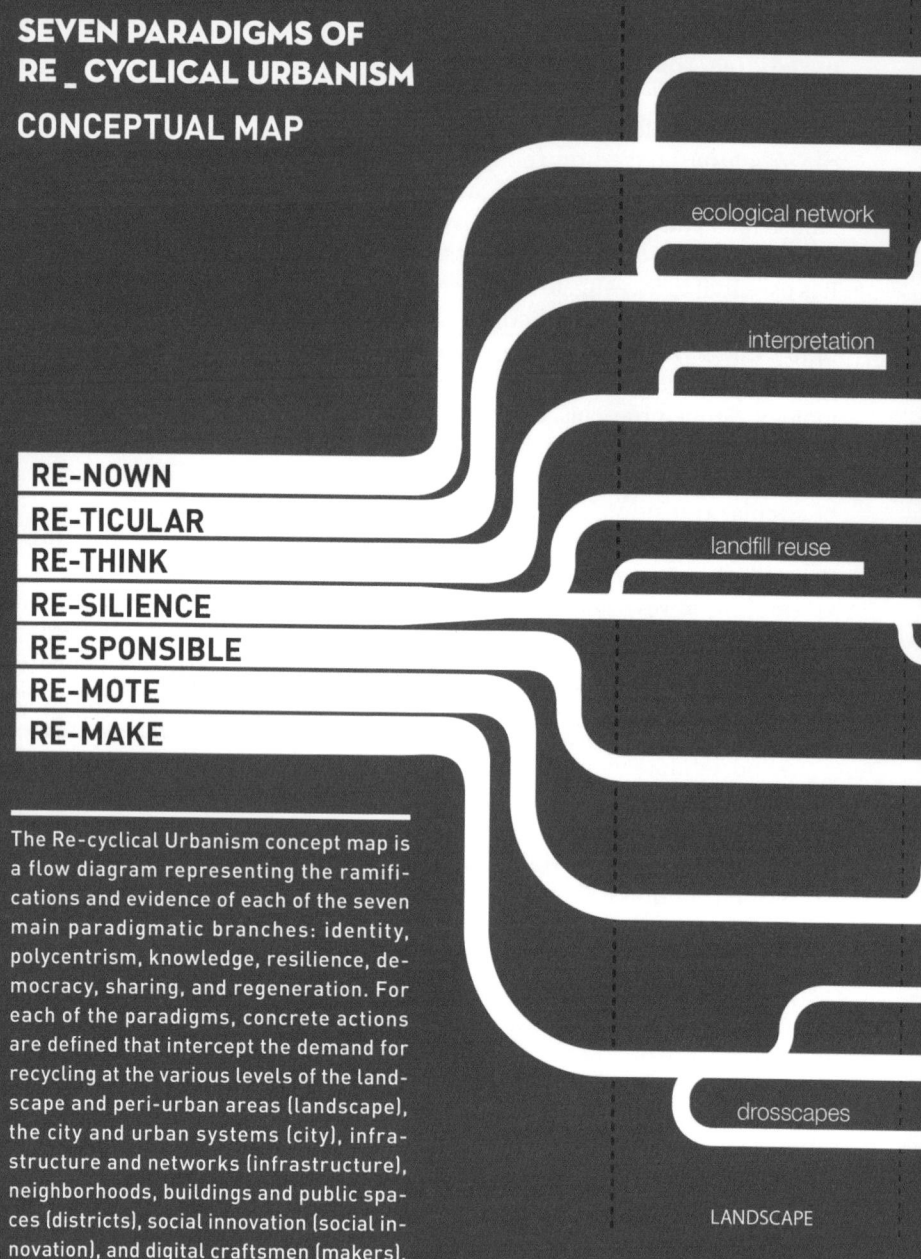

ecological network

interpretation

landfill reuse

drosscapes

LANDSCAPE

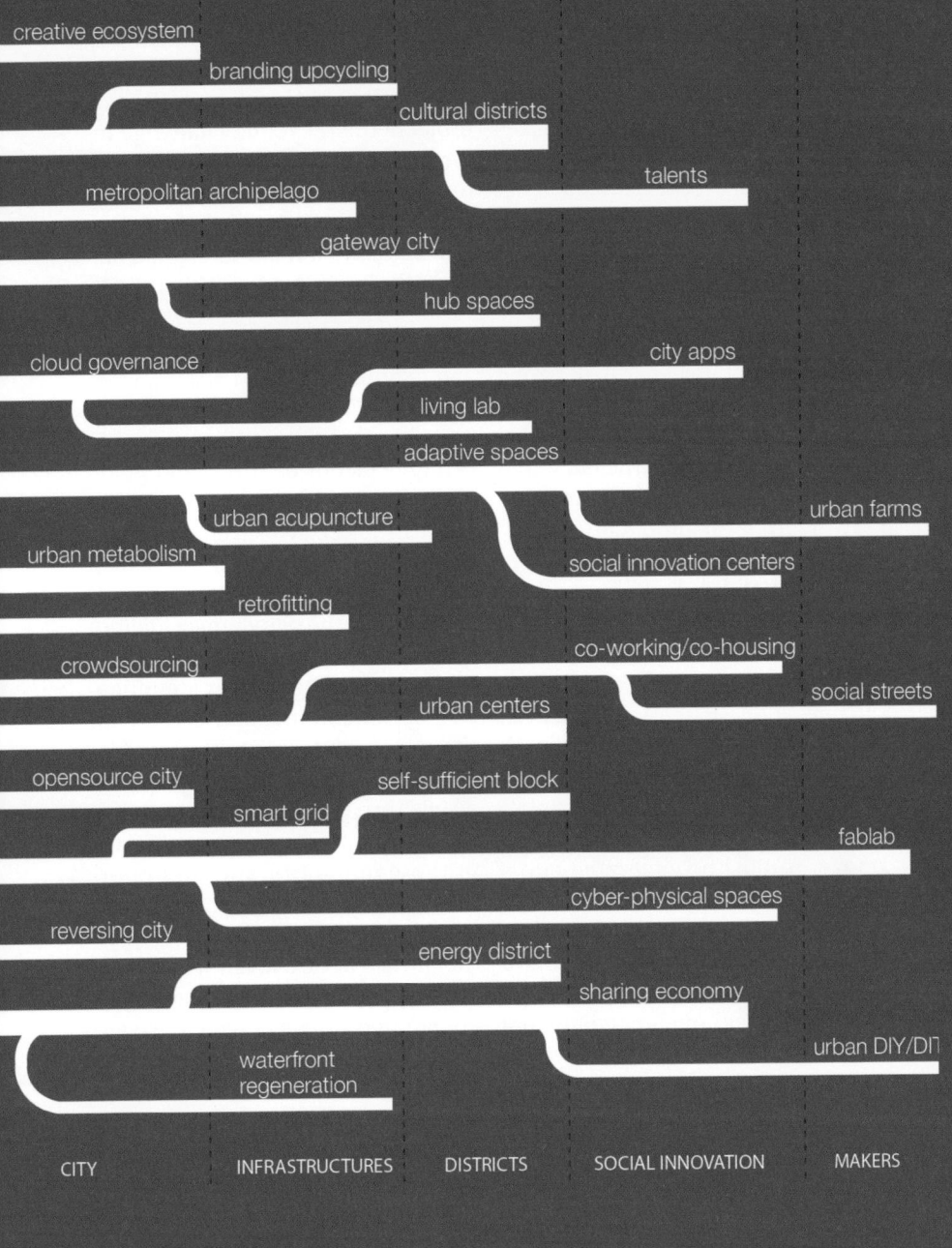

and its life cycles, but also react to deterioration scenarios. Cities of the future, particularly medium-sized Mediterranean cities — the true antidote to the world's megalopolises — must act within a new capitalism that no longer works as a linear set of financial instructions, but as an evolutionary circular system that reinvents itself and is strengthened by crisis — that learns from crisis — and is able to provide a guide to settlement processes through strong integration with ecological sustainability, regional planning, land-use management, energy efficiency, and morphology planning without withdrawing from the production of value. The new urban operating system will leave behind the linear code of the obsolete 3Rs (resources, revenue, regulation) to adopt the circular code of the new 3Rs: recycling, resilience, and reactivation. However, in order for them not to remain an ineffectual mantra and to be capable of generating new planning practices and urban devices, the three new keywords must be integrated into a renewed urban ecosystem.

For those, like myself, who take a militant approach to seeking a new urban ecosystem, there is now much empirical evidence showing the presence of re-cyclical urbanism, and to sort through it, I have developed a concept map as a flow diagram representing the ramifications and evidence of each of the seven main paradigmatic branches: identity, polycentrism, knowledge, resilience, democracy, sharing, and regeneration. To specify the traces, latent evidence and experiments underway for each of the paradigms, I have defined how, with what concrete actions, and by means of which projects the recycling challenge intercepts with the various levels of the landscape and peri-urban areas (*landscape*), the city and the urban systems (*city*), infrastructure and networks (*infrastructure*), neighborhoods, buildings and public spaces (*districts*), social innovation (*social innovation*), and digital craftsmen (*makers*), identifying ramifications, origins and offspring in order to trace a map that can give us our bearings and guide subsequent experimentation. Using the "RE-" prefix, which characterizes the re-cyclical approach, I've called the first branch RE-NOWN because it represents the paradigm of identity as urban reputation, which is essential in facilitating greater identification by inhabitants and users with the new circular metabolism. The first level on which it acts is the city, which, through creative ecosystems, is once again an educational factor in the community and an opportunity for knowledge and training (Marseille, Euroméditerranée). At the infrastructure level, we witness the branded upcycling of viaducts or abandoned railways which are enriched by urban marketing actions to strengthen their regenerative effort (Lowline Park in New York; the IM Viadukt in Zurich; the Atlanta Beltline). At the level of architecture and public space, cultural districts are increasingly re-elaborating new forms, places and relations that contain and connect the flows of information and communication the city generates with increasing frequency, scale and speed, especially starting from its latent cultural resources (Farm Cultural Park, Favara). Finally, social innovation is implemented and accelerated by the role of talents in reactivating cities, both in the redevelopment of spaces and in the notoriety and reputation of cities (Mapa del Talent, Barcelona; Mappa dei Talenti, Palermo). The second branch is RE-TICULAR and supports the paradigm of polycentrism, striving to create new social aggregation hubs that fluidize settlements, occupying places undergoing change and reusing them for social occasions as new activators. It acts firstly on the landscape, restoring ecological networks in a planning perspective that redefines functions and ways of using the natural and anthropic components, restoring the grid of agricultural production that has given structure to the European landscape throughout the centuries, reclaiming old railway routes, re-naturalizing infrastructure that has fallen into disuse and reactivating agricultural functions (Natuurbrug Zanderij Crailo Ecoduct, Netherlands). At the city and infrastructure level, metropolitan archipelagos accelerate the affirmation of new supralocal values that allow new semantic cycles to be activated in areas undergoing transformation and discontinued areas of cities transitioning from local egoism to a reticular and polycentric dimension (Randstadt Holland; Poland Reticular Strategy). Specifically, *gateway cities* of the global system belong to the infrastructure level and serve as hubs in the reactivation of local cycles by tapping into the energy produced by global flows (Amsterdam, Rotterdam, Barcelona). The consequence at the district level is the proliferation of hub spaces that facilitate the localization of urban places structured into archipelagos of competitive clusters in the various fields of development. Their task is to help new service- sector or urban manufacturing businesses revitalize the urban hubs by favouring their localization in recycled areas at a lower settlement cost (Impact Hub Global Network; Nantes, Hub Creatic).

RE-THINK is the paradigm of new forms of knowledge, which are able to act on urban communication by planning opportunities and designing places in which knowledge of the urban system arises from specialisms and becomes widespread knowledge, intersubjective competence and new collective thinking, becoming concrete material for an agreement for the co-existence of urban populations and the resulting development pact. Belonging to this paradigm are the now consolidated US and French experiences of *interpretation*, which have generated a spread of plans for the interpretation of natural and cultural landscapes to guide the use of the cultural armature, reactivating the cycles of knowledge, education and sustainable tourism (Site Unesco du Pont du Garde nella Région Languedoc-Roussillon). At the city level, sustainable development policies are defining and consolidating veritable cloud governance that systematizes the widespread knowledge constantly produced by the population and by local stakeholders to produce a new integrated system of sensors and actuators that makes urban policies more effective and less dissipative (Office for Civic Innovation in San Francisco). Living labs are a productç at the district level that increasingly enliven towns by providing places to encourage open and shared innovation, complementing technical knowledge, innovative processes and social demand with a public-private partnership (Sant Cugat LOW3 in Barcelona; the Centquatre in Paris). Social innovation is incited by the continuous creation of city apps for smartphones and mobile and wearable devices that are revolutionizing the relationship between questions and answers, sensors and actuators, active citizenship and proactive administrations (Renurban; Boskoi for mapping edible landscapes; Twitter Mapping by Fischer).

The RE-SILIENCE branch channels the lifeblood of resilience and environmental sustainability and encourages us to adopt a flexible and dialogue-based attitude in which the flexibility of functions, the permeability of spaces and the adaptability of settlements are no longer addressed as purely conceptual and spatial problems, but are examined in relation to the social, economic and technological result which today becomes part of building a city, becoming issues/instruments/regulations for planning urban resilience. New peri-urban landscapes created by recycling garbage dumps are becoming more frequent as new vital systems capable of producing places of leisure and generators of power from the waste cycle (Freshkills Park, New York). The resilience paradigm produces practices and creates neighborhoods or entire cities with a new urban metabolism, which are capable of better handling climate change or hydrogeological changes and of absorbing floods, producing new fluid urban forms especially from public spaces. Water, for example, even flood water, becomes project material to be absorbed by parks, roads and permeable squares, both to alleviate the sewage system, and to create new collective spaces in connection with water, giving them breath (Rotterdam Urban Metabolism; Saint-Kjelds Climate Adaptation District, Copenhagen; BIG U project, New York). The infrastructure level is the subject of specific resilience activities with the retrofitting of roads, railway areas, sewage systems and waterways to make them more suited to energy efficiency requirements and to the challenges of climate change. Belonging to the same level are urban acupuncture experiments aimed at reactivating the life cycles of deteriorating or stagnated neighborhoods. The reactivation of urban capital can occur by leveraging small pressure points in the city, giving rise to a positive repercussion affecting large areas, covering the functional, infrastructural, cultural and social networks of the cities (Curitiba: acupuncture strategies applied to the city were used as the best solution to solve the critical issues of the contemporary city and enabled it to win the Globe Sustainable City Award in 2010). New adaptive urban spaces are the increasingly frequent outcome of the evolution of tactical urbanism, in which the reactivation of the urban resources on a micro-scale and by micro-players is favored over large-scale programs requiring the use of large amounts of capital. The new spaces that readapt abandoned areas and buildings in a transitioning city also contribute to providing responses to a compelling demand for social resilience, leading to the creation of veritable social innovation centers in districts and communities. These encourage the sharing of spaces and skills to ease empowerment with regard to the new challenges of the future (Centre for Social Innovation in New York), as well as the rise of actual urban farms that bring agriculture back to the city beyond the rhetoric of urban horticulture, making them a powerful engine of new social relations and a power supply for renewed urban economies (Sociopolis, Valencia; Agropolis, Munich; Greening Detroit; Hackney City Farm).

The paradigm of participatory democracy upholds the RE-SPONSIBLE branch, which requires communication to nourish improvement of the collaborative dimension and efficiency of the plans themselves, fostering widespread environments of awareness/action more suited to contemporary social and environmental needs. The first effect is the extension of crowdsourcing to urban policies, by means of a new proactive use of citizenship as a permanent system of sensors/actuators. New argumentative ethics of planning must become a vehicle for interpersonal relations, a creator of responsibility and activator of the mobilization of collective intelligence surrounding the urban project through the spread of urban center networks. Less and less are these physical and institutional places, but rather, increasingly open and shared, creating social innovation around themselves by means of an increasingly widespread system of co-working and co-housing that overcomes the initial logic of the need to share costs to participate in a powerful ethics and aesthetics of sharing urban space (The Embassy Network: shared housing for people with digital and creative talent). Within this paradigm, makers are steadily emerging from their digital laboratories, and citizens from their associations, to produce social streets, with the goal of making their sensitivity, skills and professionalism available to the local community. They can, therefore, establish a bond, share necessities and exchange knowledge in order to carry out collective projects of common interest and thus reap all the benefits arising from greater social interaction (Via Fondazza in Bologna and over 300 of its followers).

RE-MOTE is the sharing paradigm that has produced the *open source city* in which we live, which requires a high level of synergy between the new poly-centrality of services, the molecular building structure required by new forms of living, and

the constant supply of increasingly wireless and cloud-based technological services. The new urban fabrics arising from reuse are increasingly imbued with digital components (sensors, apps, *social networking, civic dashboards*) that are made and remade between *producer* and consumer, *intercepting the demands of increasingly prosumer citizens* (Ratti, Claudel, 2016). The digital cycle connects the perceptions and requirements of functionality and comfort of inhabitants, complementing them with their requests for knowledge and experience and with the demand for democracy and supply of cooperation (Smart Citizen Initiative for the shared monitoring of environmental quality; Place Pulse, an experiment of open source mapping of urban perception). At the infrastructure and district level, the increasingly consolidated and effective testing of smart grids for intelligent energy management is changing the traditional model of delocalized energy production with inefficient and costly distribution in favor of a model that not only brings production closer to consumption but also sustainably synchronizes supply and demand. Experiments regarding energetically self-sufficient blocks are of great interest. They reshape the settlement space using a multi-purpose solution that involves the interaction of the residential space, the production space related to new urban factories, and the space related to the return of urban agriculture, connected by new collection and self-recycling of waste, with the self-production of photovoltaic, micro wind power or even power from the photosynthesis of algae (Solarschiff in Freiburg; the Bed Zed Pavilion in London; the Algae-Powered Building in Hamburg). All this contributes to deep social innovation, produced by the union between the digital and physical space, creating the conditions to reactivate the new collective city by means of new forms and ways of using public space. Fab labs and digital craftsmen increasingly take the new leading role in the contemporary city that once again becomes a productive and manufacturing city (KPMG, 2016). They present themselves as an archipelago of micro-players in the economy – but also in politics and society – in the third industrial revolution, contributing to the return of manufacturing in abandoned warehouses, reactivating craftsmanship and establishing cooperative networks with research and industry, often forming actual *makers quarters*. Today there are over 350 fab labs throughout the world and Italy has the third highest number of them, following the United States and France (the Fab Lab at MIT in Cambridge, the Fab City project in Barcelona and the new Manifattura in Rovereto give us three different interpretations of the urban role of *makers*).
Finally, RE-MAKE is the branch concerning the regeneration of public space. It not only activates places of social interaction, but also provides incentives for the rebirth of new professions and revived urban factories alongside the traditional ones that have survived extensive industri-

alization, revitalizing them, adjusting ancient artisan knowledge and adapting it to the changed demands of new and more aware consumers. The city of innovative professions and the productive city of the manufacturing renaissance will require, more and more often, not only the use of creativity, strategic vision, economic and fiscal support, and innovative management, but also integrated projects and urban planning tactics for the collective space, accompanied by a constant assessment of the effects of choices and performance monitoring. The new creative and innovative ecosystem of cities more and more often arises firstly from new public spaces, from landscapes of agricultural transformation, and from parasitic structures that colonize abandoned, idle or underused urban areas with increasing frequency, producing new and more attractive urban lattices that can be accessed in multiple ways and which connect the new cultural, educational, and ecological functions to production. These are drosscapes, formed from the scraps produced by the evolution of cities, considered interstitial, in-between spaces in the urban fabric, free strips along the roads, archipelagos of parking lots, unused land, areas waiting for development, waste dumping sites, cargo storage districts: an endless and pervasive stretch of breaks and perimeters that frame the residential neighborhoods. They are areas that accumulate in the process of post-Fordist deindustrialization and technological innovation and which can once again accommodate the new urban factories. They are sites of the reversing city (Secchi, 1999), made up of places of transition and less and less residual spaces, and increasingly the new protagonists in the re-cycle oriented project. Infrastructure subject to review and recycling increasingly includes those of ports and peri-portal areas — urban waterfronts as activators of fluid cities (Ronsivalle, 2016), as urban regenerators through the energy of flows crossing them (an example is Hafencity in Hamburg). Playing a leading role in the regeneration paradigm are the new energy districts, capable of integrating and promoting public demand, reduced consumption, energy and fiscal incentives, and private requirements for redevelopment projects. Their feasibility will have to be substantiated by drawing up energy agreements in support of the districts, in the face of environmental sustainability and social projects, assessed on recycling parameters regarding the buildings, public spaces, mobility, the waste cycle and digital infrastructure (the EcoQuartier de Bonne in Grenoble or the Eco-quartiers Flaubert et Luciline in Rouen). Social innovation is encouraged through the pervasiveness of the *sharing economy*, which is reaching significant results and dimensions, whether it be the sharing of goods, services, information, spaes, time or skills, *bartering* between individuals or companies, *crowding*, or *making*, that is, self-production from hobbies to digital fabrication, radically transforming the fields of

7 projects for 7 paradigms of Re-cyclical Urbanism

RE-NOWN: Farm Cultural Park, Favara
RE-TICULAR: Hub Creatic, Nantes
RE-THINK: LOW 3 Living Lab, Sant Cugat
RE-SILIENCE: Dryline Project, New York
RE-SPONSIBLE: Casa Netural, Matera
RE-MOTE: Bed Zed Pavilion, London
RE-MAKE: FabHouse, Barcelona

tourism (Airbnb), transport (car and bike sharing; Uber), energy, food (Food sharing initiatives) and design. Urban making is also being strongly driven by DIY (Do It Yourself) and DIT (Do It Together) urban practices by means of which groups of citizens, residents, temporary users, travellers, urban hackers and urban farmers reactivate places, manage abandoned sites, take care of public spaces, and maintain or co-manage collective services (*tactical urbanism; pop-up city*).

A planning agenda for re-cyclical urbanism

To ensure it does not wither away into a tempting conceptualization, *Re-cyclical Urbanism* requires us to verify the accuracy of its intuitions, the robustness of its hypotheses and the sustainability of its proposals. We must yield to the responsibility of translating the numerous process and project experiments that dot the map of recyclical-based planning into general rules so that they are not just local and episodic responses or winning tactics that cannot be replicated outside of the experimentation contexts or beyond the talent of the planner. We are faced with an intellectual challenge that needs to result in a planning, cultural and political challenge. The first challenge concerns legislation because I believe it necessary to incentivize recycling so that it is not just affordable but preferable, even acting within the existing legal framework. This should obviously not prevent us from attempting to identify regulatory innovations or new legal frameworks that make the recycling paradigm even more structural in the actions of territorial governance and urban planning, adding an additional thematic implementation layer to the practices put in place, which works by combining law and taxation. The second challenge is operational and asks us to choose whether recycling, both functionally and in terms of planning, must be molecular, that is, whether it should settle for acting precisely where it is applied by means of specific planning devices, or whether it needs to be systemic, and therefore metabolic, pervasive and perturbative. The second option enables the driving force of the first phases of an urbanism based on local recycling not to run out of steam, risking a sort of mannerism. We must overcome an approach in which recycling appears merely to be a successful lexical innovation that re-semanticizes already known methods, to experience a new paradigm that destroys — by proposing an alternative — consolidated habits, but now so weakened as to seem illusions. To me, systemic recycling is a new way of seeing the world that surrounds us, steering action so that it is relevant to the new demands and is, above all, timely with respect to the questions being formed: this is the strength of a new urban planning paradigm — that it can provide answers ahead of time. The creative, intelligent and resilient planning of city, territory and landscape transformation requires a multi-scale and multi-player approach, in which not just the urban planner's contribution is relevant, but also that of the legal expert, the economist, the development manager, and active citizens. In this type of approach, we must be action-oriented, producing real effects on cities, infrastructure, and landscapes, and not just convincing rhetoric. Experimentation islands based on the application of recycling in traditional contexts no longer work, as they do not initiate the radical metamorphosis of development that we need. What I demand — and beseech — is an archipelago of recycling involving not only areas naturally inclined towards recycling — places of often dramatic productive and infrastructural discontinuance —, but also those areas which, although not directly engaged by recycling actions, are involved in a process of transformation by means of other approaches and project tools, making them more efficient, safer, more attractive, and even more beautiful. Recycling is more a conditioning factor than an invariant to be coldly replicated. We must, therefore, reject a molecular approach in which, notwithstanding the parts of the territory to which recycling is applied, the rest can continue to pursue erosion, consumption, and production of expansive revenue — now just based on paperwork and therefore parasitic. To innovate the re-cyclical — adaptive, re-user and circular — metabolism, we cannot wait to revise the current regulatory system but should act with practices, from which to extract rules, which will then become laws. I thus prefer a pragmatic approach, based on a vision like the one that brings our research to life, a germinal way of acting that operates via amendments, extension, creative interpretation of the existing instruments and regulations from which to extract the standards that will be make up future regulations. Acting within the regulations, plans, and measures at their respective levels of cogency and jurisdiction, crossing scales and subjects in search of new connections.

Obviously, the question is how? In my opinion, we should develop a provision that makes the effects of re-cyclical urbanism tangible, which shares the advantages, bringing them into people's everyday lives. We need a real *"Re-cyclical Dividend"*, a collective dividend produced by territorial recycling processes. Either we turn recycling into a new "currency" in circular capitalism, a factor that comes into play in valuation, capital that acts in a new market of cultural values, or recycling will remain confined to local practices regarding sustainability instead of becoming its constitutive matrix[7]. The ethical challenge that the recycling dividend offers us is to make its effects collective and inter-subjective. We need to prevent recycling from being experienced as a game of the elite, as an interest of a few instead of being demanded as a new right of citizenship, capable of extending its effects to the whole community, even the parts not involved in the direct actions. It must become part of the daily life, even of those who think they can't afford the burden of recycling, who prefer the consolation of consumption.

Land use has been the new comforting "absinthe" of contemporary cities, and we are responsible for awakening, by showing the regenerative effects of a circular metabolism compared to the erosive effects of linear development. It is our duty to show that the disappearance of a sizeable system of economic resources compels us to change our vision before our instruments, to change actions before regulations. Our duty to show that the disappearance of a hierarchical decision-making system must coincide with a widespread ethic of responsibility that imposes a circular, adaptive and non-erosive approach with regard to the few available resources. The atomization of the decision-making power of public figures entails awareness of the wealth of distribution of powers within a true principle of subsidiarity, which is shared responsibility above all. We need to break the illusion that a dead frog can be resuscitated by applying an external electrical current.

We need to show that its jerking movements are not a dance of resurrection, but the spasms of a zombie. Gone are the days in which the eruption of an urban project funded with European resources was hailed as the birth of a renewed vitality instead of reading the omen of an end created by consumption of the last truly vital resources: identity, community, and the environment.

I thus propose a new path for regeneration, which our research and many activities underway[8] have clearly shown: acting on identity life cycles, working on components of the urban metabolism that are still alive, finding out which vital factors to reactivate, the materials of a fertile *bricolage* which, as in a coral reef, create new life from raw materials fallen into disuse from other life cycles in a creative circularity that produces the necessary leaps to generate energy. We need to design places that can accommodate temporary functions within a scheduled cycle that looks at the whole day or year as inspiration for functions, as an attractor of uses with a strong charge of innovation. Let's return to talking about the city's timeframes and cycles, which we had too soon abandoned, believing it was only an issue concerning the conciliation of time for living, equal opportunities or gender differences. Today it is also a problem of ergonomics, of a metabolic view of the city that shows us that during the day, there are inevitably different cycles in which different stakeholders play depending on the uses most suited to the time. Our life has become fluid, multi-layered and multi-scale. Social segregation itself has crumbled in favor of diversity, which requires multiple and plural metabolisms, a true hypermetabolism that demands greater circularity of the city itself.

I'm certain that after having published the *"Re-cycle Manifesto"*[9] — which clarified our not only scientific positions, but also political positions — we need to push the proactive dimension even further with regard to territorial governance and urban policies, particularly at a time in which the country is engaged in redesigning the metropolitan armature and the rural settlement ecosystems, in an attempt to innovate urban planning legislation, and in testing better-performing procedures for reducing land use and mitigating climate change. Indeed, recycling requires a plan of actions punctuated over time that is not only able to produce immediate solutions for the reuse of abandoned spaces, but is at the same time capable of enabling the conditions for reducing the production of new residue or for preventing the disruption of cycles, by planning and designing the reversibility of uses. Re-cyclical urbanism outlines a shared project to counter the crisis, so that in the circular and shared economy, the resources of scrap, residue and disuse contribute in a more creative and less erosive manner to redefining the way we move, to closing energy cycles, to fuelling creativity, to producing new ecologies, and to feeding urban intelligence. Recycling is thus militant and is not limited to a cultural approach, ecological sensitivity, or social action. It requires strong ethics of responsibility oriented towards change and it requires concrete actions. I consider it essential to extract an "urban recycling agenda" from the numerous analyses and experiments we carried out within the scope of our National Interest Research Project Re-cycle Italy. This agenda will be made up of specific actions to be presented or addressed to urban policies capable of responding to the demands of a circular society[10], which are able to infect specific points of our instruments and regulations, which we can consider to be the pillars of a line of reasoning, on which we will together have to subsequently build the architecture of our action. The first changes to the rules in force call for action in the "identity" domain because the places we are talking about often hold powerful symbolic connotations and are the reserves of identity in the changing city. They may have lost their latest layer of identity but they have salvaged the deeper underlying layer of their palimpsest. Reactivating identity cycles means asking ourselves, first of all, what cycle the particular place, artifact, infrastructure or landscape belongs to, what metabolism fed its function. This is so we can ask ourselves, before taking any replacement action — daughter of the obsolete concept of industrial archaeology as a universal receptacle — whether it is more appropriate to reactivate an identity function, which costs less in terms of resources because of its predisposition, is functional at the end of a production, energy, infrastructure, or environmental cycle, and restores circularity to the territorial metabolism of the area. Other actions will need to be taken in the field of "social dynamism" characterizing the areas to be recycled, as a result of the community's dissatisfaction with the present state and its desire for a potentially different future. *Drosscapes*, the voids of the reverse city, are often places that catalyze associations, civic-mindedness, and social protagonism, first as a reaction to the neglect and then as resolved proactive behavior. Sometimes we are still in the phase of civic effervescence, of tactics of reappropriation of places, a phase that must be dynamically channelled through system actions that define a common vision connecting the tactics, without however, reducing their energy: an *open source approach that works s multaneously by coding and hacking, with intuition and rules.*

We thus need actions that facilitate "interaction" — between sectors, places, and people — and which contribute to the essential multi-sector, multi-timeframe, and multi-scale nature typical of urban policies based on circularity. Specifically, the multi-scale nature of recycling doesn't just connote a crossing of scales — in which all the components are already present, but become visible progressively — but the application of a true scaling up process that is able to manage the growing complexity of space, time, stakeholders and resources that materialize and come into play to include interactions and their effects among the social, physical, cultural, economic and environmental dimensions. Other rules concern the "potential" contained in these places, that is, acknowledgement of disparity between reality and project, between gaze and vision, which allows the potential energy to be transformed into an essential mechanism for the generat ion of tangible and intangible resources, which nourish the project for the area's future in a self-sustainable way. Moreover, the potential energy of recycling areas, drosscapes, and urban ruins is high, both in term of stock, geographical location and symbolic reputation. So rules and regulations that are able to act on this principle of potentiality are fundamental in attributing a value to them, which can be calculated even when it acts in the field of intangibles, and which can be offset in an urban regeneration operation that recognizes their existence and provides for their urban equalization. Some actions must operate on the "administrative" dimension, innovating the regime of ownership and powers in favor of a collaborative approach, streamlining procedures for authorization and control of transformations in the exchange rate of the intended use, subject to monumental, stability and structural constraints. Re-cyclical urbanism must facilitate change in internal configurations and the splitting of buildings to meet the continuously changing settlement needs, but above all, it must be able to supplement the new housing and production requirements with new energy opportunities. Other changes to the rules concern the "economic sustainability" of the transformations, not as a point of balance between a mixture of resources, but as the identification of the new values to be reactivated, closing the residence-production-new lifestyle cycle as the essential lifeblood of creative cities. The re-cyclical city becomes a veritable *Fab City*[11], a place of widespread micro-production, of district manufacturing supply chains and circular economies corresponding to the neighborhood. Finally, we need "perturbative" actions because recycled areas are never neutral, sterile places in a stable equilibrium, but places with a constant vibration, places infected with the virus of change, places in a constantly precarious equilibrium in relation to a new state. They are principally resilient places if we consider resilience as the constant force of adaptation towards new evolutionary states. It is from this state of disruption that we can extract the vital endogenous factors that can revitalize the area and reactivate the metabolism without waiting for an illusory external energy. All this must naturally be converted into planning devices. We have already launched some proposals on other occasions and here, I would like to propose them again in light of the regulatory actions needed to put them into effect[12]. Firstly, I consider it fundamental to propose urban regeneration plans based on "urban recycling districts", within which to integrate and take advantage of public demand, reduced consumption, energy and taxation incentives and the private need for redevelopment projects. Recycling districts are places, mostly the size of a neighborhood, in which forms of re-cyclical life are experienced, a sort of urban "coral reef" in which everything is recycled to become the constitutive basis of another life cycle. Districts in which the cyclical nature shares places, but also functions — the social streets model shows us some interesting examples. A community that finds roles and responsibilities in the new, more sustainable urban metabolisms. The recycling districts, however, cannot be subjected to regeneration projects that adopt ineffective masterplans based on the prediction of long-term effects founded on the inflexibility of the decisions and actions envisaged. Recyclical urbanism requires an incremental and adaptive approach of colonizing tactics, of the resulting entrenchment and of development scenarios: a protocol of urban regeneration that I have called the *Cityforming© Protocol*[13], based on a strategic masterprogram approach hinging on the flexibility of actions and timeframes, rather than a fanciful instant masterplan based on control, which is often ineffective and impracticable in weak, fluid and fragmented territorial conditions in which the urban planning of transitioning cities operates. To support the districts, "recycling agreements" will need to be entered into in view of environmentally and socially sustainable projects, benchmarked on the basis of recycling indicators regarding the buildings, public spaces, mobility, the waste cycle and digital infrastructure. The recycling agreements, among the increasing forms of agreement between parties in pursuit of common objectives, need regulations that si plify their implementation and give incentives for their activation, operating, for example, in the domain of tax, administrative or management compensation. A true recycling governance that provides for recycling as a rewarding component in the relationship between administration and citizenship, but in the perspective of a large area so as to be able to count on greater leverage instead of higher rates, difficult to obtain in the tax progression hibernation we have been plunged into. It is essential to activate "agencies of shared responsibility" — for design, economics, urban planning, and management — between the public and individuals, connected to a responsible simplification and greater efficacy of administrative action. They will have to be agencies/laboratories of circular urban development that don't settle for managing, controlling and maintaining, but which co-plan: a sort of "urban recycling company" that brings together the owners of areas, service managers, institutional stakeholders and economic players looking towards the transformation of the areas, which is re-cyclical in terms of what we've said so far. Finally, we repeat, innovation of the instruments of public-private-civil society partnership is necessary through the principles of compensation and urban equalization, fiscal leverage and incentives. We need urban planning taxation that rewards and assists those who build on recycled land, for example, by burdening or charging higher taxes to those who build settlements on greenfields, and providing incentives and removing duties for those who create settl ments that reactivate brownfields and who lighten the ecological footprint of grayfields. Although not exhaustive, these appear to me to be the main points of an agenda for multiple rules for multiple stakeholders — which is also an agenda within the community of the urban and territorial project. Recyclical urbanism is thus a planning and regulatory action that requires a shared commitment, so that recycling does not remain within the scope of individual decisions or i stitutional willingness, but has the explosive force of a new or remade regulatory mechanism that guides public action, facilitates private behaviour, and consolidates the informal practices which characterize the new operational instruments. Re-cyclical urbanism calls us to be committed to a new social responsibility and a new hermeneutics of the project as a result of planned circularity, of a creativity generator made up of treatment, reclamation and reactivation of cities which once again become social devices to feed life cycles, nurturers and pasture of the talents of inhabitants (to quote Plato), magnets to attract ideas, engines to generate innovation and produce new economies and armature to strengthen cooperation networks: what I call the "augmented city" (Carta, 2016). The circular economy and new forms of production must fuel new habitat projects capable of refocusing the principles of balance, continuity, and cognizance of eco-systemic limits. From a critique of the "production-con sumption-waste" linear models, the transition towards a circular society dictates that the circularity is transferred on a programmatic basis to the processes, plans, and projects, that it fuels the reclamation of abandoned areas and abandoned or underused infrastructures, that it activates the recycling of land-waste and reactivates the metabolism of drosscapes, but above all, that it produces the planned recycling, to which we have already referred, for a territory that evolves without producing inert waste and that develops without the erosion of resources. Re-cyclical urbanism needs to design, activate and preside over systemic processes and actions oriented towards recycling, through the reactivation of buildings in disuse, dormant areas and neglected infrastructure, valuable resources excluded from the choices of a development model addicted to a modern *kykeon*[14] extracted from the mixture of revenue and public funding. Above all, it imposes a radical innovation of urban policies so that we are more effective and creative, sensitive to cultural and landscape capital, and capable of generating new value, which is not just financial, but also territorial. A systemic re-cyclical action requires urban planners not to settle for handling the strategic retreat from compulsive urbanization, effectively governing the contraction, being objectors of growth or legally imposing the reduction of land use, but will have to adopt a way of thinking/ acting that turns scrap stone into the new "cornerstones" of the city in the time of metamorphosis. I am certain that this is the necessary challenge if urban planning wishes to be effectively re-cyclical, contributing to the implementation of a planning agenda for the circular metamorphosis in which we already live and to which we need to adapt forms and functions of the settlement, planning and regulatory instruments, planning processes and governance.

Bibliography

Angel, S. (2012), *Planet of Cities*. Cambridge: Lincoln Institute of Land Policy.

Badami, A. (2012), *Metamorfosi urbane*. Firenze: Alinea.

Bergevoet, T., van Tuijl, M. (2016), *The Flexible City. Sustainable Solutions for a Europe in Transition*. Rotterdam: nai010 publishers.

Bianchetti, C., Cogato Lanza, E., Kercuku, A., eds. (2015), *Territories in Crisis. Architecture and Urbanism Facing Changes in Europe*. Berlin: Jovis.

Bonomi, A., Masiero, R., Della Puppa, F. (2016), *La società circolare. Fordismo, capitalismo molecolare, sharing economy*, Roma: DeriveApprodi.

Brugmans, G., Strien, J., eds. (2014), *IABR 2014. Urban by Nature*, Rotterdam: IABR.

Brugmans, G., van Dinteren, J., Hajer, M., eds. (2016), *IABR 2016. The Next Economy*, Rotterdam: IABR.

Campbell, K. (2011), *Massive Small. The Operating Programme for Smart Urbanism*. London: Urban Exchange.

Carta, M. (2014a), *Reimagining Urbanism. Creative, Smart and Green Cities for the Changing Times*. Barcelona-Trento: ListLab.

Carta, M. (2014b), "Smart Planning and Intelligent Cities: A New Cambrian Explosion", in Riva Sanseverino, E., Riva Sanseverino, R., Vaccaro, V., Zizzo, G. (eds.) *Smart Rules for Smart Cities. Managing Efficient Cities in Euro-Mediterranean Countries.* Zurich: Springer.

Carta, M. (2015), "Iper-strategie del riciclo: Cityforming © Protocol", in Carta, M., Lino, B., a cura di, *Urban Hyper-Metabolism.* Roma: Aracne Int.le.

Carta, M. (2016), "Augmented City is Where the Ideas have Sex: Urbanism as Connection", in Nava, C., ed., *The Laboratory_City: sustainable recycle and key enabling technologies.* Roma: Aracne Int.le.

Carta, M., Lino, B., a cura di (2015), *Urban Hyper-Metabolism.* Roma: Aracne Int.le.

Carta, M., Ronsivalle, D., a cura di (2015), *Territori interni. La pianificazione integrata per lo sviluppo circolare: metodologie, approcci, applicazioni per nuovi stili di vita.* Roma: Aracne Int.le.

Carta, M., Ronsivalle, D., eds. (2016) *The Fluid City Paradigm. Waterfront Regeneration as an Urban Renewal Strategy.* Cham (Zug, CH): Springer International Publishing AG.

Chakrabarti, V. (2013), *A Country of Cities. A Manifesto for an Urban America.* New York: Metropolis Books.

Ciorra, P., Marini, S., a cura di (2011), *Re-cycle. Strategie per l'architettura, la città e il pianeta.* Milano: Electa.

Crutzen, P.J., Stoermer, E.F. (2000), "The Anthropocene", *Global Change Newsletter,* 41, pp. 17-18.

Ellen MacArthur Foundation (2012), *Towards the Circular Economy: Economic and business rationale for an accelerated transition.* Chicago: EMF.

European Climate Foundation (2010) *Roadmap 2050. A practical guide to a prosperous, low-carbon Europe.* Den Haag: ECF.

European Commission-Regional Policy (2011), *Cities of Tomorrow. Challenges, Visions, Ways Forward.* Brussels: European Commission.

European Commission, Directorate-General for Research and Innovation (2012), *Global Europe 2050.* Luxembourg: Publications Office of the European Union.

Gasparrini, C. (2015), I*n the City. On the City.* Barcelona-Trento: ListLab. Goldsmith, S., Crawford, S. (2014), *The Responsive City: Engaging Communities Through Data-Smart Governance.* San Francisco: Jossey-Bass.

Hall, P. (2014), *Good Cities, Better Lives. How Europe Discovered the Lost Art of Urbanism.* London: Routledge.

Kaletsky, A. (2010), *Capitalism 4.0: The Birth of a New Economy in the Aftermath of Crisis.* New York: Perseus.

KPMG (2016), *Innovation through craft: opportunities for growth.* London: Kpmg.

Lino, B. (2013), *Periferie in trasform-azione. Riflessioni dai "margini" delle città.* Firenze: Alinea.

Marini, S., Rosselli, C. (2014), *Re-cycle Op_positions I, II.* Roma: Aracne.

Mehrotra, R., Vera, F., Mayoral, J. (2016), *Ephemeral Urbanism. Cities in constant flux.* Santiago: Ediciones ARQ.

Owen, D. (2009), *Green Metropolis, Why Living Smaller, Living Closer, and Driving Less Are the Keys to Sustainability.* New York: Riverhead Books.

Ratti, C. (2015), *Open Source Architecture.* New York: Thames & Hudson.

Ratti, C., Claudel, M. (2016), *The City of Tomorrow: Sensors, Networks, Hackers, and the Future of Urban Life.* New Heaven: Yale University Press.

Ricci, M. (2012), *New Paradigms.* Barcelona-Trento: ListLab.

Ricci M., Schroeder J., eds. (2015), *Towards a Pro-active Manifesto.* Roma: Aracne.

Rockström, J., Klum, M., eds. (2015), *Big World, Small Planet: Abundance within Planetary Boundaries.* New Heaven (CT): Yale University Press.

Rodin, J. (2014), *The Resilience Dividend: Being Strong in a World Where Things Go Wrong.* New York: PublicAffairs.

Ronsivalle, D. (2016), "The fluid city experience: an update", in Carta, M., Ronsivalle, D., eds., The Fluid City Paradigm. Waterfront Regeneration as an Urban Renewal Strategy. Cham (Zug, CH): Springer International Publishing AG.

Sijmons, D. (2014a), "Waking up in the Anthropocene", in Brugmans, G., Strien, J., eds., *IABR 2014. Urban by Nature*. Rotterdam: IABR.

Sijmons, D. (2014b), "The Urban Metabolism", in Brugmans, G., Strien, J., eds., *IABR 2014. Urban by Nature*. Rotterdam: IABR.

Swilling, M., Hajer, M. (2016), "The future of the city and the Next Economy", in Brugmans, G., van Dinteren, J., Hajer, M., eds., *IABR 2016. The Next Economy*. Rotterdam: IABR.

United Nations Environment Programme (2013), *City-Level Decoupling: urban resource flows and the governance of infrastructure transitions*. Paris: UNEP.

UN-Habitat (2016), *Urbanization and Development: Emerging Futures. World Cities Report 2016*. Nairobi: UN-Habitat.

1. The word Anthropocene was coined in the 1980s by Eugene Stoermer to indicate the geological epoch which began following the industrial revolution and in which the main causes of territorial, structural and climate changes originate from humankind and its activities. The word was then made popular in the early 21st century by Nobel Prize winner Paul J. Crutzen (Crutzen, Stoermer, 2000).
2. The operational challenges to proactively address the Anthropocene are described in Rockström, Klum (2015).
3. The planning challenge of a renewed alliance between humankind and nature, between urban settlement and natural system, was the key topic of the International Architecture Biennale in Rotterdam in 2014, whose emblematic title was "Urban by Nature". The guiding vision promoted by curator Dirk Sijmons is that "we are urban by nature" and that we must recognize that most of the processes surrounding us are a combination of natural and man-made forces acting at the same time, producing one of the most visible hybrid forms on the planet: the urban landscape (Brugmans, Strien, 2014).
4. Renewed focus on the active role of cities in the challenge of climate change has resulted in numerous studies and documents that confirm the need for cities, the predominant form of settlement on the planet, to be the new "ecological engines" of development (Owen, 2009). Some of the most interesting practices of cities that have implemented projects based on creativity, intelligence and resilience can be found in Hall (2013). See also UNEP (2013) and UN-Habitat (2016).
5. The *Circular Growth* movement aims to change the current linear system on which our industrial society is based, into a cyclical system, replacing the "produce, use and throw away" process with a more fertile one of "produce, use and reuse" (Ellen MacArthur Foundation, 2012). The principles of the circular economy raise the fundamental question of how the recycling of materials, semi-finished products, scraps, products at the end of the cycle of use and biomass could contribute to the growth of a more responsible and less erosive GDP, so that the production value would be maintained for longer through reuse and, where possible, *up-cycling*,

triggering a new cycle of sustainable prosperity that generates new services in a fertile combination of new products, lower environmental impact and the elimination of toxicity.
6. I describe paradigms and operational instruments of the emerging recycling urbanism in my text "Re-cycling Urbanism nell'era circolare", published in Carta, Lino (editor), 2015.
7. The plea for a recycling dividend is borrowed from the proposals developed by the Rockefeller Foundation for the worldwide program *100 Resilient Cities to incite the adoption of strategies and instruments to boost and extend urban resilience* (Rodin, 2014).
8. Not only good practices, but increasingly widespread effective protocols and performing processes are characterizing the urban policies of European cities such as Freiburg (described by Peter Hall as "the city that did it all"), Rotterdam, Copenhagen, Amsterdam, Barcelona, Lyon, Marseille and Nantes, or Turin and Faenza to mention a few exemplary cases in Italy.
9. The Re-cycle Manifesto was drawn up on the 21st September 2014 during the "Superelevata" workshop in Genoa as a collective contribution of experiences and proposals, later edited by Bocchi, Carta and Ricci to draft the final version published in Ricci, Schroeder (eds.), 2015.
10. The characteristics of the circular society and of the sharing economy are described in Bonomi, Masiero, Della Puppa (2016).
11. The Fab City is an urban model of a self-sufficient city that is locally productive and globally connected. The Fab City program was initiated by the IAAC in Barcelona, the Center for Bits and Atoms at MIT and the Fab Foundation. See the report *Fab City Whitepaper. Locally productive, globally connected self-sufficient cities*, edited by Tomas Diez in 2016.
12. The vision, paradigms and planning tools of a re-cyclical urbanism capable of guiding and designing more creative, intelligent and resilient cities to overcome the challenges of change have been examined in Carta (2014a). Further investigations of the characteristics of an urbanism based on planned recycling as a project option have been published in: Carta, M., "Re-imagine, Re-load, Re-cycle: New Urbanism for the City of Future", in Calcatinge, A. (ed.), *Critical Spaces. Contemporary Perspectives in Urban, Spatial and Landscape Studies*, Zurich, LIT, 2014; Carta, M., "Postfazione. Re-cycling Urbanism: orizzonti, paradigmi e strumenti", in Scavone, V. (editor), *Consumo di suolo. Un approccio multidisciplinare ad un tema trasversale*, Milan, FrancoAngeli, 2014.
13. The theoretical and conceptual principles, and the operational contents and practices of *Cityforming* have been described in Carta (2015) and brought over to this book in the chapter "The Cityforming Protocol: incremental and adaptive strategies".
14. In Ancient Greece, the *kykeon* was a psychotropic drink extracted from the ergot fungus, which enabled the out-of-body experiences linked to the Eleusinian Mysteries.

CULTURAL COMMONS
PARTICIPATORY GOVERNANCE OF CULTURAL HERITAGE

ANGELA ALESSANDRA BADAMI

Until the 1990s, Italian policy for cultural heritage, when compared to that of other European states, was characterized by a greater focus on safeguarding measures, accompanied by legislative instruments centered mainly on legal and administrative protection directives. While on one hand, the protective attitude of the restrictions preserved the integrity of much of Italy's cultural heritage, on the other, it too often confined it within a legal status of immutability that excluded it from transformation processes affecting evolving societies and territories. The failure to invest the cultural heritage in activities recognized by contemporary socio-economic processes as being useful has often resulted in the liability of the State and public administrations, contributing to the widespread abandonment and consequential degradation of these cultural assets. It would appear that the time has now come again to assess the "advantage and disadvantage of history for life"[1]. The cultural and environmental assets, in their capacity as resources — important resources of the *Bel Paese* as they characterize the historic identity of the Italian regions —, must be used productively and in a way that is compatible with their nature and conservation requirements. This will allow them to creatively take part in processes of cultural, social, and economic development, making explicit their role as power sources of a culturally based evolution. Italian policy regarding cultural heritage has been rerouted, from the last decade of the last century[2], more and more towards strengthening the necessary union between protection and promotion, introducing new categories of potential actions concerning the cultural assets, as well as "protection measures" and "conservation measures". The new "principles" for the promotion of cultural assets, introduced by the Cultural and Landscape Heritage Code (Italian Legislative Decree 42/2004), are given substance in new forms of authorized management that envisage the involvement of the private sector, cultural assistance services of various nature, promotion of studies and research in collaboration with universities and research centers, dissemination of knowledge through new media, cultural activities focused on the production of new cultural heritage, the definition of landscape quality objectives, the reclamation of neglected landscapes, etc. With an approach that is no longer just repressive, but proactive, the Code suggests new categories of action regarding cultural heritage. We need, therefore, to redirect cultural assets policies so that the reclaimed, promoted, perceived, and experienced heritage, reintroduced into its current use, becomes a vehicle for cultural evolution, improved quality of life, social progress, and civil conquest. We need to assign a new dimension to cultural policies, which are not limited to the role of "custodians", but are able to reactivate disrupted or completed cycles by inserting the heritage into active development processes by means of a resemanti-

Thanks to the mobilization of the inhabitants of the La Chapelle district (Paris, 18th arrondissement), who formed the CEPA collective, the *Halle Pajol* and the *Halle des Messageries* were salvaged (in a project by Jourda Architectes) and restored to the community, complete with services requested by the residents: a library, a gym, a youth hostel, a hall for performances and assemblies, a branch of IUT Paris Diderot, a middle school, business venues (concept stores, American fast food, coffee shops, bars, and restaurants), a fablab, the Rosa Luxemburg garden, and a garden sheltered by a 3,500 square-meter photovoltaic roof. In 2013, the district received the eco-district award from the Ministry of Ecology, Sustainable Development, and Energy.

Mercat del Ninot (Barcelona), a new model of urban market promoted by the IMMB, refurbished in 2009 with sales counters on the ground floor, a supermarket on the floor below, next-generation services, and the open-kitchen restaurant El Ninot Cuina, with a menu dedicated to revised traditional Catalan dishes. In the renovated markets, to complete the product range and ensure the economic sustainability of the traditional supplies, supermarkets have been included to supply packaged products (the supermarkets have the opportunity to distribute in the city's major trade centers and reciprocate with services and incentives to maintain the historic markets).

cizing operation. As Malraux warns, *"que nous importe l'identité de l'Homme au Casque, de l'Homme au Gant? Ils s'appellent Rembrandt et Titien"*[3]. Just as a painting or sculpture undergoes metamorphosis by ceasing to be the portrait of someone and becoming a work of art, likewise, the heritage features cease to have their useful value and become the metaphor of eternal cultural values.

Metamorphosis, as rebirth in a new form, modernizes the values of the heritage in a planning dimension that is educated and conscious of the tangible and intangible evidence of the past as being values of civilization. The traditional keywords of cultural policies centred on protection will be replaced by a "modern cult of monuments"[4] laid down on the chains of "conserve — pass on — increase the value of the heritage"; "protect — enhance — promote its use"; "reclaim — redevelop — reuse" to ensure their social usage.

The effective governance of heritage, however, requires deep social involvement for shared participation in the protection and promotion actions. Responsibility is transferred to local communities, which also means rethinking the operational dimension of territorial governance instruments to strengthen the local dimension and democratic participation in making planning choices, promoting appreciation, appropriating the values of

the cultural heritage, and collectively taking part in their management.

The Council of Europe Framework Convention on the Value of Cultural Heritage for Society (Faro Convention[5]) developed a more extended definition of cultural heritage: "culture heritage comprises a set of resources inherited from the past which some people identify, regardless of their ownership, as a reflection and expression of their continuously evolving values, beliefs, knowledge, and traditions. This includes all aspects of the environment arising from the interaction between humankind and the environment over time" (Faro Conv., Article 2a).

The approach is no longer centered on the object of protection but is addressed to the subject that identifies it as such, recognizing in it the values of his/her own cultural identity. A new subject — the heritage community — is thus identified, which establishes a protection project: "a heritage community is made up of people who attribute value to some specific aspects of the cultural heritage that they would like to uphold and pass on to future generations, within the framework of public action" (Faro Con., Article 2b). Cultural heritage is, therefore, a metaphor for the harbored values that we wish to pass on to future generations, with a view not just to protect, but also enrich them and create

The Marseille History Museum, created as a result of archaeological finds discovered during excavations for the building of the Centre Bourse in the historic center, is built inside the shopping centre and traces the historical stages of its evolution.

new heritage that is representative of societies in the making[6]. Among the cases of bottom-up mobilization in defense of heritage pinpointed as identity-forming for a community, or representative of the history of a place or part of the city, was the formation in 2002 of the CEPA collective (Coordination Espace Pajol). The collective was founded by inhabitants, local associations, and artists and endorsed by professional volunteers including architects, urban planners, landscape designers, and sociologists to defend a railway wasteland in the 18th arrondissement of Paris.

The setting, strongly characterized by abandoned railway infrastructure in a neighbourhood with high-density public housing and strong social problems (unemployment, school dropouts, immigration, drug addiction, and crime), was turned from an emergency scenario into the most important opportunity area in the neighborhood, thanks to cooperation between the institutions, associations, inhabitants, and families.

In opposition to the municipal administration plan to demolish the railway facilities and create more public housing, the inhabitants of the neighbourhood set up the CEPA collective, whose mission was to support, as a precondition to any new project for the area, the maintenance and reuse of the abandoned facilities to create equipment, spaces, and community services from a perspective of environmentally sustainable development.

For more than 10 years, from 2002 to 2013, an unprecedented negotiation process saw the collaboration of different institutional players (administration, public operators, architects, and landscape designers) with civil society (residents, associations, collectives, and district councils) to develop the urban project that saw the participation of around 200 people between the ages of 12 and 82.

At the end of this process, the former railway buildings were salvaged to accommodate facilities and services, including a youth hostel, a library, businesses, a middle school, a university campus, a gym with adjoining career guidance center for young people, an office building housing a business center, and the largest urban solar plant in France, guaranteeing the complex a sustainable energy supply. Local administrations have also implemented policies for the conservation and promotion of heritage recognized as identity-forming and vital for the community. This is the case of the Barcelona City Council, which established an autonomous office for the management and direct administration of historic markets, the IMMB (*Institut Municipal de Mercats de Barcelona*) in 1991. The IMMB also provides for the modernization of markets by improving infrastructure and personal services, the upgrade of product ranges based on new consumer demands, and the enactment of policies for the promotion of markets as centers of social cohesion and cultural development.

The Jesuits' College (Alcamo, TP) is a monumental complex in the historic center of the city. It was repurposed in 2103 as the Museum of Contemporary Art and headquarters of Creative LAB, an integrated system of cultural services supporting activities related to contemporary artistic production, craft production, visual-tactile arts, museum education, and contemporary architecture, by means of cultural projects focused on the juxtaposition of contemporary art and the identity of the area.

The project "Creative LAB Alcamo. A creative center at the former Jesuits' College of Alcamo as a cultural pole of reference for the territory", ERDF OP Sicily 2007/13, Priority Axis III, Operational Objective 3.1.3, Line of action 3; head of research A. Badami.

Markets are not only powerful driving forces of the urban economy as places of local trade, employment, and entrepreneurship but play an important role in social integration and cultural promotion, which contributes to urban regeneration processes. Over the past 10 years, 20 markets in Barcelona have been refurbished, with an investment of over 150 million euros. Among the most successful examples is the Santa Caterina Market in the historic centre, restored by Miralles and Tagliabue, which, with an original pop composition, created using multicoloured tiles on the "fifth facade", evokes the colours of the fruit and vegetables sold in the market and has today become an icon of the city's contemporary urban landscape. Another example of urban regeneration in Barcelona started from the Mercat del Born, housed in an iron and glass building dating back to the late 1800s. In 2013, its commercial function having died out, it was given new life in a project by Enric Sòria and Rafael de Càceres as the Born Cultural Center. This exhibition center, complete with bar and bookshop, focuses on the promotion of the eighteenth-century archaeological finds which resurfaced during its refurbishment, on divulgation of the historic events related to the siege of Barcelona in 1714, and on the promotion of cultural events.

To complete the product range and ensure the economic sustainability of the traditional supplies, supermarkets have also been integrated into the renovated markets to supply packaged products (the supermarkets have the opportunity to distribute in the city's major trade centers and reciprocate with services and incentives to maintain the historic markets). An example is El Ninot Market, which was refurbished in 2009 and represents the new model of urban market promoted by the IMMB, supplying next-generation services.

Even medium-sized towns such as Alcamo (TP, with a population of approximately 45,000) are now heading in the direction of an active policy for cultural assets. From the turn of the century, Alcamo has been committed to an economic and cultural revamp of the city by means of redevelopment and repurposing projects conceived from the area's historic, architectural, urban planning, and landscape heritage. The regeneration principle has been based on a specific desire to protect the historical identity by reaffirming it through innovative interpretations capable of responding to the new demands of contemporary society. A reinterpretation of the city, starting both from the needs of its inhabitants and anticipating new demands, with the introduction of functions capable of repositioning the city's rank in a wider supra-local context. On the strength of a historic centre that is still perfectly recognizable and largely intact but, like many other centers, subject to residential and, above all, commercial abandonment, the Municipality has invested in urban attractiveness actions by improving the quality of public spaces, creating pedestrian and restricted traffic areas, and introducing new functions within the historic fabric, capable of reactivating the disrupted cycles of economic productivity and introducing new cultural activities. A catalyst in the urban regeneration process was the European project Creative LAB (2010-2016)[7], arising from a synergy between the Municipality, the Department of Architecture of the University of Palermo, and cooperatives representing the local business community. The project encouraged the introduction of a new innovative function within one of the architectural heritage sites most important to the city's history. The monumental building of the former Jesuits' College, which opens onto the main square in the historic center, has inaugurated a new Museum of Contemporary Art, whose collection is sourced from within the territory. In this way, the former Jesuits' College has become the testing ground for a new museum concept based on local identity.

To begin the process of building the new collection of artworks, the project provided for the involvement of prominent and emerging artists, who created site-specific artworks for Alcamo in Alcamo, working in contact amongst themselves and, above all, with the public, providing the chance to enjoy the artistic products, not only upon their completion, but throughout the course of their conception and creation.

The Creative LAB project also acted from urban redevelopment and territorial development support devices for the purpose of interpreting, creatively promoting, and effectively communicating the identity of the territory through an integrated system of cultural services.

The process saw the active involvement of both cooperatives of local entrepreneurs, for the promotion of food production, winemaking, and crafts of the tradition of Alcamo, and the population, through the promotion of cultural activities in which different age groups took part: primary school children with museum education workshops, young architects and architecture students with design workshops involving the city, and elderly women of Alcamo — depositories of the ancient embroidery traditions applied to the production of contemporary artworks.

The fortuitous discovery of archaeological remains dur ing upgrading operations of historic centers also becomes an opportunity for their reinterpretation from an urban regeneration viewpoint: by mishap, the ar t i fact undergoes metamorphosis from a residue of time to a mold for the cultural rebirth of the city's historical memory.

A landmark case was the Centre Bourse in Marseille, the first large shopping center built within the historic center of the city in the 1970s. During the building of the project, which included the creation of underground parking lots and new architectural facilities including residential towers and office buildings, port structures of the original Greek settlement were unearthed, raising the issue of the choice between conservation and transformation.

The Centre Bourse case in Marseille was fundamental in French law for defining options in the event of the chance discovery of archaeological finds in areas undergoing urban transformation, giving rise to the intervention categories "rescue archaeology" and, subsequently, "preventive archaeology".

Awareness of the importance of the discovery convinced administrators and investors of the need to modify the project and of the opportunity to create a museum to exhibit the artifacts. The new project built an exemplary case of virtuous integration between different needs, modified so as to accommodate both the archaeological area of the immovable artifacts to be conserved on site and the rediscovered archaeological assets that found a space within the shopping center, enriching it with an unprecedented cultural function.

The added value of the Marseille History Museum consists of a new interpretation of space and time dedicated to cultural experiences: being located in a shopping centre, the museum, a *"confrontation de métamorphoses [...] d'une recréation de l'univers qui donne la plus haute idée de l'homme"*[8], is contained within one of the most visited places in the city (with an average of 7 million visitors per year) and proposes the enjoyment of cultural assets as one of the many moments of everyday life, bringing the community closer to its historic heritage.

1. Nietzsche, F., *Vom Nutzen und Nachteil der Historie für das Leben*, Leipzig, 1874. In the second of the four *Untimely Meditations*, Nietzsche insists on the need to replace historiographic hypertrophy, a trend of late 19th-century historical thinking, a history-life tropism, or rather, a virtuous transfer of nourishment that history must provide to life, in which the historical sense consists of transforming past history into present history.
2. See, specifically, Italian Legislative Decree 112/98.
3. "What does the identity of the *Man with the helmet* or the *Man with a glove* matter to us? Their names are Rembrandt and Titian", Malraux, A., *Le Musée Imaginaire*, Lausanne, Albert Skira, 1947. The museum imposes a new relationship with the artwork, repositioning it on a different level than its original function and causing a semantic metamorphosis of its meaning.
4. Riegl, A., *Der moderne Denkmalkultus: Sein Wesen und seine entstehung*, Vienna, 1903. Recognition of the cultural asset (of the monument, in Riegl) occurs in accordance with the values shared by a certain society and attributed to certain elements of the past; the conservation of their original integrity or their transformation for a current use depends on the relationship with the perception of the collective identity and is a determining factor of social change.
5. *Framework Convention on the Value of Cultural Heritage for Society* adopted by the Committee of Ministers of the Council of Europe on the 13th October 2005 and opened for signing by the Member States in Faro (Portugal).
6. Badami, A., *Metamorfosi urbane*, Florence, Alinea, 2012. The planning application of cultural heritage to urban metamorphosis is the goal of a quest for re-signification, more than a just repurposing, of the inheritance of the past in a current scenario and in the projection to the future of the ways in which we experience our environment.
7. The project *Creative LAB Alcamo. A creative center at the former Jesuits' College of Alcamo as a cultural pole of reference for the territory*, financed with funds from the ERDF OP Sicily 2007/13, Priority Axis III, Operational Objective 3.1.3, Line of action 3 – "Development of cultural services to the territory and to artistic and craft production (documentation, communication, and promotion) working in the field of art and contemporary architecture"; head of research A. Badami.
8. Malraux A., *Le Musée Imaginaire,* Lausanne, Albert Skira, 1947.

METROPOLITAN PERSPECTIVES AND NEW LIFECYCLES FOR THE OUTSKIRTS

BARBARA LINO

RE-CYCLICAL URBANISM

A taxonomic gap: the liminal identity of the outskirts and the suburban revolution

In 1961, Lewis Mumford described the American outskirts as "a multitude of uniform, unidentifiable houses, lined up inflexibly, at uniform distances, on uniform roads, in a treeless communal waste, inhabited by people of the same class, the same income, the same age group, witnessing the same television performances, eating the same tasteless prefabricated foods, from the same freezers, conforming in every outward and inward respect to a common mould" (Mumford, 1961, 486).

The dull image of unidentifiable houses, at uniform distances on uniform roads, single-class social groups, and standardized lifestyles describes a very different suburban scenario from that of Europe during the same years and even more different when compared to the contemporary one. Now, the most macroscopic outcomes of the social and spatial trajectories of transformation are evident in the narratives dominating the media and political arenas, which describe the outskirts as problem spaces, where issues of safety and social inequality are intensified.

In the periodic uprisings of Parisian *banlieues* and the episodes of violence, intolerance, and complicated civil coexistence in the outskirts of Marseille, Brussels, Munich, and the many districts of Rome, Milan or other Italian cities, social inequalities are establishing themselves as a "new urban issue" (Secchi, 2013, 59). They remind us of the city's role as a selection and separation machine for integration or social exclusion, in which the temporal nature and ways of using the urban space by various social groups are not only articulated by the effects of social and economic policies, but also by the stratification of infrastructural and urban planning choices. "The city has always been a machine regulating idiorhythms: using physical, spatial, legal, and institutional devices, it has constantly turned the various idiorhymths into articulate and often very complex spatial, economic, and social relations" (Secchi, 2013, IX).

Separated by infrastructure belts, the fences of industrial areas, or large unused green spaces, the outskirts carry out their own daily activities and social rhythms among unsold property, large business districts, overspecialized enclaves of consumption and leisure time, outlets, factories, service stations, and playgrounds, separated by in-between spaces, such as clearings, car parks, debris areas on the fringes of infrastructure, viaducts, and interchanges.

Investigating the suburbanization phenomenon at a global level in "Suburban Constellations" (2013), Roger Keil has attempted to define what is global in a phenomenon that is one of the most "shared" experiences on the planet and which occurs "globally", but is structured "locally" as a function of specific consumer choices, the real estate market, production, and the distribution of goods. Specifically, according to Keil, three interrelated components should be governed to guide the way outskirts form: the land market; the governance dimension, where the ability of public action to regulate the market is crucial in counteracting forms of spatial and social segregation; and infrastructure, which has a clear consequence on the spatial structure of the territory. Keil's most interesting theoretical contribution, however, lies in the formulation of a new urban theory. By shifting the focus from a taxonomic and defining problem to the building of a new theory, Keil invokes the "urban revolution" that Lefebvre spoke of in the 1970s, and talks about a "suburban revolution", recognizing in suburban settings the creative potential traditionally attributed to more central areas, which instead emerge exponentially in the activities and different lifestyles that occur there.

Overturning a dominant view, which identifies in the more central areas a level of creativity capable of producing innovation, Keil highlights the rapid change that the social "factory" of the outskirts is undergoing and draws attention to the huge potential for social innovation contained in the various lifestyles that suburban settings produce as innovation hot spots.

Being the product and, at the same time, "waste" of a haphazard transformation "model", urban outskirts are muscling in as landscapes laden with ambiguity and problems, but also possibilities and latency at the same time. They are liminal landscapes (Turner, 1969), on one hand due to the conflictual conditions generated by the market and by the formal and informal stakeholders pushing for transformation; on the other, due to the sense of indeterminacy of border spaces and, at the same time, their potential and suspension between the past and future. They are spaces of destabilization and transformation, in which micro and macro forces collide, driven by order and disorder; formal pushes for transformation resulting from planning processes and informal pushes resulting from the new routines and lifestyles of the communities that inhabit them.

Metropolitan cities and the new "Copernican revolution"

The updated governance model of the territorial phenomena being experienced as much in various European urban contexts as nationally, within the scope of defining new metropolitan cities, is radically changing the governance system at a metropolitan scale and is subjecting the outskirts to significant further transformative tension, with repercussions on spatial and functional relationships, especially between suburban areas of the city core and the municipalities of the first belt. As Copernicus placed the Sun at the center of the universe and not the Earth, likewise the future action proposed by new metropolitan cities places the suburban areas at the center of a new functional and relational system, overturning their traditional condition of physical marginality.

Extensive and varied literature has unhinged the established idea of urbanized space (Dematteis, 1988 and 2005; Lanzani 1991), altered the terms of the urban issue (Secchi, 2010), and interpreted new post-metropolitan settlement forms (Balducci, 2015; Soja, 2011). Beyond the various positions, the emerging territory model facing metropolitan cities is characterized by very complex phenomena already in place, which implicate overriding the image of a city traditionally described as a compact urban structure that develops around a center and thins out (in density, functions, and urban values) along centre-outskirts trajectories. The spatial dynamics in place are actually the result of a combination of border crossing by the central city into other municipal areas, true conurbation between adjacent centers, and phenomena characterized by variable geometry.

The features most deeply affecting the disarticulation of the organizational and socio-spatial forms by unhinging the urban operating model as we have traditionally known it are social and economic fragmentation, the accelerated movement of people, goods, and information, and the building of new networks (Balducci, 2015).

At a metropolitan scale, polycentrism replaces traditional monocentric and polarized structures characterized by a single large dominant centre with reticular structures, in which the conurbation trends are accompanied by infrastructural and functional specialization policies based on the self-organizational capacity of the local communities. It is the metaphor of the "super-organism" city, "that is, a set of individuals organized into cohesive societies, where everyone has a clear and defined role and — like the components of a perfect mechanism — moves in unison, contributing in a differential and incremental way to the pursuit of the organism's development" (Carta, 2013, p. 248). At a national level, legislative innovations regarding the reform of metropolitan cities introduced by the Delrio Law[1] have opened a theoretical and political context that calls for, on one hand, general rethinking of the administrative and governance system and testing of a decision-making system that is as participatory as possible and capable of engaging the multiplicity of the territory's stakeholders, and, on the other, a profound cultural, social, and disciplinary challenge aimed at shaping new tools to respond to the spatial dynamics of territorialisation and cross-scale urban phenomena affecting new metropolitan cities.

Omitting the extensive debate underway regarding both the political dimension, relating to the formation and operation of the metropolitan Government, and the administrative dimension, on the suitability of the border configuration of the metropolitan city which, by law, includes the municipalities of the former province of the same name; it is good to note how the complex future action of the metropolitan city is not facing new phenomena, nor completely new administrative boundaries (the phenomena involved are already underway and the administrative boundaries coincide with the previous borders of the province) but, rather, requires renewed action instruments for new visions: the instruments involved (strategic planning, territorial planning and coordination of infrastructure, environmental policies and services) must be able to unhinge the dependence of gravitational centres on the city core and define general guidelines for the structural and strategic layout based on overall rethinking of the territorial imbalances, counteracting deconcentration phenomena, reorganizing the mobility system, counter-balancing dispersive phenomena, and differentiation and promotion of local contexts (Lino, 2013).

What are the roles?
Centers, joints, filters

The delicate transition caused by the emergence of metropolitan cities is radically changing the role that suburban areas located on the fringes of city cores can take on.

From a broader perspective, these areas stand to play a key role in building a metropolitan territorial agenda, as a result of new spatial centrality and their potential roles as toothing joints between neighboring territories, places for new social living activities, and rur-urban filter areas.

The role of the outskirts of the city core is that of a "new center". The decentralization process underway in the main large cities and the demographic decline caused by the population abandoning central areas to settle in the municipalities of the first belt in search of a more accessible housing market, is accompanied by commuter gravitation of city users who travel to the large centers on a daily basis, using private vehicles or, in the best cases, public transport. Commuters cross the suburban areas to reach business districts, universities, hospitals, as well as places of leisure and culture (museums, restaurants, nightclubs, etc.). The suburban areas are crossed by commuter flows and take on a new aspect of centrality in relation to them. Decentralization strategies, on one hand, and policies of integrated management of collective mobility services on the other — in terms of integration between urban and extra-urban mobility and fare integration for example — can play a crucial role in facilitating settlement forms based on a better quality of life and more sustainable mobility models.

The role of the outskirts of the city core is that of "new joints". According to a new spatial centrality, the outskirts provide privileged areas for the decentralization of major services: new territorial authorities will need to be able to coordinate themselves at the various levels, as well as on issues such as the distribution of infrastructure, mobility and environmental policies, and the identification of poles and joining areas where services of common interest can be localized. The marginal position of the municipal territory gives suburban areas greater potential for an easier convergence of localizing interests between neighboring subjects/ municipalities. The strengthening of forms of cooperation, sharing, and coordination and the activation of compensation mechanisms for territorial equalization could accompany the transition from a hierarchical, traditionally monocentric model, to a poly-centric and reticular layout. The role of the outskirts of the city core is that of "workshops for new social living practices". The growing problems of polarization of social inequality and of the "new urban issue" (Secchi, 2013, IX) require us to implement strategies of social cohesion and place-based initiatives aimed at uniting communities around shared projects. The outskirts provide privileged and, at the same time, priority ground, not just for the containment of commuting and revenue — key factors in the process of urbanization — but also as a location for public housing and for support to policies for the home and forms of co-production and co-management that express a new protagonism, a renewed request for social cohesion, and a greater awareness of the right to the city.

The role of the outskirts of the city core is that of a "rur-urban filter". Being areas of rur-urban transition, the outskirts are often places in which rural and urban can no longer be dichotomous elements, but terms of a strategic alliance: forms of innovative and multipurpose agriculture and productivity of the agricultural space are strategic elements for the generation of new economies and ways of living.

Variable geometry strategies. From the XL scale to forms of local resilience

The perspectives outlining the new roles and potential identities of the outskirts can contribute to defining a new urban agenda promoted by the metropolitan city as a set of actions, tactics, projects, and, above all, shared visions and strategies of variable geometry, aimed at rebalancing the weights of settlements and at facing the challenges of urban quality, social cohesion, and livability. In an article published in Limes magazine in May 2016, Luca Molinari identifies three scales of transformation of the outskirts: the "XL" (extra large) scale, characterized by a resort to architectural mega-structures, typical of the 1960s, as a way of tackling the migratory pressure felt in all major Western metropolises; the "M" (*medium*) scale, linked to good urban practices managed by public administrations; and, finally, the "S" (*small*) scale, identified as potentially the most innovative intervention scale, in which action is taken by the cities' micro-communities, who work together to reshape abandoned suburban areas. Distorting Molinari's "XL scale", the extra large view of the outskirts recalls the metropolitan dimension, which provides a privileged perspective for intervention on the center-outskirts dynamics, identifying action fronts shared between neighboring areas and broadening the view of the urban community to territories in which the inhabitants of the metropolitan area carry out their daily lives. Working in this direction are several strategic planning experiences in Barcelona, Lyon, Munich, and Turin, with the activation of agencies that manage common metropolitan services, capable of influencing the territorial metabolism, for example by controlling the cycles of waste, energy, and mobility.

On the intermediate "M" scale, on the other hand, actions take place in the grooves of integrated place-based public policies for urban regeneration. After an intense season of complex planning, the "National Plan for the Social and Cultural Requalification of Degraded Urban Areas", announced in October 2015, the results of which cannot yet be assessed, awards advanced redevelopment projects for degraded urban areas, defined according to a summary score based on ISTAT data and statistical indicators, such as the unemployment rate, employment rate, rate of youth concentration, and level of schooling.

The closest range, the "S" (small) scale, includes practices of spatial and functional micro-densification which, starting from the recycling of disused or underused spaces, act on alternative ways of modifying the space and new ways of managing common resources.

The fixed capital of cessation, sedimented on the territory as a result of the change in economic and urban cycles, becomes a valuable resource to support new social practices and new forms of production and use, such as the sharing economy and new manufacturing. From this perspective, abandoned public properties become enabling platforms for collective action, spatial devices in which spatial innovation can be channeled. In practice, the need arises to build overall views capable of overcoming the shattering of initiatives and to build a framework within which to guide processes, recognize, enable, and involve the players who bring innovation.

In the re-balance between emerging social energies and public policy, experiences such as those of Bologna (Collaboration Agreements) and Milan (incubators in the suburbs and the Council of the suburbs) are encouraging and supporting different forms of management of public goods in the outskirts.

One device that is currently being tested, whose huge potential is easy to imagine, are "collaboration agreements" — an instrument envisaged by the "Regulation on Collaboration Between Citizens and the City for the Care and Regeneration of Urban Commons"[2] to shape collaboration between municipal or district administrations and active citizens. The agreements, which are the instrument by means of which the municipality and citizens work together to carry out projects to care for and regenerate common assets (Article 8), aim to promote social innovation (Article 7), urban creativity (Article 8), and digital innovation (Article 9).

The first collaboration agreement governing the accord between citizens and administration for the care of and regeneration of urban commons was signed in September 2014 in Bologna, in the San Donato district, by a group of associations and individual citizens forming the Graf San Donato committee, and the Municipality of Bologna. The purpose of the collaboration regulated by the agreement is the implementation of co-designed interventions for the care and management of certain spaces in the district. These include the Piazza Spadolini area and the Bentivogli e Vittime di Marcinelle gardens, in which stands a publically-owned property, the former registry office, assigned to the committee for management at no charge and for which the municipality will bear the utility expenses for the first year. The activities envisaged by the agreement include events open to artistic, cultural, educational, historical, and civic content and self-funding initiatives. Together with Bologna, other cities (Siena, Ivrea, L'Aquila and Bari) are also working to draft guidelines for the care and regeneration of urban commons and to give a concrete structure to the new relationship emerging between citizens and administration, in a less and less authoritative, and more shared form. Another experience that combines the capitalization of unused public assets and public support in the form of urban reactivation for social and entrepreneurial innovation is being promoted in certain districts of the outskirts of Milan. Becoming part, together with Rome, of the 100 Resilient Cities international network — a project supported by the Rockefeller Foundation to help cities become more resilient in connection with current social, economic, and environmental challenges — Milan has stated its intention to work towards an urban redevelopment strategy, starting from the outskirts, to pursue its goal of resilience and quality development, understood as ability to learn, flexibility, integration between players, and adaptation. In order to promote urban development and community welfare in four suburban areas, the Municipality of Milan, with the collaboration of associations, has launched the creation of four business incubators: Fabriq, a social innovation incubator in Quarto Oggiaro; an incubator of creative enterprises (fashion, design, multimedia production) in the Tortona-ex Ansaldo area; an incubator specializing in the themes of the smart city and new technologies with an ICT and green economy vocation in Bovisa, where the Politecnico incubator already has a campus; and finally, an incubator of lightweight enterprises and coworking for professionals in the Palmanova/ via Bottego area. In Quarto Oggiaro, where Fondazione Welfare is already based, the incubator has arisen in a refurbished space within the scope of the Urban Community Initiative Program. Its purpose is to support entrepreneurship with social value, such as third sector enterprises, non-profit organizations, and community services. The incubator provides services to new or established non-profit entrepreneurial businesses at subsidized rates, as well as workspaces, sharing areas, mentoring, development support, administrative-management-taxation advice, communication activities, educational seminars, and meetings between potential social entrepreneurs. Also dealing with sensitivity at a micro scale is the much criticized "patching" of the outskirts desired by Renzo Piano and his work group G124, made up of young architects who, thanks to the salary of the senator for life, devote themselves to the urban outskirts, identified as "the city of the future" and "future of the city". The value of "patching" should be sought in the ability to evoke, in a context in which the lack of exogenous resources is compounded by the crisis, the minimal logic of repair and intervention devices such as self-construction, lightweight construction sites, and collaborative forms of managing resources and spaces. These projects do not radically transform the settings, but they do input operations that work on the existing and with the existing, using human and physical materials.

Finally, "Taking Care - Designing for the Common Good", an exhibition curated by the TAMassociati team for the Italian Pavilion at the 15th International Architecture Exhibition of the Venice Biennale, which spawned, more recently, the first civic crowdfunding project for the Italian outskirts, is an additional reflection focusing on the close scale and on the collaborative paradigm as a style of action for marginal and outlying settings.

The devices and strategies defined on the various scales "XL", "M", and "S" become fields within which to test different styles of action, but, whatever the instruments involved, the new reticular metropolitan dimension is certain, and therefore the directives will need to be multi-scale and of variable geometry and, in pursuing a shared and participatory vision, will need to implement multi-level policies, achievable pilot projects, and agreements founded on the use of more or less formalized elements, such as pacts, networks, and local coalitions.

Bibliography

Balducci, A. (2015), "Le trasformazioni post-metropolitane e il modificarsi del legame tra spazio, forme dell'urbano e confini amministrativi", in Lodigiani, R., a cura di, *Milano 2015 Rapporto sulla città. La città metropolitana sfide, contraddizioni*. Milano: Ambrosianeum Fondazione Culturale, FrancoAngeli, pp. 41-54.

Carta, M. (2013), *Reimagining Urbanism. Città creative, intelligenti ed ecologiche per i tempi che cambiano*. Barcelona-Trento: ListLab.

Dematteis, G. (1988), "La scomposizione metropolitana", in Mazza G., a cura di, *XVII Triennale, partecipazioni internazionali*. Milano: Electa.

Dematteis, G. (2005), *La citta nell'era della conoscenza: un sistema territoriale irragionevole*. Pisa: Irme.

Keil, R., ed., (2013), *Suburban Constellations: Governance, Land and Infrastructure in the 21st Century*. Berlin: Jovis.

Lanzani, A. (1991), *Il territorio al plurale*. Milano: FrancoAngeli.

Lefebvre, E. (1970), *La Révolution urbaine*. Paris: Gallimard.

Lino, B. (2013), *Periferie in trasform-azione. Riflessioni dai "margini" delle città*. Firenze: Alinea.

Mumford, L. (1961), *The City in History: Its Origins, Its Transformations, and Its Prospects*. New York: Harcourt, Brace and World, Inc..

Molinari, L. (2016), "La periferia dopo la periferia", *Limes - Indagine sulle periferie*, n. 4, pp.309-323.

Secchi, B. (2010), "A new urban question", *Territorio*, n. 53, pp. 8-18.

Secchi, B. (2013), *La città dei ricchi e la città dei poveri*. Roma-Bari: Laterza.

Soja, E. (2011), "Regional Urbanization and the End of the Metropolitan Era", in Bridge, G., Watson, S., eds., *The New Blackwell Companion to the City*. New York: John Wiley & Sons, pp. 679-689. Turner, V. (1969), *The Ritual Process*. Chicago: Aldine.

1. Italian Law no. 56 of 7th April 2014 "Provisions regarding metropolitan cities, provinces, and the union and fusions of municipalities".

2. The Regulation, approved on 19th May 2014 by the Municipal Council of Bologna, is the result of the project "Cities as Common Assets", carried out thanks to a partnership between the Municipality of Bologna, the Fondazione del Monte di Bologna and Ravenna for economic support, the Centro Antartide, and Labsus-Laboratorio for the scientific direction of the project.

BREAKING THE SIEGE

FROM THE PALEO- TO THE NEO-ANTHROPOCENE

DANIELE RONSIVALLE

Crutzen's view[1] regarding the geological significance of the actions taken by humankind is well-established and accepted by many in the field of natural sciences and sciences studying the transformation induced by the presence of humankind. Moreover, even the recycling approach[2] itself aims to limit the subtractive and reductive transformation action that humankind exercises on the Earth. It is basically a view centered on the geological crisis and other crises induced by humankind.

Since the MAXXI exhibition curated by Sara Marini and Pippo Ciorra[3], however, every time that the problem arises of defining what recycling is and what rules oversee it, a state of uncertainty is substantiated — very similar to that created during a siege. The difference is that those dealing with recycling are both the besieger and the besieged, as the decision-making process that ought to be activated to limit consumption of the Earth's scarce resources; including land first and foremost, cannot find an actionable way out of an evident deadlock condition. However, one can get out of a besieged city[4] as a winner in due ways:

- by using skillful tactics to make the besieger believe that the siege could be long and arduous due to the plentiful supplies accumulated in the city (the sheep tactic of the Thracians);
- by attacking the besieger front on, even at the cost of using the very walls of the city as projectiles (defense to the bitter end).

Or, one can escape from a besieged city by night from the opposite side, hoping the enemy is paying excess attention to just one attack front. Or, again, one may risk being the victim of psychological stress from the siege and begin a long phase of crisis that could give rise to the extreme situations of cannibalism and coprophagia and, obviously, to unconditional surrender.

The first metaphor suggests a "bulletproof" plan conceived against speculators, and against all those who lay siege to the land resource with whom urbanism refuses to converse: the land resource is still present, perhaps in different forms from decades past, and is conserved to avoid new extensive and indistinct speculation conditions, but we pretend that land is abundant and that the city's government thus has a large capacity for negotiation.

The second metaphor is the total closure of regulatory planning against property speculation, but both urbanized and agricultural unused land easily loses its value when wielded in an attempt at extreme defense.

If we imagine a refusal to converse with the stakeholders, it is possible to escape from the siege, but it will be difficult to achieve lasting peace. The last inauspicious chance is given by the heartfelt defense of quality, history, and the landscape by those who, locked within the enclosure of protection, no longer see that outside of the siege, there is still a lot to be done to rebuild the patterns and qualities of the landscapes. Instead, they gnaw at each other while crookery and revenue thrives outside of the protective enclosure.

Metaphors aside, the condition of those testing instruments for the development of new life cycles for the city, landscapes, and infrastructure is that they often remain enclosed within behavioral, linguistic, and lexical frameworks that do not allow them to move beyond the starting conditions from which their work begins.

The following are several actionable proposals for the victorious resolution of the siege.

Contingency in the crisis condition leads us to reflect on the fact that, after the crisis, the world will never be the same again and, therefore, by extension, it is a mistake to think that the instruments, approaches and working procedures can be identical to those of the past.

Let's try to understand why.

At the dawning of urban civilization, the articulation into social classes and the specialization of labour were defined. The time freed up for superior activities (science, literature, art, etc.) for each individual in relation to their specific occupations gradually increased and the city became enlivened with a collective intelligence. This activated processes of urban development, causing the progressive urbanization of the population and the definition of life cycles ranging from the production of chemical energy (food, agricultural production, extraction of raw materials, etc.) in the countryside, to the transformation of intellectual energy (artifacts, liberal arts, politics, etc.) in the cities. Thanks to the exchange between photosynthetic chemical energy and intellectual energy, a single life cycle was developed, which was able to counteract the irreversible force of heat energy degradation defined by the Second Law of Thermodynamics. The current crisis condition[5] — about which, moreover, we hear less and less, as through wishing to distance ourselves from the problem without solving it — can be studied from various points of view:
- Is it just a financial problem?
- Is it just capitalism now devoid of its sources of liquidity supply (the war as an anti-cyclical condition and the State as bestower and redistributor of wealth)?
- Is it just an ecological matter of over-riding energy processes too tied to non-photosynthetic chemical energy?
- Is it just a demographic issue regarding the increase in urban population?
- Is it just a question of governance and absence of authoriality in choices?
If we analyse just one of the viewpoints shown above, which have been proposed in various ways throughout the 20th and early 21st century, it appears that we are not able to emerge from the siege[6].

The post-industrial urban reality, an economy based on capitalism, production processes based on hydrocarbons, the demographic processes of irreversible urbanization, and the generalized crisis of authorial capacity have slowed down the city-countryside cycle that arises with the city. Only one feature has never changed throughout the history of the city: its ability to create added intellectual value, culture, and liberal arts and to block energy dispersal through processes of "negative entropy", or cultural development[7].

This condition is the true basis to allow us to emerge from the conceptual siege of recycling made up of the reuse of tangible products and scraps and to give an overall definition of the new life cycle of our cities by rethinking cyclical approaches and the application of new languages and operational approaches[8].

1. The photosynthetic energy cycle as a generator of city planning

The first feature that should be brought into focus is the way in which the planning of cities, infrastructure and landscape relates to the solar energy which must be acquired as a reference for urban development. Which doesn't mean just making existing buildings more technological or covering the city with photovoltaic surfaces, but rather, activating processes by which the form of the city itself finds in solar energy (strong, abundant, and sudden in the south of the world or weak, limited, and continuous in the north) a way of redesigning itself.

2. Circadian time as a new urban planning timeframe and a place for celebrating urban rituals.

As a consequence of the urban planning vision oriented on energy, urban transformation — and the disciplines dealing with it — must add circadian time to the life timeline of the project carried out so as to accentuate the competitive urban advantage of its use of spaces and distribution of services.

3. Priority of public and/or public-private intervention.

The areas available within compact urban systems (neglected or underused areas, abandoned fragments of the city, etc.) are the raw material on which a new life cycle can ensure innovation of the urban system starting from the resources present[9].

We must emphasize the need to also apply priority criteria to the location and project choices in order to redefine how some places should preferentially be the subjects of transformation (also with public intervention if possible) to activate more complex and extensive transformation processes. Equalization and compensation processes can also be adopted to make some interventions more useful.

4. Treating waste and scrap as inevitable in entropic processes.

This assumption supposes that it is necessary to ensure that scrap "doesn't exist" as a concept, but the production process envisages a long life cycle that is devoid of gaps and easy to activate at a local level.

5. Recycling as a language.

The recycling of materials thus becomes a linguistic mode[10], in which discarded materials are used as meaningless bricks in new construction and production processes. These are thus five ways to escape from the siege, which can be nodes to develop within the various cores of recycling, but which can guide a new cyclical vision in the experimental work resulting from research — the outcome of a broad and shared vision on the issues of local territory development, which take into account all the techniques required for the balance of urban development. Here, therefore, is a sign of discontinuity in the Anthropocene: the neo-Anthropocene of Ecological Urbanism, of the closure of life cycles, and of non-erosive economies.

1. Crutzen, P., *Benvenuti nell'Antropocene!*. Milan: Mondadori, 2005.
2. Marini, S., Santangelo, V., editor, *Re-cycle Italy. Nuovi cicli di vita per architetture e infrastrutture della città e del paesaggio* [English edition: *Re-cycle Italy. New Life Cycles for Architecture and Infrastructure of City and Landscape*], Rome: Aracne, 2013.
3. Ciorra, P., Marini, S., editor, *Re-cycle. Strategie per la casa, la città e il pianeta* [English edition: *Re-cycle. Strategies for the Home, the City and the Planet*], Milan: Electa, 2011.
4. Sun Tzu, *L'arte della guerra* [English edition: *The Art of War*], Rome: e-Newton classici, 2011, (e-book edition), Pos. 168.
5. Carta, M., *Reimagining Urbanism, Città creative, intelligenti ed ecologiche per i tempi che cambiano* [English edition: *Reimagining Urbanism. Creative, Smart and Green Cities for the Changing Times*], Barcelona-Trento: ListLab, 2013.
6. See, in this regard, the problematic relationship between economics and ecology described and articulated in Ravaioli, C., *Il pianeta degli economisti ovvero l'economia contro il pianeta*. Turin: Isedi, 1992.
7. Rizzo, F., *Economia del patrimonio architettonico- ambientale*. Milan: FrancoAngeli, 1992.
8. Mostafavi, M., Doherty, G., *Ecological Urbanism*. Zurich: Lars Müller Publishers, 2010.
9. Stanghellini, S., *Perequazione, Compensazione, Fattibilità*. Rome: INU Edizioni, 2013.
10. Ciorra, P., Marini, S., op.cit.

Poggioreale Nuova: signs of the siege.
With the disruption of the photosynthetic energy cycle, city and country no longer recognize the reciprocal functions of production and innovation.

Can Batlló, Barcelona.
The prevalence of private or public/private intervention does not always entirely produce the desired effects.
To escape from the siege, often diversionary action leads to an initial phase of redevelopment at no cost to the community.

Urban business activities.
Storage, logistics, delivery: the timeframes of the city and the rebuilding of urban rituals.

RE-CYCLICAL URBANISM

THE CITYFORMING© PROTOCOL
INCREMENTAL AND ADAPTIVE STRATEGIES

MAURIZIO CARTA

The pathologies of top-down urban regeneration — autism, schizophrenia, sterility, and addiction — cannot be solved by simply revising the participatory procedures, improving planning devices or innovating implementation processes. Instead, the viewpoint must be turned on its head. A concrete and effective process for the regeneration of urban areas characterized by marginalization and decline, by the disposal of buildings and infrastructure, by functional underuse or by cycles undergoing weak reactivation (mobility, water, waste) must adopt an approach that doesn't just reject the traditional and now ineffectual *topdown*, but which neither surrenders superficially to the comforting rhetoric of bottom-up. We need a hyper- strategic, incremental, recursive and flexible approach, rather than a closed and simultaneous strategy. The traditional rigid and instantaneous masterplan, unchangeable during its implementation – ineffective in areas that do not benefit from enormous amounts of public or private resources — must be replaced by a consciously temporalized and adaptive Masterprogram, capable of composing an overall vision through the implementation of partial visions, capable of timely and temporary actions but which have the force to generate new futures.

The sustainability of the urban metamorphosis, particularly in a time of development model crisis, of the transition of settlement models, and of the reduction of public resources, must be implemented through a regenerative process that moves forward in subsequent cycles, guided by a general vision, and capable of adapting to the real effects of the implementation process. Hyper-strategic urban regeneration must itself create the conditions of success to fuel the subsequent phases. It must produce a part of value on which to trigger the subsequent investment. It must generate the oxygen that brings to life the new housing, productive, commercial and cultural functions that can regenerate the area. A sort of "terraforming" (a term coined by Jack Williamson in the novel *Collision Orbit* of 1942, which then became one of NASA's protocols for the colonization of other planets): a process designed to make the abandoned or deteriorated area once again liveable for a new community, working on the territorial components that are still active – creating new ones or changing their composition – so that it is able to support a new ecosystem. I define this process Cityforming©, a planning protocol that is able to reactivate the metabolism of an area in subsequent stages, starting from its latent regenerative components, activating multiple cycles with increasing intensity to create a new urban ecosystem that is sustainable over time. Strategic Cityforming works in incremental and adaptive phases required to produce partial results that become the generative basis of the subsequent phases. Cityforming, by progressing through the phases of "colonisation", "consolidation" and "development", produces the necessary "urban oxygen" for the formation of an ecosystem that is adequate enough to generate a new urban metabolism to reactivate inactive cycles, reconnect disrupted ones, or activate new ones that are more suited to the new identity of the places. The figure on page 65 shows the sequence of the three phases and their characteristics.

1) The colonisation phase contains several initial functions that act as oxygen reserves for the formation of the new atmosphere. We can define these as new functions or reclamation of buildings or spaces as "stem cells" because, although grafted through planning action, their characteristics and functions are not dissimilar to the pre-existing tissue. These urban stem cells serve as activators of new urban aspects — in the various forms by which the city expresses itself today — and can be ecological areas of re-naturalization, plug-in energy devices, low cost and smart blocks, living labs and productive micro-districts for digital manufacturing, redevelopment of public spaces, etc. Colonisation can also take place through the removal of some infrastructural or environmental detractors that reduce the vitality of the area in order to facilitate the reconnection of ecological networks for the reconstitution of environmental connections. Regeneration colonies are characterized by a high level of self-sufficiency due to their ability to be energetically autonomous by using renewable sources, by their ability to produce sufficient profitability to sustain maintenance costs, and by their ability to activate forms of widespread partnership for their management. Colonies must also be strongly recognizable in relation to the territorial context, since, although involving low-intensity transformation, they serve as transformation landmarks. They act as witnesses to the new reputation of the area and agents of urban marketing. The predominant urban planning paradigm that is used in this phase is that of Tactical Urbanism with a three-year time frame, within which the subsequent phase must be activated. In the USA, initiatives to test incremental and adaptive forms of urban regeneration are spreading, including, for instance, *Better Block Urban Design*, founded in Dallas Oak Cliff by Jason Roberts and Andrew Howards and trialled in Memphis, St. Louis, New York and Boston as an exemplary tool to produce new temporary visions of a space to show its transformative potential in creating a neighborhood that is safe to pass through, lively and creative. The urban planning tactics or the varied forms of Pop-up Cities and DIY regeneration, however, are almost always self-consistent, satisfied with redeveloping the space of their action, without avoiding the risk of the sterility of the structural effects and the risk of their premature breakdown. Cityforming colonisation, on the other hand, believes in a subsequent territorial entrenchment and creates the conditions to trigger a chain reaction consolidating its effects.

2) Consolidation acts on the new ecosystem being formed by grafting some of the more valuable and powerful functions from a profit and value generation viewpoint, suppor ted economically by the increase in value and attractiveness of the area. Ecological and intelligent neighborhoods, makers districts and energy communities, green manufacturing and attractors for the new metropolitan archipelagos or infrastructural gateways operate through a process of hyper-cycling that activates various cycles in order to achieve a sufficient endowment of attractive and productive functions. Consol idat ion also work s by reactivating latent resources already present in the area, which have been stimulated

CITYFORMING	MASTERPLANNING
is incremental	is instantaneous
is open	is closed
is planned in phases	is implemented in phases
is strategic	is regulative
is dialogic	is assertive
is adaptive	is conformative
enables urban planning tactics	defines land use
activates scenarios	prefigures scenarios
produces new metabolisms	acts on separate sectors
generates resources	uses resources
acts on programs	acts on projects
generates communities	settles inhabitants

and positively perturbed by the colonisat ion phase. The consolidation phase acts more via networks than nodes and loses a bit of its self-sufficiency and autonomy, often starting to use the tangible — but more often intangible — urban resources of the place to take root and spread, also initiating a process of camouf lage with the context, which reinforces its presence. It is often the pre-existing inhabitants who help the new users attracted by the colony in the process of integration. In this phase, several tactics or several "third landscape" actions of the previous phase are involved in a process of Opensource Urbanism that changes them, hybridizes them with local intelligence, and integrates them with the actions of urban acupuncture, in order to transform their strategies to deepen their effects of reactivating the urban cycles.

In this phase, with a timeframe of five years, the initial attractiveness of the flows of users is replaced by the stability of new inhabitants who contribute to the growth in demand for services and to enhanced care of the places, also through forms of agreement and based on cooperation.

3) Finally, development is the longterm phase with a timeframe of at least ten years, in which the new metabolism of the area is put into operation to create new urban value. In this phase, following the metamor-

phosis produced by the first two, a Masterplan of the whole area is drawn up based on the new identity of the place, made more fertile by the success of the previous phases, being able to tap into a stronger investment multiplier, capable of supporting the sizeable investments required for the complete transformation of the area. In this phase, a Masterplan makes sense as it acts in a time of more advanced change and in a phase in which the robustness of the development vision can be better confirmed. It isn't, therefore, a masterplan that assumes the conditions of its implementation in advance or which intercepts economic and entrepreneurial resources already given, but a Landuse Urbanism that acts on the new urban ecosystem and is specified starting from the changed conditions of the recolonised and consolidated area. In this phase, the deep innovation required is generated and is capable of enabling the creation of eco-cities, low&high cost creative districts, new metropolitan municipalities, urban development projects, extensive regional parks connecting urban and rural areas, and new integrated platforms of development within the new scenarios enabled by the completion of the Cityforming process. The Cityforming approach, therefore, is not limited to implementing a predefined vision for extracts of time, a vision that is the result of a preliminary planning process presuming enormous economic resources for its complete implementation or requiring the activation of high land or real estate revenue in order to carry out all its works. Rather, Cityforming generates a program of actions that are put together and defined as a function of partial results, based on the consolidation of new urban roles of the area and on the values and expectations generated by new inhabitants, new services and forms of collaboration, taxation opportunities and new urban economies generated in the first two phases, which are capable of triggering the third.

Cityforming works constantly within the dimensions of the project and process and activates actions within a predicted scenario whose effects make up their specification and definition, consolidating the trend scenario or contributing to forming a new programmatic scenario. An exemplary case of Cityforming is the High Line in New York. In the colonisation phase, it was the inhabitants of the neighborhood who reactivated the old railway line, now inherent in their landscape identity, by means of a recycling project that turned it into a public space of connection. Subsequently, consolidation occurred through the intervention of real estate promoters who acted to extend the effects of the renewed attractiveness of the area and to entrench the results, activating the redevelopment of other buildings and places to restore residence, professional activities, and trade, and to introduce the services to tourism. Finally, the development phase has recently begun with the creation of the new Whitney Museum, designed by Renzo Piano, which ratifies the

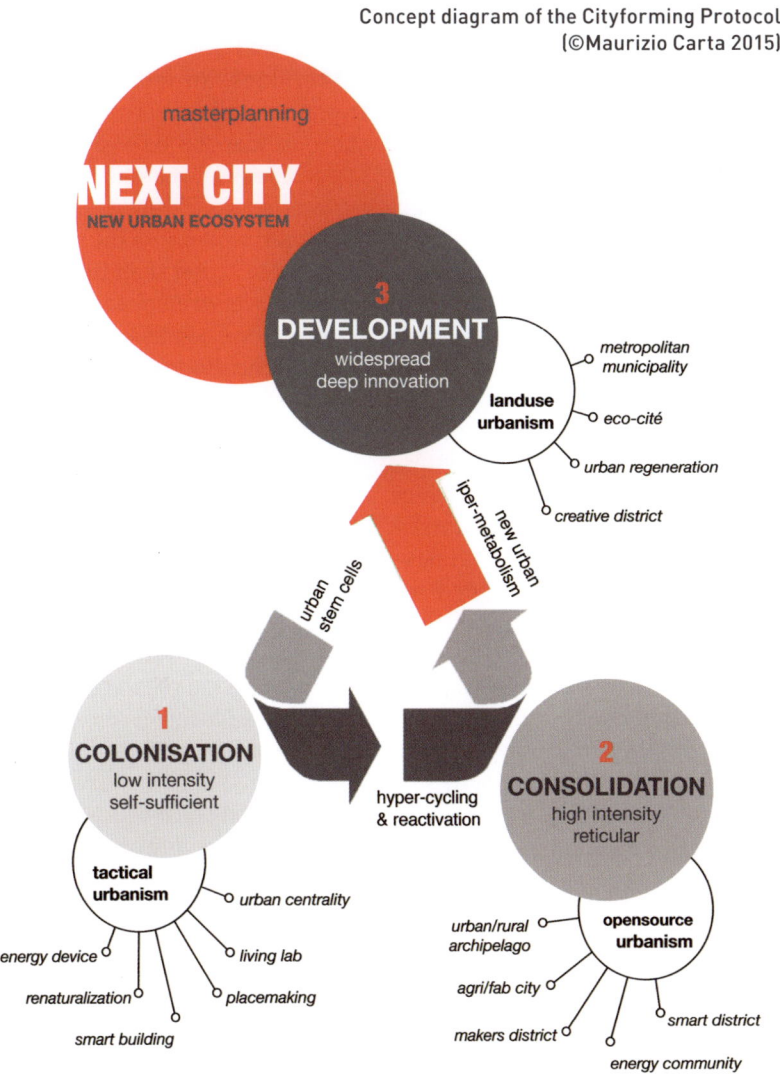

Concept diagram of the Cityforming Protocol. (©Maurizio Carta 2015).

transformation of the Meatpacking District into a neighborhood of creativity and innovation. Not by chance, Samsung has opened a representative office here, Google its New York office, and Apple one of its stores, but urban horticulture also proliferates and the Center for Social Innovation is increasingly filled with new activities. The completion of the development phase is represented by the masterplan for the construction of the Hudson Yard Development, the largest private urban regeneration operation in New York after the Rockefeller Center: 158 hectares of commercial, office and residential spaces (half of which are public spaces), and cultural centres, including the extraordinary Culture Shed designed by Diller Scofidio + Renfro. The High Line, with its colonising effect, has completely redesigned the socio-cultural map of New York firstly, then redefining the map of talents, creativity, and innovation, as well as the real estate map that generates the profits for its management and maintenance. The incremental and generative action of the Cityforming prevented a saturation of the market and spaces, which would not have left any opportunities for the inhabitants, but would have expelled them instead, as occurred in SoHo in the 1970s and Chelsea in the 1980s.

Instead, it was the colonising action of the inhabitants of the neighborhood, joined together in the association Friends of the High Line, which prevented the planned real estate speculation, replacing it with care for the spaces, re-naturalization of infrastructure, and safe places: actions which reinforced the social fabric and the human capital of the area, upon which the interventions of greater added value were consolidated.

The Cityforming process, therefore, is not limited to incrementally planning actions for the transformation and reactivation of disrupted cycles and latent resources but acts as an antidote to the gentrification connected to urban regeneration. In fact, precisely because of its low transformational intensity and stemcell function as a generator of new spatial and social tissues, colonisation does not induce an instant transformation that would uproot the local identity in favor of external attractiveness. Instead, colonising actions act as catalysts of identity resources, working on the palimpsest of the area rather than on its standardizing overwritten text.

Furthermore, consolidation acts just like osmotic action between the local population and traditional customs of the area and the new inhabitants, who contribute to social diversity without replacing or expelling others. Finally, the development phase cannot have the disruptive and disidentifying force that it would have had at the beginning in the phase of full decline of the area as it is introduced in a new urban configuration and with a more active role of local players.

The Cityforming© Protocol has been applied to Palermo in an experimental phase during the international planning workshop for the regeneration of the South Coast. It demonstrates awareness that the redevelopment, reconnection and development strategies of the area cannot be activated by a traditional urban project without risking its economic unsustainability or, worse, a gentrification effect in a delicate and valuable area of the city, which is rich in social capital, areas to be recycled, agricultural landscape, and identity- forming aspects. Starting from the areas with the greatest regenerative capacity, some low-intensity actions have been identified that could serve as colonies to reactivate the latent or disrupted cycles and, subsequently, actions capable of triggering their consolidation by tapping into local vital energy.

The programmatic development scenario is proposed as a hyper-cyclical planning timeframe, which will be defined in a collaborative process with the players that have shown the greatest strength and in places that have expressed the greatest propensity for transformation. Belonging to the colonisation phase, for example, are coastal re-naturalization actions, urban acupuncture operations, and the activation of social innovation sites. Consolidation will occur by working on the residential space and on public space, on the provision of neighborhood services and on the proposition of new lifestyles and mobility. The development phase will comprise the actions of greatest metropolitan relevance, with the localization of big attractors (the energy district, the aquarium, and the sports center), around which new residential neighborhoods will develop, together with the commercial and production activities supported by the new urban values produced in the previous phases.

Cityforming, therefore, is not limited to a planning strategy or to the innovation of urban policies but acts as a powerful creative disruptor of territorial systems undergoing metabolic arrest, reduced energy, and developmental crisis.

It does not input external energy, which could not keep a compromised metabolism active for long, but takes care of the vital factors already present, recomposes latent ecological resources, and reactivates the resilient social networks to generate the indispensable basis of territorial and social capital on which the fertile seed of the self-sustainable urban regeneration project can take root.

Dell'Arte by Jaume Plensa. Courtyard of the Can Framis Museum, Fundació Vila Casas, Barcelona).

2

SMART CIRCULAR PLANNING

2.1 **HYPER-METROPOLITAN PALERMO**
UNCONVENTIONAL STRATEGIES AND MAPPING
FOR CIRCULAR METROPOLITAN SCENARIOS
Maurizio Carta

2.2 **INNOVATION, CIRCULARITY AND LOCAL DEVELOPMENT**
Maurizio Carta

2.3 **A SMART LAND TO REACTIVATE TERRITORIAL WEALTH**
Marilena Orlando

2.4 **NO EXTERNALITIES FOR CLOSED-CYCLE CITIES:**
STRATEGIC ENVIRONMENTAL ASSESSMENT AND PLANNING
Daniele Ronsivalle

HYPER-METROPOLITAN PALERMO

UNCONVENTIONAL STRATEGIES AND MAPPING FOR CIRCULAR METROPOLITAN SCENARIOS

MAURIZIO CARTA

Palermo metropolis of cities

Local Sicilian administrations in search of a new role in the metropolitan scenario that Italy has set itself in compliance with the Delrio Law (Law no. 56 of 7th April 2014) are today debating between a renewed necessarily reticular metropolitan dimension and a response to contingent local needs, fluctuating between vision and mission. After numerous fruitless attempts (the main measure being Regional Law no. 15 of 4/08/2015, as modified by Regional Law no. 5 of 1/04/2016 and finally amended by Article 23 of Regional Law no. 8 of 17/05/2016), the three Sicilian Metropolitan Cities (Catania, Messina and Palermo) are today called upon to play a role that goes beyond the asphyxiating boundaries of the law, to carry out new and more extensive functions than in the past through the use of increasingly multilevel and circular factual procedures of government/planning/ action. They are committed, therefore, to testing a new approach to decisions and actions regarding the numerous flows and cycles involving metropolitan systems. An approach that effectively uses scale crossing, flexibility, and circularity as paradigms/ instruments of new largescale territorial policies rather than traditional gravitations that are no longer able to represent the complex metropolitan relations (as shown by studies of Soja's Postmetropolis and Moretti's New Geography of Jobs).

The scenarios of economic competitiveness, ecological sustainability, cultural creativity and social cohesion envisioned in the face of the new metropolitan administrations require an awareness of the need to launch innovative policies against crisis and decline by innovating decision-making processes, permanently assessing effects, planning choices, and co-planning actions.

In this context, in 2015, the Municipality of Palermo, even before the institution of the metropolitan city, clearly chose not to limit itself to being a service provider to citizens and businesses of a large area, avoiding the reproduction of now obsolete gravitational models surpassed in more mature European experiences: see the reflections and data contained in Urban@it (2016) *Rapporto sulle città. Metropoli attraverso la crisi*, Bologna, Il Mulino. It chose, instead, to act as the protagonist in the post-metropolitan transition of European cities, being an active player in the production of environmental and cultural quality, social cohesion and ethnic integration, economic sustainability and attractiveness of resources for the overall future project in the urban Anthropocene we have entered into. The result was the decision to act within a strategic scenario that is not just metropolitan (the belt of municipalities or the former province), but overtly "metapolitan" (for a broader regional area stretching from Cefalù to Marsala) to guide the processes of regeneration and development through the preparation of the Strategic Plan for Palermo Capital (drawn up with my advice, together with that of Stefano Stanghellini and

The multilevel system of governance for the metropolitan area of Palermo. The functional relations are represented in a systemic vision that aligns the planning tools to the various contexts and scales and identifies the subjects who exercise their powers in relation to spheres of influence. Metropolitan governance, therefore, acts within a flexible and scalable system of tools and powers, regulating a metropolitan ecosystem in which each component interacts with the others through various instrumental interfaces.

The images in this chapter have been extracted from the Strategic Plan for Palermo Capital (Municipality of Palermo, with the scientific advice of Creta srl, Maurizio Carta, Stefano Stanghellini, 2015)

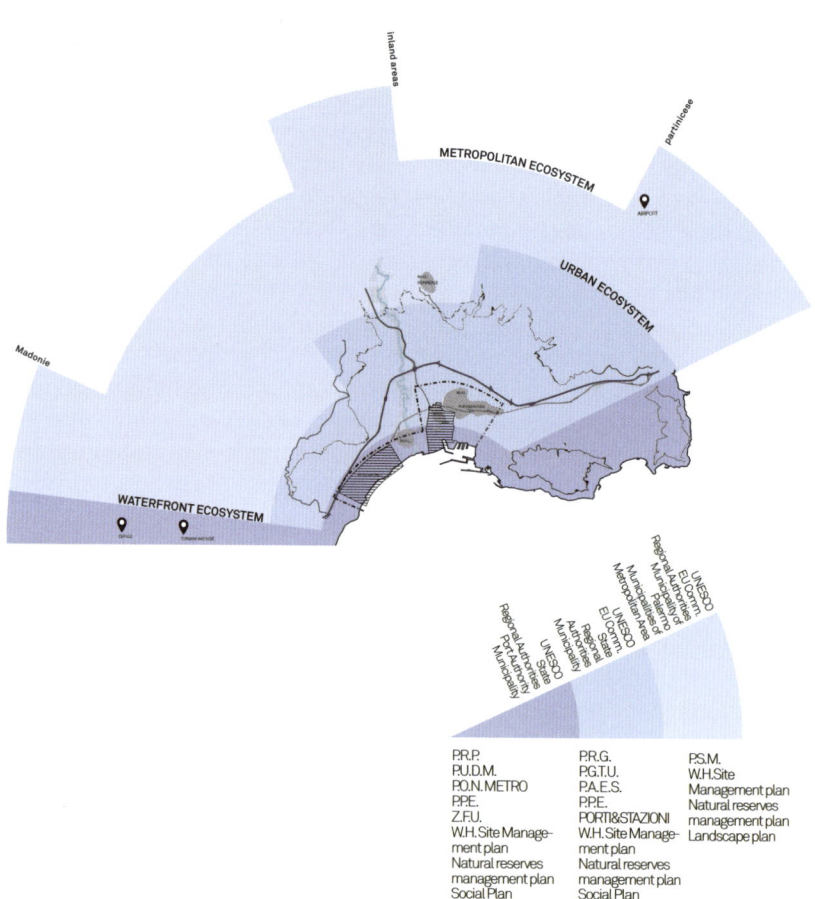

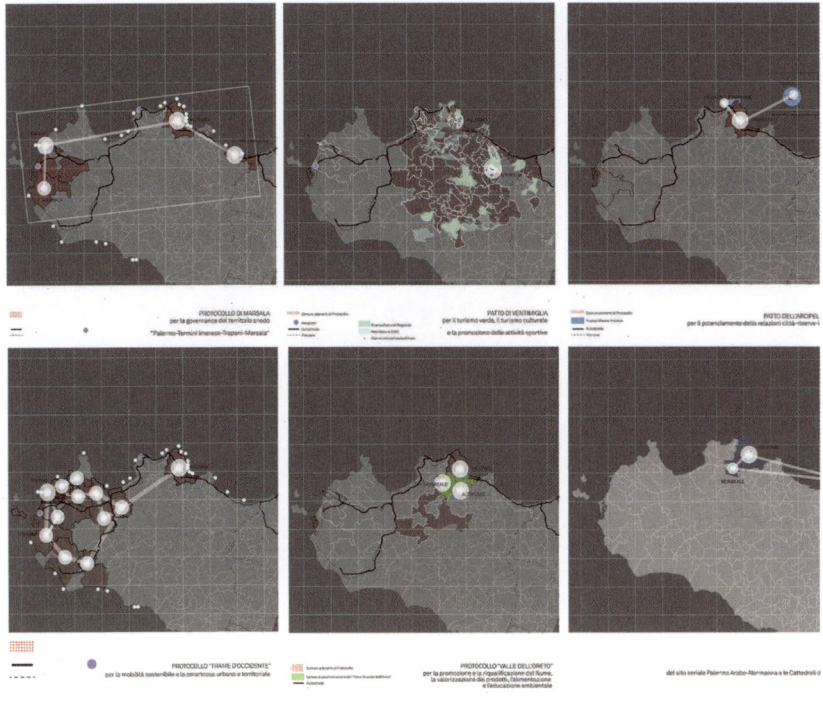

The agreements and large area networks that build patterns of relations and policies in force for rethinking the territorial structure and for the enhancement of the resources of the Western Sicily Platform.

From left to right from top to bottom, the agreements entered into: 1) Marsala protocol for the infrastructural governance of the Palermo-Termini Imerese-Trapani-Marsala Hub-Territory; 2) Ventimiglia Agreement for green, cultural and sports tourism; 3) Archipelago Agreement to strengthen relations between cities, nature reserves, and islands; 4) "Trame d'Occidente" Agreement for sustainable mobility and urban and territorial smartness; 5) "Valle dell'Oreto" Agreement for the promotion and redevelopment of the river; 6) UNESCO serial site of Arab-Norman Palermo network and the cathedrals of Cefalù and Monreale.

SMART CIRCULAR PLANNING

URBAN DROSSCAPES

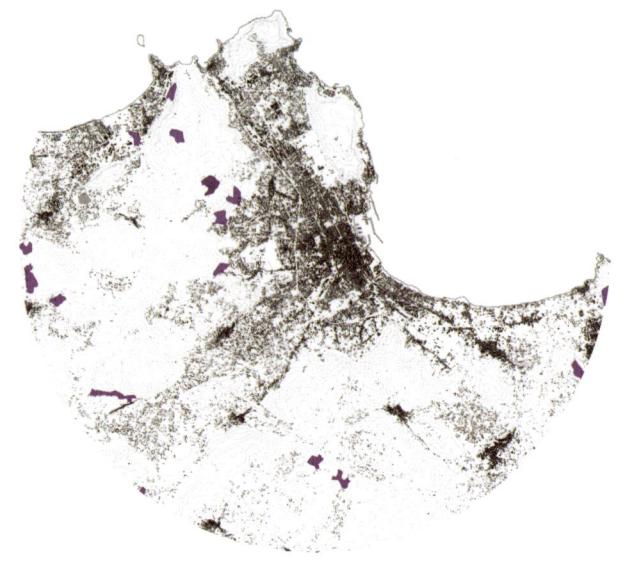

METROPOLITAN DROSSCAPES

RE-CYCLICAL URBANISM

URBAN PRODUCTIVE
AND SETTLEMENT SYSTEM

URBAN NATURAL
SYSTEM

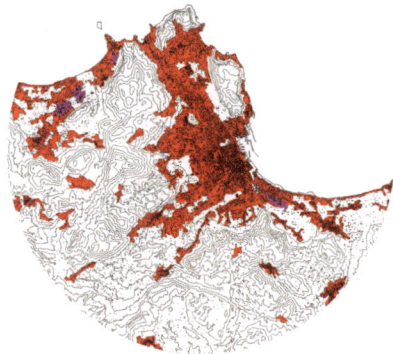
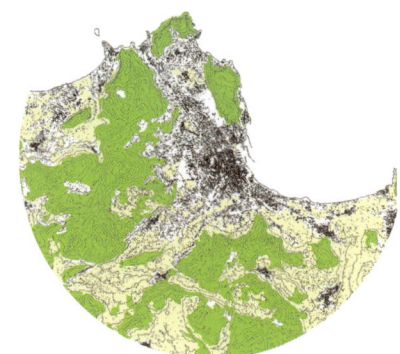

METROPOLITAN PRODUCTIVE
AND SETTLEMENT SYSTEM

METROPOLITAN NATURAL
SYSTEM

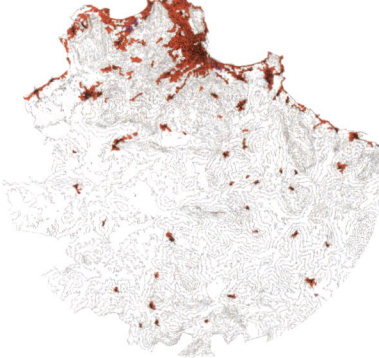
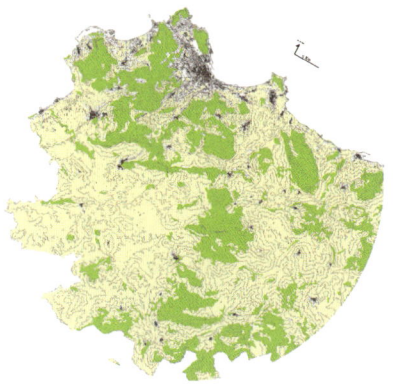

The evaluation of urban systems allows three key issues of re-cyclical development to be briefly analyzed: drosscapes as resilience reserves; the compact city as a place for the reactivation of the urban cycle; the agro-natural system as a place for capturing CO_2 and energy reactivation of the life cycle of the city. Given the hyper-metropolitan nature of the analysis, the display of results is always multiscale, crystallized in these maps of the urban belt and metropolitan visions.

Creta srl) for the purpose of orientation, guidance and coherence of territorial transformations, with a 2025 scenario, and of the future governance of the city and involved territories through voluntary agreements. The Strategic Plan thus ascribes spatial and infrastructural dimension to the "city-region" of western Sicily, of which Palermo, in recent years, has acted as catalyst of its role in the European and Mediterranean context, as activator of its competitive factors and as provider of social, economic and cultural policies, as well as those relating to mobility (see the feasibility studies of the Ministry of Infrastructure and Transport on the Western-Tyrrhenian Platform and the Hub-Territory). The Strategic Plan proposes to all stakeholders – institutional and otherwise – a process capable of acting at the same time on the capital city and on the large hyper-metropolitan and sub-regional area of territorial relations, identifying the required strategies, activating the relative cross-sector urban policies, drawing up working plans for regeneration, and identifying the resulting rules that allow the implementation of the strategies and projects, balancing the certainty/flexibility of decisions, timeframes and the most effective procedures. Strategic innovation of the planning, decision-making, and implementation processes acts in accordance with a principle of circularity that fuels the metropolitan metabolism (as explicitly placed as a foundation of the new strategic plan of Barcelona), which favours reuse, sharing, and integration of projects to enhance some areas that are already the subject of planning or transformation processes underway by the Municipal Administrations involved or by the private sector.

The circular and shared approach makes the territorial system more creative and sparks the interest of the multiple players involved in governing the territory to take part with the public players in the creation and management of regeneration and transformation projects, in the improvement of efficiency and performance of collective services, as well as in the pursuit of the European strategic goals of sustainable development, above all with regard to mobility and climate change, which require circular policies.

Palermo metropolis wants to once again play an active role as a regional, national and Mediterranean gateway-city: capable of intercepting the flow of people, goods and services which cross the medium and long networks and of turning them into resources to fertilize local territorial settings and, at the same time, capable of extending its own life cycles to a broader context, especially those related to culture, creativity, and education (a strategy for this is the Strategic Cooperation Agreement with the University of Palermo, signed in 2016). Palermo metropolis wants to once again play a pivotal role between Europe and the Mediterranean, acting forcefully within its natural cosmopolitan vision, which is able to connect the various

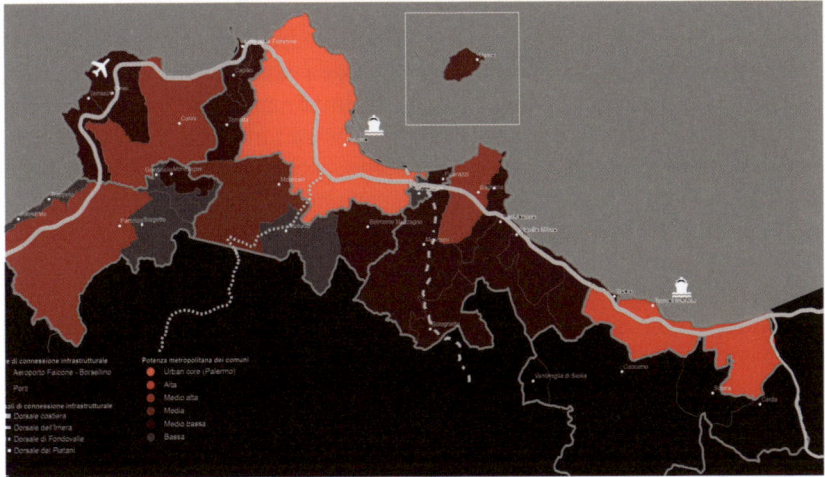

The metropolitan power index: the traditional analysis of metropolization conditions has been enriched by a synthetic analysis of the presence and localization of some of the activities of greatest metropolitan significance in the municipalities making up the metropolitan system. The presence of those activities in the municipalities allows us to extract a synthetic index (not contemplated in this phase) of the "metropolitan power" of the municipalities, divided into five classes and highlighting the distribution over the metropolitan territory of the centers of greatest centrality, attractiveness, and specialization.

life cycles of its numerous communities. Palermo Metropolis 2025 offers itself, thus, as the experiment of a new generation of metropolitan city: a metropolis of cities, not just physical ones — the municipalities comprising it and those with which specific agreements have been entered into — but above all, social, economic and cultural cities. A *hyper-metropolitan city* articulated by specific objectives that fuel its territorial metabolism. Palermo Metropolis 2025 is first of all an *educating city*, as it is capable of informing, teaching, and empowering through its own tangible and intangible cultural heritage (the UNESCO recognition of the global value of the Arab-Norman architecture is crucial evidence of this, albeit partial, in light of the extraordinary palimpsest of Palermo, in which high-quality cultural records can still be read), as well as through its own scholastic, university and associative tissue. Moreover, the Strategic Plan itself takes on a "pedagogical" function, as it is capable of extracting potential for transformation from the human and urban identity resources. It is a *welcoming city* as, throughout its history and even today, it has welcomed migrants, travellers, and cultures capable of integrating, hybridizing, and reciprocally mutating to produce extraordinary results and innovation, recognizing mobility as an inalienable human right: that of asserting the connection between the rights of citizenship, residence, and access to services.

It is an *inclusive city*, as it does not stigmatize, separate or produce effects of social and cultural explosion and fragmentation, but recomposes the tissue of the city to include diversity, combine functions, and enrich the metropolitan experience with the other municipalities with which it shares its vision.

It is a *resilient city* that creatively, fluidly and innovatively adapts to climate change, social changes, and economic bradyseism, producing new sustainable development from those changes. A city that reactivates the cycles of its coastal metabolism as an ecological matrix of its future. Palermo Met ropol is 2025 is a *next-generation metropolitan city* that doesn't limit itself to being the gravitational center of the flows of the other municipalities and does not settle for sharing higher ranking services but is a metropolis of neighborhoods, small and medium towns, farmland and production areas, nature and culture. It's a metropolis of cities, a hyper-metropolis, in fact, capable of guiding people and territories towards circular development, within the scope of renewed integral ecology and contributing to care for the common home.

Palermo between metropolitan super-organism and territorial archipelago

The vision of Palermo Metropolis 2025 is thus twofold. On one hand, it is to pursue its primary function as metropolitan super-organism, that is, a geo-eco-system of urban and rur-urban settlements of sub-provincial dimensions, organized as a single cohesive community, where each settlement and production system has a clear and defined role, and all — like the components of a perfect mechanism — act in unison, contributing in a differential and incremental manner in pursuit of the development of the organism. On the other hand, the Palermo metropolitan city is not content with consolidating its role as new eco-systemic (non-gravitational) settlement system but aspires to test — in its regional metapolis dimension — the activation of a territorial archipelago involving western Sicily.

It will not, therefore, limit its function to the provincial dimension circumscribed by the Delrio Law, but will configure as a polycentric territory of the reticular specialization of functions, which gives value to the nodes and networks, the islands of excellence and the connectors of identity, within a new hyper-rur-urban relationship. It will be, therefore, a hyper- metropolis of multiple opportunities favoring the reclamation of the existing and the recycling of resources, which reduces the waste of land, buildings, and infrastructure, making it an opportunity for diversification. It will be a hyper-metropolis that is sensitive to the landscape and which tends towards urban regeneration to strengthen diversified centralities capable of activating social innovation and economic vitality.

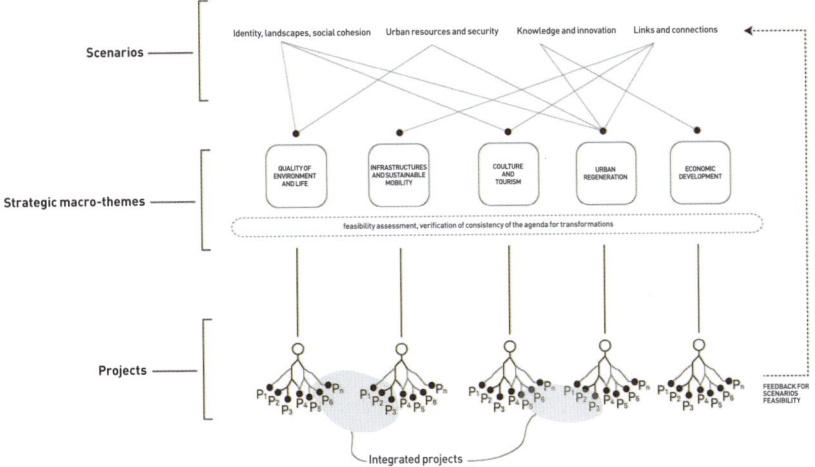

From scenarios to integrated projects: the logical planning structure for the Hyper-cycling city.

The hyper-metropolitan city of Palermo — a western Sicily metropolitan area

The hyper-metropolitan city of Palermo — a western Sicily metropolitan area — aims to carry out functions and tasks concerning the population and the regional territory in the cross-scale integration of services to individuals and the community, territorial and urban planning and infrastructure networks, the layout and use of the territory with reference to the localization of production activities and mobility, environmental, ecological and energy sustainability, the management and organization of public services of general interest, and economic and social planning and development.

These tasks will not remain within the domain of governance but are intended to move to the spatial domain to reshape urban and territorial policies.

The hyper-metropolitan city as a device enabling intelligence

Palermo Metropolitan City, therefore, by means of its Strategic Plan — practicing Re-cyclical Urbanism — will carry out several macro-functions that contribute to the intelligence, creativity, and resilience of the regional system:

- Firstly, it will be a Gateway City of tangible and intangible cycles (of goods, people, and services) that interconnects and interchanges the short regional networks and the long national and international ones through connective and interface functions;

- It will be a Knowledge City, an accelerator of innovation, by means of involvement with the university and research centers and the strengthening of innovation services;

- It will be a Productive City, a business incubator — particularly for micro-enterprises which will become

SMART CIRCULAR PLANNING

urban — due to the presence of clustering services and facilitation to the mature districts (the two urban duty-free zones and the National funds for Metropolitan cities are an example) and the provision of suitable enabling tangible and intangible infrastructure;
- It will be a Smart City, which provides metropolitan services of high added value to individuals and businesses (knowledge-based, culture- oriented, creative-driven), comparable to the homologous European metropolitan cities with which it acts competitively and in collaboration (see, for example, the recent agreement signed with Montpellier for the exchange of practices for the incubation of innovative enterprises);
- Finally, it will be a Circular City, as its polycentric settlement system, no longer concentrated in the dense city or just in Palermo, reactivates the metropolitan metabolism by intervening on the energy and waste cycles and regenerates the life cycles of the cities, infrastructure, and landscapes by reassembling the connections between urban and natural, residential and productive systems.

The performance of these strategic macro-functions is influenced by the optimized articulation of some pivotal functions already carried out by the territorial systems involved in the large-area agreements, which represent their settlement, social, economic and infrastructural concretization. To transfer the metropolitan macro- functions to urban policies and planning of the capital city and hyper- metropolitan centres, these must be characterized by a flexible settlement system that adheres to the more mature processes of post-metropolization in Europe, based on macro- territorial agreements, metropolitan pacts, and territorial districts, rather than predefined boundaries (the French "metropolitan poles" experience or the Polish national system of metropolises of specialization are examples). Palermo next-generation hyper-Metropolitan City intends to equip itself with a system of multilevel governance and metropolitan-level planning tools that allow nodes and networks of development to be standardized in distributive forms that do not erode the more valuable territorial resources.

The Metropolitan City provides high-ranking services, above all related to the innovation of development, the competitiveness of production, cultural attractiveness and urban metabolism cycles. It is also a community aggregator for shared projects which, while maintaining diversity, demonstrate a high degree of collective identity, weaving connective networks between the various municipalities involved.

Finally, it contributes to the creation of an ecologically sustainable urban system by reducing land use and promoting the principles and practices of urban regeneration, reuse, and recycling, as well as the improvement of the cities' life cycles (energy, water, and waste).

The challenge thus requires the ability to manage the city as a vibrantorganism of collective questions and

collaborative answers, shared data and information, distributed sensors and actuators, actions and reactions of its human metabolism before its urban one, that which Mario Soldati called "the sweet human vortex". Palermo hyper-metropolis wishes to be an enabling device of new creative habitats and connection platforms between tangible and intangible, human and spatial elements.
Each new connection — each new agreement — produces territorial innovation, generating new ideas to explore, share and expand, capable of generating new territorial connections that extend and strengthen the territorial archipelago.
This new urban intelligence naturally requires new analytical and diagnostic instruments, and is based not only on consolidated cognitive layers but also on unconventional maps of flexible metropolitan scenarios, able to represent the new hyper-lifecycles of the metropolitan metabolism. It offers a stimulating analytical, interpretative, legislative and planning challenge and requires hyper-maps to comprehend and lead the metropolitan metabolism.

Action Plan of the "Palermo Capital of the Mediterranean" Strategic Plan

Municipality of Palermo
Leoluca Orlando, *Mayor of Palermo*

Project manager
Margherita Amato

Vice President of Cabinet to the Mayor for Strategic Development
Licia Romano

Internal working group
Giuseppe Rizzo, Giuseppe Pecorella.

External consultants
Maurizio Carta, Stefano Stanghellini, Creta srl.

Working group of the consultants
Sandra Vecchietti, Sergio Copiello, Valentina Cosmi, David Casagrande, Stefano Fatone, Barbara Lino, Daniele Ronsivalle.

Activities carried out from November 2014 to November 2015

Cross-scale reticularity for the metropolitan functions. The Strategic Plan identifies some abandoned or disused property to accommodate the "neighborhood centers", district living labs which, for each municipality, like a distributed urban center, can accommodate and facilitate forms of active citizenship and urban manufacture to reactivate the metabolism from the inside.

District 1 | San Basilio; District 2 | Former Slaughterhouse; District 3 | Borgo Ulivia; District 4 | Former Psychiatric hospital; District 5 | Cultural Building Sites (5a) and Villa Turrisi (5b); District 6 | Via Ugo La Malfa; District 7 | Fondo Raffo (7a) and former Chimica Arenella (7b); District 8 | Borgo Vecchio.

The ecological matrix of the project
Green&blue infrastructure in the project of the metropolitan core of Palermo

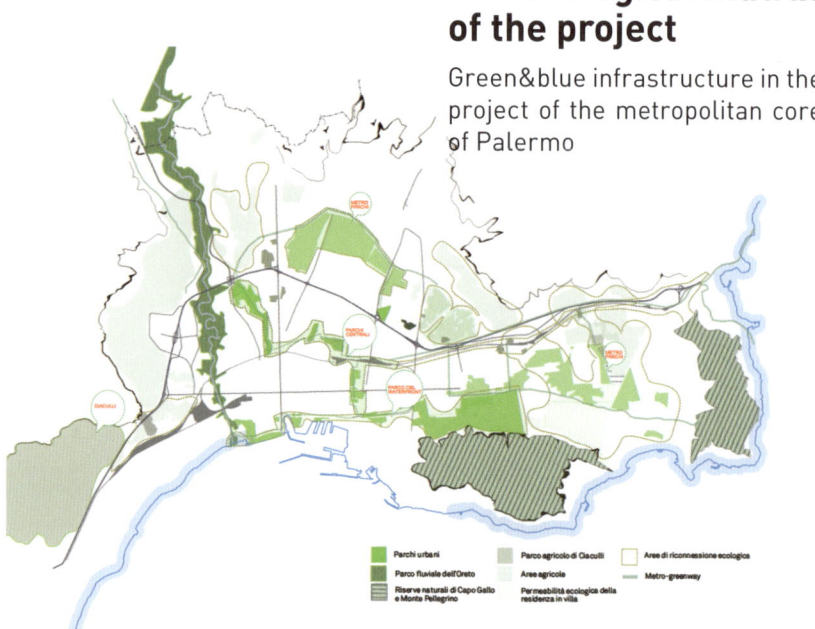

The strategy to connect ecological networks: the map represents the dynamism of relations between the green cores and the urban patterns to be reconnected, forming a true ecological matrix on which the regeneration choices of the involved neighborhoods are structured.

The ecological matrix of the strategic plan presents itself as project armature for the green and blue infrastructures on which to fasten several new centralities connected with the objective of the progressive demineralization of the city to increase its resiience on one hand, and on the other, the creativity generated by rethinking various uses of the urban ecological network, rediscovered as a common asset. In the planning perspective in which the strategic plan moves, the ecological matrix is characterized by the identification of a potential ring of parks, gardens, allotments and avenues that surrounds the compact city and goes beyond the barrier of the ring road.

The strategy thus identifies it as a "Green Ring", a large annular park made up of various types of vegetation and just as many different types of uses (production, recreation, sport, reflection, conservation or uses related to soft mobility). The vegetation aspects of the green ring and their ability to infiltrate the residential fabric also increases its function as an innovative feature of the housing systems, bringing some rarefactions and porosities typical of a rur-urban dimension — which many European cities today tend to ambitiously test out — back to the fringes of the dense city.

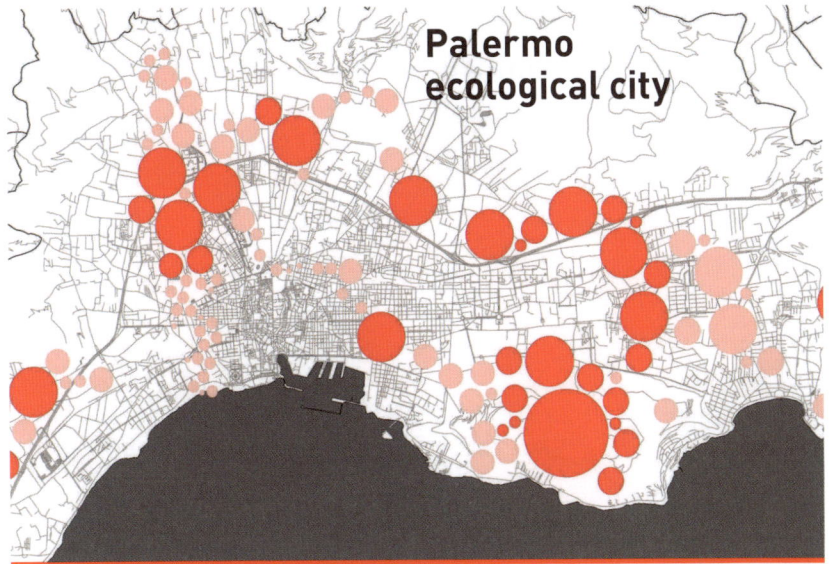

Strategy to connect the ecological networks.
The dynamism of relations between the green cores and the urban patterns to be reconnected is made explicit in the provision of an integrated framework of development of the large protected natural areas and natural urban patterns.

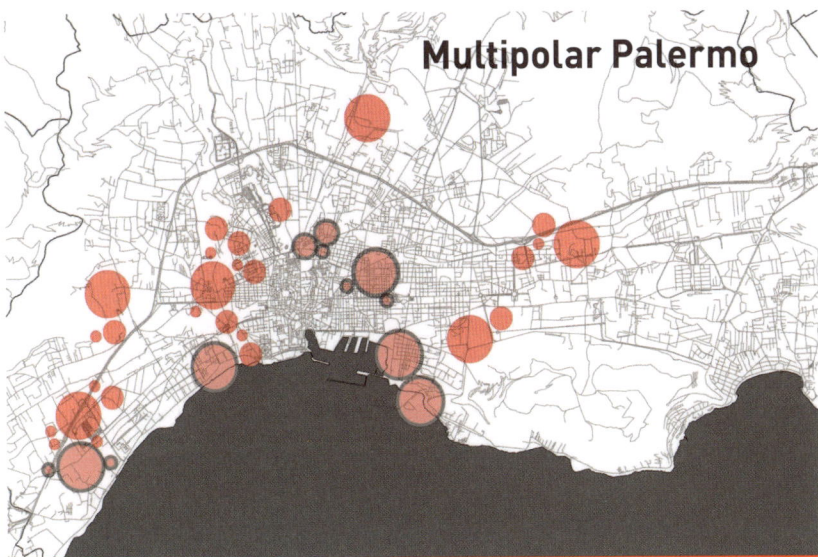

The large metropolitan attractors and the macro-areas of transformation are represented as cellular aggregates, capable of weaving new patterns for induced effects of proximity and revitalization.

SMART CIRCULAR PLANNING

The matrix of transforming mobility
Individual, shared, and collective mobility

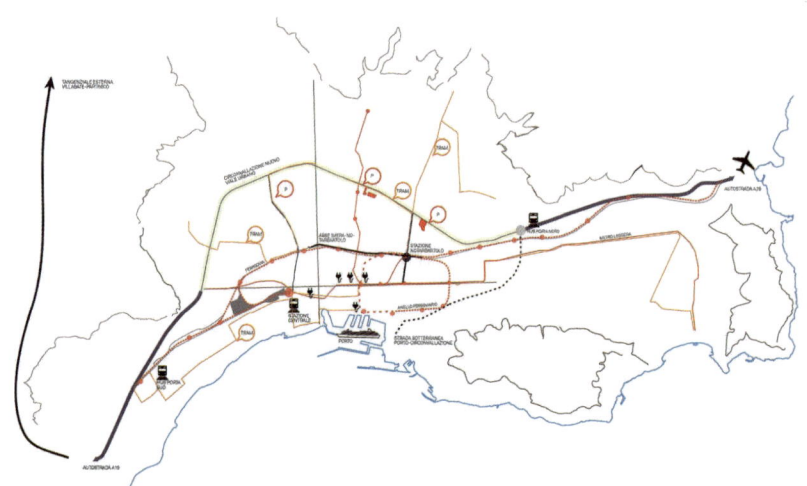

The strategy for mobility represents the way the urban core is evolving on the horizon of multimodality: collective transport and shared services (car sharing and bike sharing, electric people movers) are connected in a system that opens itself to the Mediterranean and national scale with port, airport, and railway gateways and on the local scale with road connections of the metropolitan city with the internal archipelagos closest to Palermo.
The new collective and shared mobility armature is not limited to changing the accessibility to existing attractors by favoring current origins, but radically rethinks the localization of the urban and metropolitan functions of Palermo, contributing substantially to its necessary polycentrism. Along the new major south-north longitudinal axes and around the sea-mountain transversal axes, valuable functions can be re-dislocated in the metropolitan and regional hierarchy which, enjoying a non-erosive and congestion generating mobility, can reach the user threshold needed to balance the investment and operation costs. The redistribution of residency, commerce and production is also facilitated and reshaped by the new mobility armature, allowing the large external, outlying districts to reactivate an indispensable multifunctional metabolism that can boost attractiveness, especially from a metropolitan perspective.

Palermo
& the Fluid City Paradigm

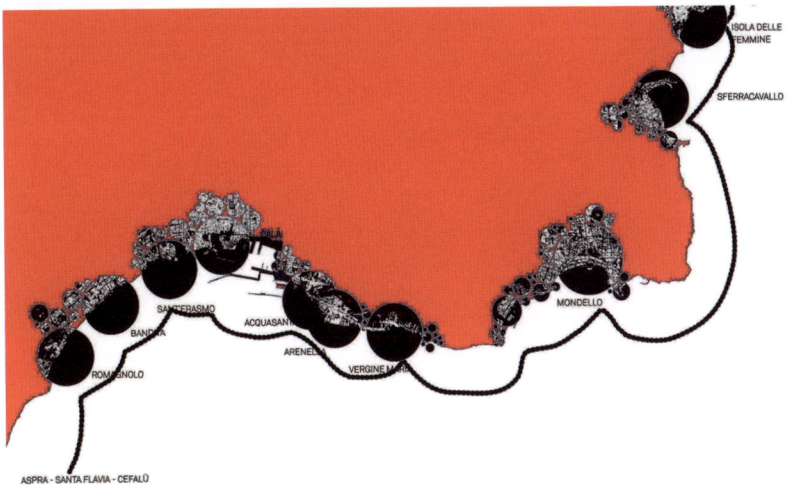

Reverse city-sea relations.
The old fishing villages, connected in the metro-sea project, assume the highest level of urban fluidity by serving as fluid gateways of the new settlement and mobility system, reactivating the urban metabolism from the sea cycle viewpoint.
From "all port" (the Greek name), Palermo becomes "fluid city", reintroducing the sea into its everyday metabolism and its future project with its nine tourist ports (some of which to be reactivated), which provide gateways that reshape the uses of the city around the ancient fishing villages.
Romagnolo, Bandita, Sant'Erasmo, Cala, Acquasanta, Arenella, Vergine Maria, Mondello, and Sferracavallo are no longer forgotten names or broken pieces of a mosaic, but once again become living, moving and productive places strongly tied to the water cycle that configures their forms and characterizes their functions. In the Fluid City paradigm, they offer themselves as parts of the porous city-port in which harbor functions and urban functions intersect in a richer fluid geography that becomes the new city.
Even in the graphical representation, the mainland takes on the fluid consistency of the sea, while, conversely, the place of connections and transformations becomes the sea with its spongy fringes.

Strategic nodes and areas of transformation

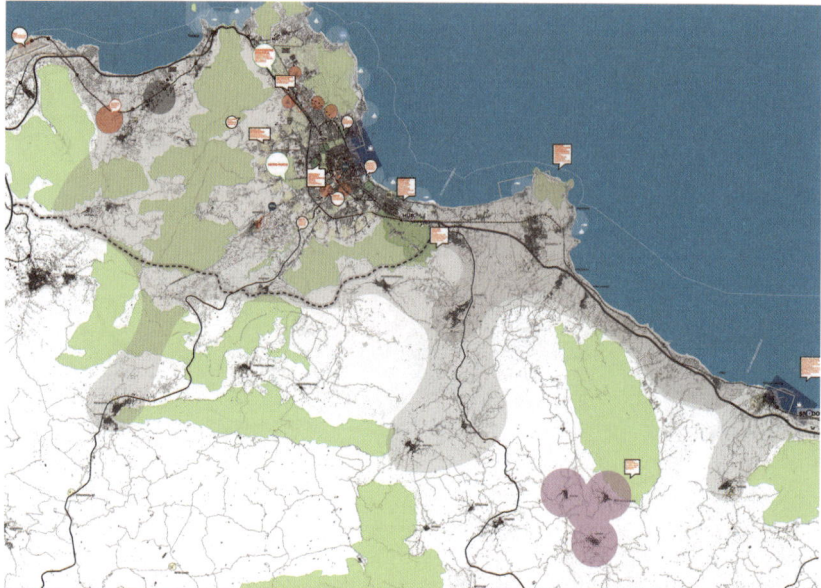

The large-area vision and the definition of the areas of transformation of the urban core of Palermo are complementary and respond to the need to close life cycles connected on scales and with multi-scale territorial relations.
The Urban level concerns the actions falling entirely within the municipal boundary (at the current state of administrative boundaries of reference), which, while having effects on the metropolitan scale, relate entirely to the urban level.
The strategic nodes and the areas of integrated transformation constitute the new centers of reticular polycentrism of the city, which allow new cycles of redevelopment and development, residency and production, mobility and services to be activated from a circular perspective. The pilot projects, in particular, are placed at the densest and richest intersection between the ecological matrix, the matrix of drosscapes and the matrix of collective and shared mobility that have been placed at the foundations of the Strategic Plan. Around each of the new urban centres, especially the larger ones (Lolli-Notarbartolo, Ortofrutticolo-Sampolo, Cascino-Fiera, Gasometro-Macello, Orléans-Oreto), recyclable urbanism will activate all the actions that will allow the birth and development of the functions corresponding to most of its paradigmatic axes, so as to stimulate the reactivation of the settlement metabolism required for the consolidation of the new urban centres, in favor of a reduction of the overly dense and concentrated central functions.

New vision for metropolitan super-organism level

The metropolitan super-organism level concerns the actions falling within the metropolitan area of reference, from Cefalù to Balestrate, which are relevant for the construction of the "metropolitan super-organism".
The polycentric reticular view that characterizes urban regeneration strategies finds a greater relevance and specificity in the metropolitan dimension, as it contributes to substantiating the passage from the obsolete gravitation metropolitan model to the super-organism model in which all the nodes perform precise vocational functions and the connections no longer follow the old server-clients logic but the more innovative and effective cloud-based logic, in which hierarchies are reduced in favour of a more effective distribution of roles and specializations. The same model of innovation cells that generate ecosystems of development is also applied to the metropolitan dimension through a logic of districts and clusters that provide the first step towards the desired vocational specialization of the metropolitan territory of Palermo.

SMART CIRCULAR PLANNING

Connection scenarios

The connection scenario acts on the urban territorial relations and their relations with the outside. This is true in a physical sense but also in an intangible sense due to the changes in behaviors produced from the diffusion of information technology and telematics. The goal of the scenario is to promote new networks of relations between and within territories: between the urban poles that comprise it, between the historic centre and its relative contexts, between parts of the city, and between elements of the urban and rural system, improving relations between its inhabitants, activities, users, and visitors.

Scenarios for the landscapes, identity, and social cohesion

Urban and rural landscapes represent elements with strong identity values. Greater focus on their quality allows us to strengthen the people's sense of belonging to the places, favoring social cohesion. The scenario begins with a consideration that the strong residential and production growth that has characterized the urban expansion of cities has not always been accompanied by a focus on the quality of the settlements and that, specifically, there has been a lack in suitable quality of the "public city".

The knowledge and urban innovation scenario promotes intelligent growth by developing a more efficient and competitive economy. It seeks to create synergies between companies and research, favoring diffusion and technological transfer, to facilitate the development and growth of companies even by means of spin-off processes. The keyword identifying this scenario is "excellence".

Reduced consumption (land, water, air, non-renewable energies, and waste) and an increase in safety (seismic, hydraulic, hydrogeological, social and gender) are the goals pursued by this scenario, which aims to promote sustainable growth. The redevelopment and repurposing of abandoned areas and buildings and the regeneration of residential districts starting from social housing are actions conveying a strong message of change. The central feature of the scenario looks at closing the water and waste cycles.

INNOVATION, CIRCULARITY AND LOCAL DEVELOPMENT

MAURIZIO CARTA

The metamorphosis of the local in the circular economy

The inland areas of Sicily, the hilly and mountainous historic centers, the villages of the land reform, the extraordinary crop mosaics of the hinterland, the productive landscapes, and the new factories of agri-food excellence should no longer be seen and managed — or more often assisted — as marginalities or as reduced versions of the urban model, inexorably destined to lose their population in a conflict with major cities. Rather, they offer themselves as significant components within the scope of the local development metamorphosis we must pass through as an antidote to the deterioration and desertification of rural areas. From places to be abandoned or surrendered to the tired memory of the elderly, they are beginning to be transformed into active subjects for proposals, into new centers that are local in identity and global in attractiveness, into places that are identity-building in form and innovative in functions[1]. In a Sicily still unable to become metropolitan, new territorial archipelagos are taking shape between the Madonie, the Sicanians and Val di Noto. The multi-award-winning rural villages of Gangi and Montalbano Elicona are turned from resistant heresies to the modernist paradigm of the hyper-competitive city into the new avant-garde of settlement quality, cultural diversity, environmental sustainability, and social innovation as categories of the future project[2].

Favara, with its Farm Cultural Park, which is now a global destination of creativity, art and design, Cianciana, with its strategies of residential attractiveness, Menfi, with a new landscape culture of wine, the seven UNESCO WHL sites (22,000 hectares of world heritage sites with their relative buffer and protection zones) with their long networks of global tourism — just to give several examples — are not isolated cases, but are generating a cultural ecosystem from the bottom up, providing proof that a potentially different future can still be imagined, as advocated by Danilo Dolci.

They generate imitations, stimulate emulation, push for legislative and management innovation, ignite the interest of investors, and intercept financial resources. The inland areas are structured from multiple perspectives, are intrinsically accustomed to predicting the fluctuation of environmental conditions, and have been prepared to address the unforeseen events and uncertainties that dot their history: they are resilient.

Today, their reserves of resilience are essential for a Sicily that resolutely wants to pursue the path of quality generation and care of common assets. The distance of inland areas from the driving forces of the coast — consumers of land and resources in many cases, but not all — has preserved some settlements, community, landscape and identity values that can today be a valuable reserve for rethinking small cities which, starting from the need to absorb the crisis and adapt to climate and energy changes, wish to think over their form and their relationships with the rural dimension, and propose new creativity[3]. The commitment to imagining a potentially different future requires the issue of care for and regeneration of the inland areas, not limiting itself to their physical reclamation, to environmental redevelopment or to the indispensable improvement of road access, but also calling for action on the more overall regenerative capacity of the social, economic, and productive tissues[4]. We need a new vision of small cities and villages that stop consuming land, returning respectfully to a dialogue with nature, recycle everything they produce, and fight building deterioration through the retrieval of ancient architectural wisdom or self-building by the inhabitants. We can only take effective action through operations that are also capable of intervening on the social capital, involving the women and men who live there. We need to activate processes to revitalize the production activities, repositioning these centers as new agricultural community nodes or as places of artisan or innovative manufacturing related to the digital realm. We need to use the low building densities and identity-forming palimpsests to provide a housing alternative to the congestion of the coastal cities for more responsible communities of citizens in search of living places that are more in harmony with their ecological life cycles[5]. In the inland areas undergoing a metamorphosis of development, new ecological and creative, more resilient, intelligent, dialogue-based, and sensitive settlements are being tested. It is here that the dimension and capacity of the effects of the "integral ecology" referred to by Pope Francis in his Encyclical[6] are tested with greater responsibility and applied to the settlement systems of the inland areas, going beyond the strictly urban territory. The new alliance between rural and urban ecological cycles requires unconventional solutions. A renewed holistic approach shows the multi-scale need for an ecological and circular urbanism that can act on metropolitan, rur-urban and rural areas. This approach requires the functional, but also social and cultural metabolism of the territory to be the cardinal principle of planning and of the resulting planning instruments, helping to reconnect the agricultural, residential, industrial, natural, cultural, and recreational systems so that they begin to collaborate and interact within an exchange of interests between various mutually beneficial situations or between new productive relations able to determine a new organization of the settlement space.

The inland areas will have to put their territorial and social capital on the counter of a new capitalism[7] resulting from the accelerated transition produced by the manufacturing revolution of start-ups and the widespread action of makers and by the metamorphosis of the circular economy: a development model that is, yes, still capitalist, but more responsible and able to reshape the production objectives of tangible and intangible goods, but above all, capable of rethinking the settlement model in support of new economic relations. A holistic and strategic way of thinking is generating temporally differentiated uses, pervasive reuses, programmed recycling, explosive innovations, and creative evolution. The task of administrators, urban planners, architects, citizens, and enterprises is to work on rur-urban settlements characterized by the excess and overproduction generated by the development model, which caused depopulation before and is now stimulating attractiveness. Discontinued or shrinking settlement systems, health or sports services that have fallen into disuse, and infrastructural networks undergoing transformation must be addressed through actions of functional change, clustering, or reinvention, thanks to which unused components are recreated without destroying them, but by changing their functions, pursuing a generative perspective, and increasing their creative resilience.

Recycling is not just one of the main keywords of more advanced urban planning action[8] and of high-performing architecture and design, but is one of the most powerful guiding thoughts for the transformation from a consumerist linear economy to a creative circular economy for cities and landscapes that wish to pursue the path of sustainability, quality, and creativity. As already affirmed, the circular economy puts two types of material flows back into play: organic ones, capable of being replenished in the biosphere, and technical ones, destined to increase in value in a system in which all activities, from mining of materials and manufacturing to consumption, are organized so that the scraps of one phase become a resource for the following phase[9]. Finally, the circular economy postulates the passage from ownership of the product to its use, with the smallest possible environmental impact. These principles raise the fundamental question of how much the recycling of materials, semi-finished products, scraps, products at the end of their use cycle and biomass could contribute to the increase of a more responsible and less erosive GDP, so that the value of the production would be maintained for longer through reuse and, where possible, up-cycling, triggering a new cycle of sustainable prosperity (new services, combination of new products, lower environmental impact, and reduced toxicity).

In the circular economy, responsibility for the urban planning of medium and small cities that are once again welcoming to people, attractive of ideas, generative for businesses, and supportive to the community archipelagos, requires the implementation of concrete actions to guarantee a new balance between rural, urban and developable, or between landscaping weft and infrastructural warp, not just placing limits on land use, but above all, stimulating, encouraging, and rewarding the reuse of already urbanized areas and the densification of functions. Planning cities and territories in the era of urban recycling means rejecting the consolation of a molecular approach and accepting the challenge of an organic ecosystem approach, allowing ourselves to be guided by a new long-sighted vision to look towards the innovation horizon, but also to look back and retrieve wisdom, rituals, and practices. We also need effective visions and concrete projects understood as commitments to work towards an urban planning discipline that can influence the urban metabolism, recombining the genetic code contained in the areas to be recycled, which are often fragmented or weakened but still able to generate new urban tissue if reactivated by new vital energy.

It is not enough, therefore, to pump recycling sensitivity into traditional processes of urban and territorial planning. Rather, we need a disruptive innovation of urban planning processes and instruments: we need an eco-systemic planning approach based on a paradigm shift, as it must act at the same time on production materials in disuse or abandoned ones (areas undergoing deindustrialization, factories consumed by the crisis or transitioning agricultural areas), on logistic materials (railway and industrial areas in decline or undergoing functional refurbishment), and on housing areas left empty in small depopulated towns.

We need a new hyper-dimensional development model that operates through the combined action of the various dimensions (political, social, economic, ecological, and territorial) of sustainability and of territorial governance, not just juxtaposing or integrating them, but interconnecting them in a structural relationship. In this new structural relationship, the "political dimension" first of all enables the development of a culture of understanding and recognition of ecological, social, and cultural diversity as a founding value of the new settlement relationships and of the incremental enrichment that an exchange between diversities can bring to the common good. In a political view of sustainability, local identities are pinpointed as active resources for the development of sociality and community, as opposed to a culture of social polarization that tends to reduce differences. There is, in fact, a clear relationship between the indispensable growth of the local society, the strengthening of the foundations of democracy, the development of civic networks, and growth in the effective negotiation capacity of the locals in the context of globalization. The resulting "social dimension" contributes to ensuring that negotiations between public and private stakeholders for common development objectives are sufficiently articulated to guarantee not only the presence and problems of the weakest social players, but that their identification, proposition, and accountability can be incentivized, contributing to expanding the "social metabolism" of the inland areas. In fact, the ripest expressions of local, self-sustainable development base their objectives and resulting practices on promoting the accountability of local communities, which are able to rebalance the power relationship and guarantee to the communication and participation its founding statute of the legitimacy of the subjects.

The "economic dimension" that follows from this requires increasingly intangible economies, based on access rather than ownership, sociality rather than egoism, wellbeing rather than possession, and efficiency rather than consumption, laying down the model of a future that is "prosperous even without growth"[10], calling for an integration with planning that translates into a strengthening of the generative power of the sharing economy.

The "ecological dimension", upheld by a renewed ecosophical political vision[11], contributes to a commitment to territorial projects that guarantee a reduction of the ecological footprint by means of the reappropriation of settlement models capable of simultaneously pursuing a reduction of the mobility rate, an increase in the quality and uniqueness of products (environmental and cultural, but also food), the requalification of agricultural activities towards multi-functionality and sociality as factors to regenerate the territory and cities.

Finally, the "territorial dimension" imposes on the planning of infrastructure systems, on the landscape project, on the management of agricultural systems, and on urban planning, the development/testing of integrated settlement models, capable of promoting the entrenchment of the other four dimensions of sustainability, not just by identifying thresholds of land use, but with projects for the reclamation, recycling, and relaunch of settlements. We need an actual reboot of small-medium cities and inland areas, generated by the combined action of the redesign of urban fabrics, the localization of new micro- and nano-factories, and the innovative capacity of startups based on local excellence. Above all, the territorial dimension of sustainability summons urban planners to exercise creativity to plan new areas: from tangible areas of local development or the reticular areas of the territorial archipelagos to the virtual areas of human smart cities, in which numerous collective, multicultural, and multiethnic intellects interact, producing a new community.

Local development 2.0: innovation as an enabling factor

There are now numerous suggestions that help us recognize the need for a "creative and collaborative local development 2.0", which, starting from the theoretical reflections and numerous practices in contexts that test it, not just as a reaction to the crisis, requires an adaptive approach to innovation as an enabling factor of meta-project guidelines for a new metabolism of the local territory[12].

The first and most powerful enabling innovation is that produced by resilience, as the cycles of the rur-urban metabolism of the inland areas require the ineffectual resistance to metamorphosis to be overcome.

This will allow them to adopt an elastic, dialogue-based and, indeed, metamorphic attitude, in which the flexibility of functions, the permeability of spaces, and the adaptability of settlements are no longer addressed as purely conceptual and spatial problems, but put in relation with the social, economic, and technological capacity for regeneration, becoming issues/instruments/laws of the resilience project. The paradigm of resilience produces urban practices and generates neighborhoods or whole cities with a new metabolism, capable of better managing climate change or hydrogeological changes, and capable of absorbing increasingly frequent cloudbursts by producing new porous urban forms, particularly in public spaces. Water, even flood water, in hilly areas or river valleys becomes living project material to be absorbed by parks, roads, and permeable squares, both to alleviate the sewage system, and to create new collective spaces in connection with water, which gives them breath. However, resilient is also the recovery of old seeds, artisan processing of food and objects, and pre-industrial practices in which the entire community becomes the production chain.

Cultural innovation is a second enabling factor as it acts not only on the memory of places but also on their reputation, both through a greater identification of the inhabitants and users and through a validation of the opportunities offered by the vast global community interacting with the local development projects.

In a reputation economy[13], areas of innovation based on local culture, through the fame and credibility rebuilt via national and international prizes and awards, return to being an educational factor in the community and an opportunity for knowledge and training. This innovation obligates urban planners and architects to develop new forms, places, and relationships which contain and connect the information and communication flows generated with increasing frequency, capacity, and speed. Upon the reactivation of identity capital, low impact energies can be generated to power the urban regeneration based on cultural infrastructure, on the localization of creative attractors in the historic centres, in old manor farms or in the mills that dot the river lines, or on residential training initiatives aimed at redefining the attractiveness of places through a connection between education, well-being, and environmental quality.

The innovation produced by knowledge encourages learning so that for the ecological-social systems of inland areas to grow, they must be able to address the permanent change and learn to manage it by building new equilibrium, learning from knowledge and experience. This is why we need to act on communication, planning opportunities and places in which knowledge is released from the towers of specialists to disseminate collective intelligence and generate new community thinking, becoming concrete material to renew the coexistence agreement of populations of inland areas and to fuel the

The Bivona Manifesto: innovative environments for local development.

resulting development agreement. In the inland areas of Sicily, there is an increasingly number of innovative businesses created by reactivating traditional production cycles or cycles related to new tourism and food excellence, or connected to renewable energies, which also serve as a point of encounter and creativity, as true living labs for communities increasingly based on knowledge and inclined to active participation. The knowledge metabolism contributes to promoting innovation in the creation of activities, businesses, and places and to fuelling the emergence of ideas, experimentation, and the spread of projects more suited to new lifestyles and consumption habits, the birth of new enterprises where identity, creativity, and innovation intersect.

The innovation of the economy and geography of sharing[14] produces a high level of synergy between the new poly-central nature of services, the building structure of historic centers undergoing regeneration, and the supply of digital services. In inland areas that wish to be protagonists of a new Sicily, the inhabitants, through the new forms of cooperation, return to being producers and become farmers to revive abandoned parts of the city through urban agriculture. They become knowledge workers through workshops or creative incubators, produce cultural events through crowdfunding, and manage common spaces snatched from neglect and disrepair in temporary forms. Old railway stations and booths, medieval castles, slaughterhouses, almadrabas, convents, lighthouses, and watchtowers form an armature of creative activities in Sicily which is providing young local talents opportunities to test new forms of shared management.

Finally, we need a reticular innovation that enables the cycles of the multiple centres of the new polycentric geography, as opposed to obsolete gravitational models, reaching out towards the insertion of territorial armature of new nodes of social aggregation that make it fluid, using architectural sites intercepted in their change and reused for social opportunities as new urban activators. The territories of the new archipelago economy and of the social rhizomes accelerate the affirmation of new values that permit the production of new semantic cycles in areas undergoing transformation and discontinued areas capable of steering the change.

In order for the innovations described above to be enabling factors of development, they require a paradigm shift in which the territory is understood as a resource to be preserved, both in terms of reduction of its use, and considering it a holder of development cells often forgotten, underused or mystified by the illusion of the omnipotence of progressivism. They also need a deep innovation of the protocols and, above all, of urban planning instruments so that they know how to tap into the changes and lead the future.

The largest toolbox of the planner of local development 2.0 must accommodate programs of urban and territorial regeneration based on urban recycling districts, within which to integrate and enhance public demand, reduction of consumption, energy and taxation incentives, and instances of private redevelopment projects. Their feasibility will have to be substantiated by drawing up agreements in support of district forms of management of the territorial metabolism and by effective projects of environmental and social sustainability, assessed on recycling parameters regarding the buildings, public spaces, mobility, the waste cycle, and digital infrastructure. It is essential to activate territorial development laboratories and agencies of shared responsibility for design, economics, urban planning, and management between the public and private sectors, connected to a responsible simplification and greater efficacy of administrative action. Finally, innovation of the instruments of the public-private partnership will have to be stimulated through the extension of compensation and urban equalization, fiscal leverage, and incentives.

Emerging from Bivona, where the University of Palermo and the Municipalities of Bivona and Santo Stefano Quisquina established the *SicaniLab for local development and renewable* energy15 in 2014, is the resolution to use creativity and initiative as driving factors of quality, sustainability and innovation, as new energies for a better relationship with the environment and communities. Moreover, in 2014, it trained twenty-eight new professionals, through the 2nd level University Master's Degree in "Integrated Planning for Sustainable Development", who know how to put together skills and sensitivity, technical abilities, and management professionalism for a different local development based on the principles of smart planning. In 2015, it launched the first "School of advanced training in creativity and territorial innovation", in which fifty young innovators and as many people and enterprises with already mature experience proposed projects and feasibility studies to create new business, well-being, and development for the Sicanian territory.

Gone are the days of assisted local development and of projects that last only as long as their funding. The local area of the future is itself the driver of innovation, a powerful engine of new circular and shared economies, and an effective cultural promoter of our cosmopolitan identity. However, if Sicily wishes to be a land of innovation and circularity for local development, it cannot limit itself to these numerous experiments, but needs to activate several system actions that will increase their scope. Emerging from the experiences carried out in Bivona is an "agenda for local development" – which we called, in fact, the Bivona Manifesto — which identifies seven operational actions for institutions, communities, and professionals capable of changing methods and instruments for the reactivation of inland territories. Among the proposed actions, first of all, we must demand that public spaces and services be available for use and for different users over time to facilitate the birth of innovative businesses and services, but also to distribute the costs of management, maximize efficiency, and guarantee maintenance. Moreover, we must demand that public administration data be easy to access for anyone at any time, from anywhere, and from any device. Credit and corporate financing must, therefore, be facilitated by changing the forms of guarantee and the return periods and the public-private partnership must have increasing forms of shared responsibility rather than simple co-financing.

The challenge for generative and non-dissipative local development calls us to the task of a new responsibility and a new hermeneutics of the territorial plan and of urban design as the result of a generative creativity made up of treatment, reclamation, and reactivation of urban settlements which once again fuel life cycles, cultivate the talents of the inhabitants, attract ideas, generate innovation, produce new economies, and strengthen solidarity networks. It requires us to activate actions oriented to the life cycles of the inland areas, by reactivating the latent potential or the resources excluded from the choices of a development model addicted to inefficient, standardizing urban policies, which are insensitive to the cultural capital and built on financial and, above all, qualitative deficit.

Sicily, as a land of local innovation, thus requires a new disruptive approach that positively destroys the conformism of choices and the inertia of behaviors that restrain our development.

1. The Sicilian territorial armature based on the cultural matrix provides effective opportunities and powerful instruments of local development. See: Carta, M., *L'armatura culturale del territorio. Il patrimonio culturale come matrice di identità e strumento di sviluppo*. Milan: FrancoAngeli, 2002.
2. Opportunities and threats of the metropolitan and consortium model in Sicily are described in Carta, M., "Città Metropolitane: dall'eco-sistema funzionale al super-organismo di sviluppo", in D'Amico, R., Piraino, A. (editor), *Il governo locale in Sicilia. Materiali per la riforma*. Milan: FrancoAngeli, 2014.
3. Paradigms and planning devices for rethinking urban planning in the era of the metamorphosis towards more creative, intelligent, and ecological cities and territories are explored further in Carta, M., *Reimagining Urbanism. Creative, smart and green cities for the changing times*. Barcelona- Trento: ListLab, 2014.
4. See: Emery, N., *Progettare, costruire, curare. Per una deontologia dell'architettura*. Bellinzona: Casagrande, 2010.
5. See: Carta, M., "Re-immaginare il Sud. Le sfide del buongoverno per la metamorfosi dello sviluppo", in Russo, M. (editor), *Urbanistica per una diversa crescita. Progettare il territorio contemporaneo*. Rome: Donzelli,2014.
6. See: Pope Francis, *Laudato si'. Sulla cura della casa comune*. Vatican City: Libreria Editrice Vaticana, 2015.
7. See: Kaletsky, A., *Capitalism 4.0: The Birth of a New Economy in the Aftermath of Crisis*. New York: Perseus, 2010.
8. In Italy, the theme of recycling of cities, infrastructure, and landscapes was introduced in 2011 by the exhibition "Re-cycle", curated at the MAXXI (described in Ciorra, P., Marini, S. (editor), *Re-Cycle. Strategie per l'architettura, la città e il pianeta*. Milan: Electa, 2011) and spread rapidly among the more sensitive scientific community. See: Fabian, L., Giannotti, E., Viganò, P., eds., *Recycling City. Lifecycles, Embodied Energy, Inclusion*. Pordenone: Giavedoni, 2012; D'Arienzo, R., Younès, C. (sous la direction de), *Recycler l'urbain. Pour une écologie des milieux habités*. Geneva: Metis Presses, 2014. Even the professional community has established the importance of the issues of reducing land use, reuse, and recycling (see: National Council of Architects, RI.U.SO. Rome: CNAPPC, 2012). Subsequently, the issue became the subject of a study of national interest funded by the Ministry of Universities and Research and involving 11 Italian and as many foreign universities. See: Marini, S., Santangelo, V. (editor), *Re-cycle Italy. Nuovi cicli di vita per architetture e infrastrutture della città e del paesaggio*. Rome: Aracne, 2013.
9. Regarding the circular economy, see Ellen MacArthur Foundation, *Towards the Circular Economy: Economic and business rationale for an accelerated transition*. Chicago: EMF, 2012.
10. See: Jackson, T., *Prosperity without Growth: Economics for a Finite Planet*. New York: Earthscan, 2009.
11. A new active and not purely reactive ecological dimension of urban planning has been proposed by the department of ur-

ban planning at Harvard. See: Mostafavi, M., Doherty, G. (eds.), *Ecological Urbanism*. Zurich: Lars Müller Publishers, 2010; Reed, C., Lister, N.M., *Projective Ecologies*. Barcelona: Actar, 2014. It was relaunched in Italy by several urban planners of the REDS network, as in Ricci, M., *Nuovi paradigmi*. Barcelona-Trento: ListLab, 2012. 12. See: Carta, M., Lino, B. (editor), *Urban Hyper-Metabolism*. Rome: Aracne Int.le, 2015.
13. See: Fertik, M., Thompson, D.C., *The Reputation Economy*. New York: Crown Business, 2015.
14. See: Rifkin, J., *The Zero Marginal Cost Society: The Internet of Things, the Collaborative Commons, and the Eclipse of Capitalism*. New York: palgrave Macmillan, 2014.
15. The mission and operational program of the SicaniLab are described in Carta, M., Ronsivalle, D., "I territori dell'innovazione locale", in *Aa.Vv., Atti della XXXV conferenza AISRE*. Padua, 2014. The workshop follows in the wake of the European strategy towards sustainable development and a carbon free economy. See: European Climate Foundation, *Roadmap 2050. A practical guide to a prosperous, low-carbon Europe*. Den Haag: ECF, 2010; European Commission, Directorate-General for Research and Innovation, *Global Europe 2050*. Luxembourg: Publications Office of the European Union, 2012.

2.3

A SMART LAND TO REACTIVATE TERRITORIAL WEALTH

MARILENA ORLANDO

Cities are the preferred places of modernity, speed, and movement — characteristics already imagined by the futurist Antonio Sant'Elia — which have attracted enterprises, creative human capital[1], and workers for economic growth. However, there is also a network of small-medium urban centers in the mountains or hills, rural villages, and productive landscapes, in which distance from the coastal cities has preserved the identity-forming values that live in the territorial wealth of historic centers, landscape, history, production, and local traditions. These are preferential areas for the metamorphosis of development[2], in which to pursue the goals of intelligence, sustainability, inclusion[3], and creativity to reactivate territorial capital. In these territorial areas, we can test the smart land paradigm, which, through sustainability in its social, economic, and environmental dimensions, inclusiveness and widespread prosperity, is taking on a key role in the definition of potential development paths taken by local administrators and economic, cultural and social stakeholders in order to improve quality of life and rethink urban and rural spaces, not only from a technological point of view, but according to the needs of the inhabitants, rationalization of infrastructure and services, as well as to promote local excellence and, more generally, the territorial wealth that the inland areas have preserved. In Sicily, we can identify such urban/rural territorial areas, where the smart land paradigm can be tested by means of widespread shared policies oriented to boost the competitiveness and attractiveness of the territory, paying heed to social cohesion, innovation, knowledge dissemination, creativity, accessibility, usability of the environment (natural, historic-architectural, urban, and widespread), and to the quality of the landscape and life of citizens[4].

The Sicani area in particular is the subject of attention for the Local Development Laboratory of the University Research Center of Bivona and Santo Stefano Quisquina for the energy, environment, and resources of the territory[5], which is testing, under the scientific supervision of Professor Maurizio Carta, innovative local development strategies based on the rural and cultural dimension in accordance with the smart land model. The analysed Sicani area, situated between the former provinces of Palermo and Agrigento and covering 211,526 hectares with 104,102 residents, is characterized by the fragility of its urban systems — a fragility linked to its socio-demographic situation (the population density of 71.68 people per km^2 is progressively decreasing), poor infrastructural connection (ports, airports, and motorways cannot be reached in less than 60 minutes by car), and the lack of education and health services. This conflicts with the huge potential of the territory when viewed from an ecosystem equilibrium perspective. In fact, the area has an unspoilt landscape

(12,122 ha of reserves and 43,687 ha of the Park of the Sicani Mountains), an underused system of cultural resources (159 properties including military architecture, religious, residential, and productive buildings and 82 areas of archaeological assets), and agricultural resources (98,543 ha of utilized agricultural land, amounting to 45% of the territory, and 8 food and wine trails).This conflicts with a low economic endowment index (1.9%) compared to the regional average (15.53%) despite a higher entrepreneurship index (22%) than the regional average (15%), a high rate of accommodation on the coast and a virtually inexistent one in the more inland area (the coastal municipality of Cattolica Eraclea has a rate of accommodation of 141% and a tourism density of 321.27%),and a high level of programming and planning vivacity (12 territorial coalitions activated, including community programs, thematic districts, and local development companies)[6]. Furthermore, attempts at productive specialization are practiced[7] primarily in the field of organic production, promotion of a new real estate market[8], and diversified tourism aimed at forms of experiential tourism[9], which generate potential attractions and a different quality of life for both external users and potential residents.

The analysis carried out highlighted the absence in the Sicani territory of a center to attract flows and functions and, instead, the presence of small urban centers and connecting spaces with different functional specializations, which tend to organize themselves into forms of aggregation based on the opportunities of national and EU planning. This condition makes the territory particularly suited to a smart configuration, as a smart land is characterized by the presence of "uniform configurations or configurations willing to unite" to recompose themselves from the bottom up in the desire for self-transformation (based on the characteristics of the territory and cultural and historic identities)[10] and by the role of those "intermediate players" — such as municipal aggregations — which, together with the various local forces, citizens, and associations, share a common development plan to operate in and for the territory in accordance with the principles of subsidiarity. To make this possible, the technological efficiency of bureaucracies, widespread computer literacy, and the construction of capillary information networks are becoming priority conditions and necessary actions in an overall strategy of smart development.

Therefore, considering this territory to be a fertile place, in which several of the necessary conditions for the germination of the smart seed can be found, the research has verified the existence of conditions for division into districts for the purpose of identifying local rural-urban systems based on the assessment of centrality indices — cultural, naturalistic, tourism, agricultural, productive, and local planning — aimed at completing a structural analysis of the territory according to the identities and specializations it contains and at assessing its attractiveness and/or ability to generate a new identity[11].

Specifically, the centrality indices relating to cultural heritage highlight a prevalence of medium-high centrality in relation to the numerous cultural assets, which have low centrality in relation to the endowment of cultural services (museums and libraries). The naturalistic centrality index shows the high level of nature of the whole analysed territory, whose strength lies in the presence of the Park of the Sicani Mountains; the agricultural centrality index highlights the territory's strong agricultural vocation, given the high percentage of utilized agricultural land, which, however, does not have an appropriate effect in the economy[12], due to the inadequate infrastructure system that makes transportation difficult on the one hand, and the prevalence of micro-businesses on the other[13].

A parallel analysis of the typical productivity index shows various centralities that demonstrate how various nodes of the territory analyzed are investing in prestigious productivity regardless of the high agricultural centrality.

The tourism centrality index shows an imbalance between the coastal area, equipped with adequate tourist accommodation to meet the demands of seaside tourism, and the more inland area, which despite an excellent cultural and natural heritage, has not activated alternative and diversified tourism.

A comparison of the centrality indices and the local planning index — the latter reveals the aggregational capacity of the territory as a function of its ability to adhere to plans and projects linked to national and EU programmes[14] – allowed us to recognize three areas in the territory characterized by the prevalence of several functional specializations — rural/productive, widespread specialization, and tourism — which can constitute a smart land experimental laboratory, in which to define a framework of actions and policies, starting from the issues of citizenship, development, energy, mobility, identity, knowledge, and landscape that characterize its paradigm[15].

Specifically, the territorial area characterized by rural specialization, a high level of nature, and a strong agricultural vocation, requires policies to strengthen and promote the agricultural and productive excellence it contains.

These policies intercept the economic dimension, which, in a smart land, is broken down into interaction between education and entrepreneurship, tradition and new technologies, and support to start-ups and workshops of ideas.

The territorial area characterized by widespread specialization, endowed with numerous examples of excellence and several nodes of high cultural centrality, with a strong propensity for local network planning, requires policies to fertilize neighbouring areas and to implement and network services designed for the use of the territory.

Finally, the coastal area with a high tourism centrality, but devoid of connections with the inland area requires policies to diversify tourism and network for the use of the natural, cultural, and rural excellence of the more inland area.

The policies defined for the territorial area of widespread specialization and for that of tourism specialization intercept the dimension of identity and local knowledge, which in a smart land is broken down into specific actions to promote the environmental, artisan, cultural, economic, landscape, and productive local identity through the presence and dissemination, on the web and social media, of itineraries and thematic mapping of its territory, and the creation of integrated knowledge networks, through the formation of ideas laboratories that bring together all the cultural and productive components of craftsmanship and higher education contained in the territory.

These actions are supported by new national and EU planning. The National Reform Plan for Inland Areas, which envisages the adoption of a strategy to relaunch local development using the ordinary funds of the Stability Law and the 2014-2020 EU funds, and the Rural Development Plan are an invaluable opportunity to begin a process of innovative sustainable development.

The Rural Development Plan, which identifies strategic objectives, such as competitiveness of the agricultural sector, the sustainable management of natural resources, and the balanced development of rural areas, offers an opportunity to test new models of quality of life and smart use/promotion in the Sicani territory. The aforementioned Plan identifies three long-term strategic goals (Article 4 Regulation 1305/2013)for the 2014-2020 period: competitiveness of the agricultural sector, sustainable management of natural resources, and balanced development of rural

areas, based on six intervention priorities — which recall the thematic axes of the smart land –, including the promotion of innovation in the agricultural sector, strengthening of profitability of farms by means of innovative and sustainable techniques, encouraging the organization of food supply chains, the enhancement of ecosystems linked to agriculture and forestry, incentives for an efficient use of resources and for an economy of low carbon emissions, social inclusion, reduced poverty, and economic development in rural areas.

The National Strategy of Inland Areas allows us to begin a process of acquiring citizenship services for the twelve municipalities of the "Terre Sicane" Inland Area, which can become a driving force for development, even in adjacent territories. The twelve municipalities have set up several platforms for discussion and negotiation among the various players of the local community, and involving territorial experts, to develop a strategy for the Inland Area. This strategy aims to channel the available financial resources into local priorities, which, starting from citizenship services — health, education, and mobility — also include the issues of local development, craftsmanship, sustainable tourism, land protection, and energy.

The Local Development Laboratory, in its role as "development facilitator and enabler"[16], is taking part as the coordinating party in the platform on Local Development, which engages local, institutional, economic, cultural, and social players —who can all contribute to launching a new productive economic and social cycle in the inland areas —to test smart approaches to local development and reactivate the territorial wealth of the Sicani inland area.

Bibliography

Bonomi, A., Masiero, R. (2014), *Dalla smart city alla smart land*. Venezia: Marsilio.

Carta, M. (2003), *Pianificare nel dominio culturale*. Palermo: Dipartimento Città e Territorio.

Carta, M. (2007), *CreativeCity. Dinamics, Innovation, Action*. Barcelona-Trento: List.

Carta, M. (2013), *Reimagining Urbanism. Città creative, intelligenti ed ecologiche per i tempi che cambiano*. Barcelona-Trento: ListLab.

Carta, M. (2015), "Innovazione, Circolarità e Sviluppo Locale. La sfida dei territori interni", in Carta, M., Ronsivalle, D., *Territori interni. La pianificazione integrata per lo sviluppo circolare: metodologie, approcci, applicazioni per nuovi cicli di vita*. Roma: Aracne Int.le, pp.22-35.

Carta, M., Ronsivalle, D. (2015), "I territori dell'Innovazione locale: dalla ricerca allo sviluppo sperimentale", in Carta, M., Ronsivalle, D., *Territori interni. La pianificazione integrata per lo sviluppo circolare: metodologie, approcci, applicazioni per nuovi cicli di vita*. Roma: Aracne Int.le, pp.84-103.

Commissione Europea (2010), *Comunicazione della Commissione. Europa 2020, Una strategia per una crescita intelligente, sostenibile e inclusiva*. Luxembourg: Publications Office of the European Union.

Contato, A., Orlando, M. (2015a), "Nuovi paradigmi per le aree interne. Il caso del Territorio Sicano", in *Atti della XVIII Conferenza nazionale SIU. Italia '45-'45. Radici, condizioni, prospettive*. Roma-Milano: Planum Publisher, pp.521-527. Disponibile su: http://www.planum.bedita.net/ atti-della-xviii-conferenza-nazionale-siu.

Contato, A., Orlando, M. (2015b), "Il territorio dei Monti Sicani. Il sistema delle risorse territoriali per l'attivazione di politiche di sviluppo locale", in Carta, M., Ronsivalle, D., *Territori interni. La pianificazione integrata per lo sviluppo circolare: metodologie, approcci, applicazioni per nuovi cicli di vita*. Roma: Aracne Int.le, pp.84-103.

Florida, R. (2002), *The Rise of the Creative Class. And How It's Transforming Work, Leisure and Everyday Life*. New York: Basic Books.

Istat (2011a), *Censimento della popolazione e delle abitazioni*. Roma: Istat.

Istat (2011b), *Censimento dell'agricoltura*. Roma: Istat.

Istat (2011c), *Censimento dell'industria e dei servizi*. Roma: Istat.

Mirto, A.P.M. (2014), *Atlante dell'agricoltura in Sicilia. Una lettura guidata delle mappe tematiche*. Palermo: Istat.

1. The concept of creative capital as an urban development engine is addressed in Florida (2002). An interpretation of contemporary creative cities is given by Carta (2007).
2. The role of inland areas in the metamorphosis of local development is described in Carta (2015).
3. For the three priorities of the Europe 2020 strategy, see European Commission (2010). For further information on innovative paradigms for the metamorphosis of the development towards intelligent, ecological, and creative territories, see Carta (2013).
4. The smartland paradigm is addressed in Bonomi and Masiero (2014).
5. The Research Center began in 2011 through the renewal of a Programme Agreement between the Sicily Region, the University of Palermo, the Regional Province of Agrigento and the municipalities of Bivona and Santo Stefano Quisquina. The Local Development Laboratory (SicaniLab) operates within the Research Center, under the coordination and scientific direction of Maurizio Carta and consisting of D. Ronsivalle, B. Lino, M. Marafon Pecoraro, M. Orlando, A. Contato, G. Mortellaro, A. Carrara, M. Buondonno and the scientific collaboration of A. Badami, I. Vinci, and V. Provenzano. This Agreement involved the creation of an applied Research Center featuring a connection between higher education, research and development, innovation centers, and the economic fabric of the territory.
6. The figures shown, developed from ISTAT indices (ISTAT, 2011a; 2011b; 2011c), are the result of the joint work of B. Lino, M. Marafon Pecoraro, M. Orlando, A. Contato, G. Mortellaro and A. Carrara, engaged in both the census of information and interpretative phases of knowledge, under the scientific direction of Professor Maurizio Carta. 7. The best-known quality trademarks include a PDO for the Ribera orange and a PGI for Bivona fishing.
8. This is the case of the municipality of Cianciana which, following the depopulation that occurred with the closing of the sulfur mines (1962), is promoting the purchase of homes in the historic center, combining cost-effectiveness with a better quality of life compared to that of large cities.
9. Val di Kam, a tourism promotion company based in S. Angelo Muxaro, offers nature and cave walks, touristic itineraries to discover new places and experiences of participating in the life of food and livestock farming.
10. For further information on the smartland proposal and the role of "intermediate players", see Bonomi and Masiero (2014).
11. The methodology used is based on the qualitative-quantitative methodology developed within the Research into Local Cultural Systems by Carta (2003) and uses a system of qualitative-quantitative indicators, structured into thematic areas and enriched by the centrality index which, calculated for each area, helps us to understand the structure of this territory according to its unique identity and specializations. The matrix of indicators is structured into the following topics: hotel and non-hotel accommodation, equipped woodland areas, protected natural areas, agricultural areas, typical and prestigious production, cultural heritage, cultural services, festivals and cultural events, wine trails, agri-food itineraries, and local projects. For further information regarding the centrality indices calculated for the Sicani territory, see Contato and Orlando (2015b).
12. Data relating to the effect of the agricultural sector on the local economy have been analyzed in Contato and Orlando (2015a).
13. An analysis of Sicilian farms can be found in Mirto (2014).
14. Regarding this, see Contato and Orlando (2015b).
15. The themes and field of action of the *Smart Land* are dealt with by Della Puppa and Masiero, "Less is more. Manifesto per una società smart", in Bonomi and Masiero (2014).
16. The role of the University and, specifically, of the Local Development Laboratory (Sicani-Lab) for the Sicani area has been addressed in Carta and Ronsivalle (2015).

Area of rural/productive specialization

Definition: Rural area with high naturalistic and agricultural centrality and inadequate local productivity.

Characteristics: Area with a high demand for investments and networking policies and policies of territorial marketing.

Policies: Activation of policies to strengthen and promote the landscape, agricultural, and productive excellence contained in the territory.

Area of widespread specialization

Definition: Complex area with a strong propensity for local planning, endowed with numerous examples of excellence and several nodes of high cultural centrality.

Characteristics: Area featuring high planning vivacity of the local administrations.

Policies: Activation of policies to fertilize neighboring areas, and to implement and network services designed for the use of the territory.

Area of tourism specialization

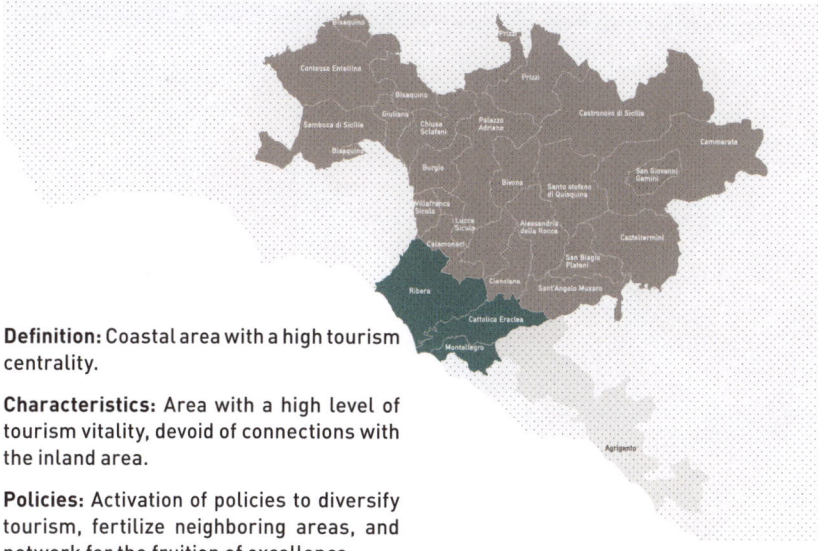

Definition: Coastal area with a high tourism centrality.

Characteristics: Area with a high level of tourism vitality, devoid of connections with the inland area.

Policies: Activation of policies to diversify tourism, fertilize neighboring areas, and network for the fruition of excellence.

The research conducted by SicaniLab recognizes three areas in the Sicani territory characterized by the prevalence of several functional specializations — rural/productive, widespread specialization, and tourism — which can constitute a smart land experimental laboratory, in which to envisage actions dealing mainly with specific issues:
- "landscape" and "identity", to boost the territorial offering and promote the cultural heritage of knowledge, places, and traditions;
- "economy", to introduce changes of a structural nature into the productive fabric;
- "energy", to create systems of energy and waste management in areas of agricultural production;
- "citizenship", as the Sicani territory, which has shown its ability to build territorial coalitions, may be considered an area in which forms of participation in and sharing of development projects can go hand in hand with interaction between administrators and local forces.

NO EXTERNALITIES FOR CLOSED-CYCLE CITIES
STRATEGIC ENVIRONMENTAL ASSESSMENT AND PLANNING

DANIELE RONSIVALLE

RE-CYCLICAL URBANISM

Contemporary landscapes in Sicily: a reference framework for active development models

Following the Second World War, contemporary Sicilian landscapes were created by the coexistence of two opposing forces: a broad convergence of the regional and national intelligentsia on issues of constitutional protection and, at the same time, a strong push towards transformation, often implemented with complete indifference to the reflections and actions aimed at conservation.

The contrasting development models have led to the formation of contemporary "third" landscapes, not like those imagined by Clément (2005)[1] in the perspective of landscape planning, but whose thirdness derives from an inability to define planning actions in the mid and long term, even when the project appears to be strong, oriented to the future, and visionary. We could say that there is a cultural chronology of these events that follows a precise line of development:
- First phase: characterized by State intervention and the production of development frameworks that were not able to create identity and continuity in the processes of identification;
- Second phase: influenced by the consumption of territorial resources and the consequential state of crisis of local communities deprived of the key resources needed for development;
- Third phase: characterized by the desire of local communities to overcome the detachment between places, cultural resources, landscapes, and the economies of the territory.

The third phase is underway, but only some areas are in a condition to develop useful plans and projects to mend the detachment generated in the preceding phases.

The Sicani case study: local replacement actions and regional planning processes

Opportunities for local development have materialized in some local areas, which, by tradition or recognition that a local identity exists, have been able to produce an alternative path or steer supra-local planning and programming: this is the case of the Sicani Mountains.

The establishment of the new Regional Park, for example, is an important piece of this protection and promotion framework, whose goal is to work not only on the protection of natural and cultural values, but also on defining local development contexts that are consistent with the existing resources and oriented to local knowledge, even when integrated with contemporary technologies and perspectives.

Local and supra-local policies already activated throughout the last decade concerning landscape planning and the enhancement strategies described above reveal the great vitality of these areas, for which the additional boost provided by the most recent landscape and environmental policies[2] plays into the hands of the possibility to integrate choices, building a complex development program that includes both the choices relating to the sector of cultural, natural, and landscape heritage, and to the settlement and compatible use of resources for economic and productive purposes. The issue, however, appears complex to resolve as, despite declarations of intent, the regional players do not currently appear ready to activate integrated policies.

The interpretation planning model, adopted in several plans for the protection and enhancement of the landscape (for example, the Landscape Plan of Partinico, Corleone, and the Monti Sicani), is currently the ideal candidate model for drafting this huge canvas, in which the Sicani landscapes become the engine of local development.

The landscape projects for the Sicani Mountains, however, will not become operational if we do not provide for the building of an integrated unified strategy using economic resources from community co-funding, where, however, a vision of integrated strategies is required, with the transformation of land uses and with the environmental qualification of the development strategies. Open issues concern the continuity of development, the availability of economies not coming from outside, and the ability to build enduring development processes that are solved bottom-up, according to a relational and cross-scale vision[3] that can be adapted to the real situations of the landscapes to be regenerated.

The solutions also concern the urban space planning review and the overall review of some strategic planning and control mechanisms regarding territorial resources that occur at the level of interaction for the approval of operational instruments, which then configure the landform.

Here, a specific condition of weakness in the planning, design, and evaluation system arises: the middle ground between territorial strategies, operational instruments for land use, and environmental assessment processes, which never relate to one another, often living in a condition of indifference or conflict. This can be solved from a planning perspective by adopting the environmental assessment frameworks which analyze some classes of content, procedural, and administrative issues and is the most suitable place to mend disjointed processes and resolve conditions of conflict.

1. The contents: local territories, such as the Sicani mountains, do not only produce development through the cartographic demonstration of static urban zoning but act through planning and funding which, as a side effect of the urban planning process, give lifeblood to the projects and urban locations assigned by the plans.

2. The procedures: territorial actions and implementation of plans are not separate and must not be if, indeed, the goal is to overcome the crisis conditions described by the first and second phases which led to the thirdness of the Sicilian landscape.

3. The administrative issue: administrations that directly or indirectly control local transformations (Regional Department of Urban Planning, Environmental Authority,

and Funding Processes Management Authorities) do not work on territorial coherence schemes capable of producing a consistent effect, except when urban planning, strategic planning, programming, and funding are actually coordinated from the bottom up by the territories producing local development frameworks.

Relevance of the strategic environmental assessment: ecological planning "without externalities"
With the scientific support of the writer, the Regional Department of Urban Planning has launched a review of the relationships between territorial planning and strategic environmental assessment with a view to:
- Adopting the assessment as an argumentative and participatory tool to increase the substantive and shareable nature of the plan;
- Integrating planning legislation and assessment processes, opening the plan to environmental, cultural, and social externalities;
- Clarifying assessment processes in urban and territorial policies with diversification and integration in planning processes;
- Reviewing the organizational processes of the plan from formulation to implementation using integrated administrative planning management tools that are more recognizable and traceable.
In the theoretical reflections and operational procedures of many Italian regions of recent years, processes of applying strategic environmental assessment to urban planning instruments have revealed a need to revise the position from which relevant players and settled communities see the assessment tool.
In rethinking the way environmental assessment and planning intersect, we can dwell on four main theoretical and methodological issues.
1. The assessment as an argumentative and participatory tool: from an argumentative and participatory perspective, planning of territorial transformations employs the assessment tools throughout the planning process to increase the substantive and shareable nature of the plan.
2. Legislative integration of the plan and assessment processes: the assessment is more and more frequently being integrated into the procedures indicated by regional urban planning laws, opening itself to environmental, cultural, and social externalities that guide the plan through its formation, and therefore bringing them into the processes.
3. Clarification of assessment processes in urban and territorial policies: the diversification of instruments and their innovation in the forms of urban policies, negotiated planning, and integrated EU planning requires assessment processes to be clarified within projects prior to their presentation, during construction, and in assessing results.
4. Clarification of the organizational processes of the plan from formulation to implementation: the building of complex planning and assessment processes requires the use of tools that make the phases of the plan-

ning processes explicit and evident, increasing their ability to be recognized and traced.

Meanwhile, the Strategic Environmental assessment (SEA) is a strategic assessment of transformations with qualification and environmental characterization, thus oriented to strategy building: the regulatory plan, for example, is not an instrument devoid of external relations and repercussions, even in the field of development strategies and strategies ensuring the ecological quality of the transformations underway. If we do not interpret the term "ecological" as the pure observation, assessment, and protection of natural and environmental resources, but as a way of interpreting the cyclical nature of territorial actions, then it is very likely that the operational connection between SEA and Planning can also be revised.

Just to give an example: the most enlightened plans currently being drafted recognize the inevitable need to cut urban expansion to zero and to restore the patterns of the peri-urban agricultural system. This intention, when carried out in the implementation of the plan, will produce induced effects that could cause extensive friction between the individual stakeholders: What economies will support agriculture that is unable to generate a market? What kinds of food production can be activated in the absence of feasibility checks on an agricultural production in areas that have been subjected to misuse for years? Can energy and agriculture once again be welded in a relationship with a low entropy profile within long energy cycles and with low thermal impact?

Only one preventive assessment — parallel to the process of drafting the plan — can define effects and orient the objectives of territorial development, avoiding conflict that destabilizes the planning processes and cripples their effects.

This vision is further enriched if we look at the territorial situation animated by life cycles that human action generates, modifies, fuels, or abandons over time: the time has ended for putting a green halftone in General Regulatory Plans to indicate the legendary "public green areas" or a wide green stroke to point out the zone E agricultural areas (with all their captious variations on the issue). The Environmental Assessment process can meet these needs to ensure that a plan is capable of reading and interpreting the life cycles of our territories.

The contents of the SEAs of urban planning instruments: synchronization or internalization?

In order to synchronize the SEA and make it useful in the drafting of urban planning instruments, it is necessary to make some considerations regarding the technical contents and complexity of the procedures:

1. The assessment process for large interventions and more complex territories and for small territorial projects is identical, while dimensional diversification between

processes could be suitable, as long as the sequence of the assessment phases remains the same;
2. The misalignment of drafting and assessment processes makes the preparation of the SEA useless;
3. The grain and scale of the environmental data are not always suited to the real territorial situations due to a normal absence of detailed data on small territorial areas;
4. The documents to be produced for the SEA process are not always prepared in a comparable way from a formal and substantial viewpoint, thus making the assessment procedure extremely subjective;
5. The publicity level of processes underway is not always transparent to the settled community through institutional channels (for example, online documents protected by passwords, websites of regional authorities that can't always be accessed, etc.).
In order to investigate and identify potential solutions, it is expedient to begin with a close examination of the regional situations: indeed, the administrative and management situation regarding the SEA issue is extremely differentiated in the various Italian regions. There are cases of total integration in planning processes, as in Lombardy, or the presence of one legislation and specific procedures, as in Apulia.
In a recent "Digest on SEA Legislation"[4], ISPRA (The Italian National Institute for Environmental Protection and Research) emphasized that only in some cases are legislation consistent and procedures standardized.

One of these cases is the Lombardy Region, in which the methodological models are differentiated according to the size, scale, and presumption of environmental impact that a given plan or program may have regardless of its specific contents.
Considering the above and looking at the ISPRA reports and regional situations, we could put forward a preliminary hypothesis of some potential solutions:
a. Interventions on the structure of the documents produced by the proceeding parties based on the territorial size of the plan/program, limiting/orienting the information required to prepare the SEA phases;
b. Reorganization of the administrative structure of the SEA service to optimize the timeframe of standard procedures (plans that are certainly eligible by law) and those requiring preventive procedures (plans and programs whose eligibility must be assessed);
c. Interventions on the procedure for preparing General Regulatory Plans and SEAs to be included together in the planning directives as two sides of the same process;
d. Production of a single drafting and assessment framework that allows the proceeding party and the relevant authorities on environmental matters to prepare, read, and assess the contents unequivocally, thus limiting – as far as possible in a text document – aleatory assessments and the response times of the Regional Department of Urban Planning Administration regarding the individual Assessment;

e. Adoption of software or an online platform/service that guides the preparation of the SEA documents and limits the timeframes for the transmission of documents[5].

The innovative contents of the Sicily Region - University of Palermo technical panel

A numerical and quantitative assessment is not sufficient to give body and shape to its urban effects: indeed, it is particularly complex to synchronize the assessment and planning processes, especially when it comes to building the urban form in accordance with an approach that could be equated to the principles of Ecological Urbanism[6].

A necessary condition for this to occur is that the SEA is really an assessment of the policies to be implemented in the urban transformation, at the level of the structural transformation scheme, so that the territorial structure proposed is assessed in strategic terms of feasibility, the consequences of choices, and the timeframes of the plan options. The sufficient condition for which the SEA makes sense, however, is that the form of the planned city responds to a series of formal checks carried out on the outcomes of the planning project. Environmental quality indicators can become the instruments to steer the formalization of urban space environmental quality. If we extract from a set of shared and recognized indicators —such as that produced by ISPRA for the SEA — a subset of the indicators which have the most territorial repercussions, and we try to understand how the project can act on the quality required by that indicator, we could propose formal solutions, rather than simple numeric targets for values devoid of meaning. The quality of transformations is assessed, therefore, on the reduction of emissions, respect for quantitative thresholds, and the capacity of the constraint to provide an opportunity for transformation.

Environmental compensation is controlled using reference planning thresholds, differing according to the type of planning instrument and the indicator proposed. It suggests to the planner how the transformation could be proposed in keeping with environmental quality and with urban planning and sustainable building regulations. Precisely for this reason, the implementation instrument, from planning by sector to urban planning and building regulations, will have to deal with the various types of environmental assessment provided for by Italian Legislative Decree 152/2006 and by D.P. Reg. Siciliana 23/2014, due to the fact that the formalization of transformations and the quantification of use inevitably intercepts the way in which urban spaces materialize.

Regional Department of Urban Planning SEA Directive 1/2014, issued by the Sicily Region and drawn up with the scientific contribution of the writer, does not attach numeric benchmark parameters but works on switch-on or switch-off modalities for the purpose of recognizing whether there is a presence, increase, reduction, or variation of urbanization interventions in the planning project that could inevitably change the level of environmental quality and which, especially with regard to inland territories or areas with reduced capacity for environmental monitoring, could have difficulty accessing really significant sets of data from a statistical and environmental point of view.

1. See Clément, G., *Manifesto del Terzo paesaggio*. Macerata: Quodlibet, 2005 for the new and proactive meaning of the Third Landscape from a planning perspective. In this case, the meaning of thirdness stops at the premises, all to be verified, of the real possibility of transforming places into material for the landscape project, which would otherwise remain in the limbo of non-use.
2. In Ronsivalle, D., *Ri-generare il paesaggio*. Milan: FrancoAngeli, 2007, the issues and possible interpretations of the landscape are studied through an interpretation centered on conservation and compatible transformation of the territorial patterns of a now pervasive landscape. Even today, the territorial planning viewpoint regarding the landscape appears not to have been resolved in a consistent form in relation to the need to integrate protection into the transformation plan and the opportunity to generate new landscapes through plans and policies that are stronger because they are more consistent with the cultural and landscape identities.
3. The vision centered on the economy of the territories (as proposed by Provenzano, V., "Marginality and Local Development: The Bivona Case". In Carta, M., Ronsivalle, D., *Territori Interni*. Rome: Aracne Int.le, 2015) is not in conflict with the condition of constitutional protection, but opens new scenarios to the integration of choices and the wise use of territorial wealth.
4. See ISPRA website, page http://www.isprambiente.gov.it/it/temi/autorizzazioni-e-valutazioni-ambientali/valutazione-ambientale-strategica-vas
5. For example, the DiVas system, developed by Abruzzo Region in 2010, is a project for the development of a GIS-based decision support system for the Strategic Environmental Assessment (SEA) of territorial plans, which follows the environmental assessor step by step in the technical assessment and process aspects.
6. See Mostafavi, M., Doherty, G., *Ecological Urbanism*. Zurich: Lars Müller Publishers, 2010.

3

PALERMO LIVING LAB

3.1 **THE FUTURE OF CITIES: BETWEEN MENDING, GRAFTING, AND RECYCLING**
Renato Bocchi

3.2 **CIRCULAR METABOLISM**
PROGETTARE LA CITTÀ RESILIENTE
Maurizio Carta

3.3 **THE NEW METROPOLITAN CITY AND THE SOUTHERN SUBURBS. XL REVERSE PALERMO**
Barbara Lino

3.4 **THE SOUTH COAST OF PALERMO**
PLANNING THE RESILIENT CITY
Daniele Ronsivalle

3.5 **FORM WHICH IS TRANSFORMED**
Vincenzo Melluso

THE FUTURE OF CITIES: BETWEEN MENDING, GRAFTING, AND RECYCLING[1]

MAURIZIO CARTA

"Breakthrough innovation arises from vision: the ability to look at the world and see what others can't see. [...] A sustainable society can only originate from visions that look beyond today, beyond immediate problems" (Norman D., Verganti R., 2014). In the face of radical changes in society and in cities — and considering the established need to not consume any more land and reduce the waste of existing resources — it appears to me that the processes of mending or restitching are totally insufficient, and that there is an ever stronger need to push for the development of visions for a radical change in mentality and, therefore, scenario[2].

There are historic moments in which we need utopias capable of swerving forward or to the side. In the architecture of the 1700s, Piranesi played this role, being able to overturn rules and spatial geometry, even starting from an antiquarian culture; in the architecture and cities of the early 1900s, perhaps a similar role was filled by the constructivist El Lisitzkij; more recently, Cedric Price embodied an analogous role as a visionary innovator, who inspired the young Piano and Rogers for the Centre Pompidou. While sharing both the ideals and architectural proposals of Renzo Piano, I find it difficult to adopt his recent rallying cry: "mending" (of the suburbs). I perfectly agree when he says, "We are all dwarfs standing on the shoulders of a giant. The giant is our humanistic culture, our ability to invent, to grasp light and dark, and to address problems laterally". I am less in agreement when he adds, "Our suburbs need a huge mending and repairing job"[3].

In the distressing outskirts of this country, I find pure "mending" an ineffective tool, despite being convinced that we must not demolish and rebuild, but rather "graft" to produce "metamorphosis", as Cino Zucchi asserted in the last Biennale of Venice[4]. In this regard, it is interesting how Zucchi refers explicitly to the concept of bricolage, used in anthropology by Claude Levi-Strauss, to whom I myself have often referred when searching for a method to address the planning issue of redeeming (recycling) discarded areas.

It should be said, however, that in the review of grafting projects proposed by Zucchi, we are still dealing with inputs in highly characterized contexts and not really within suburban contexts. They are grafts on substantially healthy plants, which are, however, revitalized by the high quality of the new interventions.

Thus, while sharing the desire expressed by Piano and by other Renzis to "change direction"; I struggle to believe it can be done without radically changing the lifestyles and ideals of Italians, especially in their ways of building cities.

In short, I think the time has come to develop new models of behavior and management, to cast future visions of re-foundation rather than mending, to develop "new paradigms" instead of simple problem-solving hypotheses. "Behaviour based on the intuition and visionary power of people is often stigmatized", explain Norman and Verganti in the article mentioned. "This myth stems from the traditional corporate culture that focuses more on problem-solving than on building a vision. This kind of approach can solve immediate problems but certainly, does not prepare for the future"[5].

This doesn't mean disregarding the potential of what exists, but using the potential of what exists as a tangible resource to be recycled and radically reinvented in favor of new life cycles. This is precisely the spirit with which the National Interest Research Project *Re-cycle Italy* developed.

Moreover, I believe that we cannot appeal to the architect-demiurge, but need to openly address the contributions arising from "bottom up" capillary action in the social realm, just as Piano himself heralds when he summons his "district laboratory" of Otranto. This cannot fail to call to mind the fundamental experiments — which are also visionary in various ways — of Danilo Dolci or De Carlo and Samonà at the Mediterranean latitudes of Sicily.

We should investigate the ways in which a structure of meaningful relations can be re-established in those suburban areas, despite starting from the "recycling" of a tangible and ideal legacy that is anything but uniform and often "desolate".

Recycling means precisely this: establishing new life cycles and thus regenerating and re-establishing things and the relationships between things, places, and landscapes. For this reason, it has very little to do with conservation and, instead, very much to do with transformation, even if it refuses to work on a blank slate. It doesn't turn up its nose at hybridization, layering, assembly, overlaying, rewriting and overwriting, just as today, the editing of so-called found footage works in recycled cinema to build new narratives[6].

It isn't enough, therefore, to proclaim the sacrosanct desire to "no longer consume land". We believe we must also, and above all, outline new strategies to recycle what has already been built. These "new paradigms", tested in the living lab of Palermo, are required of us by the time of crisis in which we are immersed. This crisis inescapably demands that we seek a new beginning, making any work of pure mending, repair, or weak modification insufficient.

1. The text is a summary of the author's contribution to the work of the PMO/Reverse workshop, organized by the Palermo Research Unit of the National Interest Research Project Re-cycle Italy, held in Palermo from the 9th to the 13th September 2014.
2. See the document www. t sm. tn. i t/ interne/interna2.aspx?Tipo=6&Anno=2014&ID=15309&IDD=6734&Cat- Vis=4
3. Piano, R., "Il rammendo delle periferie", *Il Sole 24 ore*, 26th January 2014.
4. Zucchi, C., editor, *Innesti-Grafting*. Italian Pavilion, 14th International Architecture Exhibition. Venice: Marsilio, 2014.
5. Norman, D., Verganti R., "Per costruire una visione servono nuovi contesti", *Il Sole 24 ore, Nòva*, 2014, no. 430, p.7.
6. Bertozzi, M., *Recycled cinema*. Venice: Marsilio, 2013.

CIRCULAR METABOLISM
PALERMO SOUTH COAST

MAURIZIO CARTA

Nowadays, contemporary cities are looked at through thousands of new eyes, both from improved and more sophisticated technical viewpoints, and from new and more sensitive social perspectives.

The result is not just a better and more precise analysis of existing resources but, above all, the discovery of new quality and development factors. The new views bring to the surface valuable resilience reserves in cities that find themselves facing the multiform crises we have been plunged into: they are places of reverse geography, essential in reactivating evolving vital mechanisms and necessary in redesigning cities as organisms undergoing metamorphosis, rather than as corpses to be resuscitated or fabrics to be mended. They are fragments of agricultural landscape, remnants of infrastructure, functionally recycled neighborhoods, armatures of drosscapes and systems of brownfields, social archipelagos boiling with participation, and productive microcosms in productive ferment. Moreover, they allow cities to take on less rigid and more elastic forms that are less resistant to innovation and more adaptive to evolution.

These resilience reserves are not static resources but allow processes capable of managing a larger number of interacting problems to be activated, the plurality of players and varied social networks to be involved in decisions, and forms of governance that are able to balance competition between cities to be actualized. Resilience cells — true urban stem cells — from which to reactivate a more creative, intelligent, and ecological urban metabolism, concentrated in apparently marginal areas and excluded from the rhetoric of turbo-development: in transitioning outskirts, industrial districts undergoing refurbishment, and port and railway areas going through a phase of infrastructural recycling. Places in which community, landscape, and identity values have been preserved, far from the driving forces of the compulsive urban model, which consumes land and resources. It is particularly in the new districts of stigmatized marginality that a city can start over, knowing how to put its capital back into the game after being cured of its dramatic addiction to "subprime" urban planning that numbed its ability to imagine, plan, establish roots, and lead. In new resilient, dialogue-based, and sensitive settlements, the cycles of elasticity and adaptation require renewed flexibility of functions, greater permeability of spaces, and fruitful adaptability of settlements. They are not purely conceptual and spatial problems, but relate to the social effect of a growing demand for sharing, with the economic effect increasingly oriented by circularity, and the technological effect guided by distributed intelligence: components which are now structural parts of building the city, becoming planning issues/ instruments/laws for a new urban metabolism.

PALERMO LIVING LAB

Palermo. South Coast. (Photo by Jessica Smeralda Oliva)

This was the PMO/Re-verse Workshop, a collective challenge to begin again from the reverse geography of the city, to reactivate the numerous disrupted, latent, implicit, or forgotten cycles that give structure to the South Coast of Palermo. Reversing our view allows us to generate a new future vision of the metropolitan city. Above all, the "reverse city" provides the necessary genome to allow an evolutionary leap towards an urban organism that is not only more resilient, but profitably more resistant to the metamorphosis of development protocols that the crisis imposes on us and whose effects can be reversed starting from new viewpoints, varied project languages, and the diversified tensions that emerged from the workshop.

The workshop itself, in fact, was reflection in action, an aggregate of sensors and magma of actuators: planners, decision-makers, managers, active citizens, and makers form a powerful collective intelligence that tightens the new viewpoints to transform them into projects and resulting action, orients decisions but steers action, improves management but distributes responsibility. The South Coast is not content with a necessary but insufficient reactivation of cycles but calls for a strategic Hyper-Cycling action, a succession of life cycle reboots that gradually reactivates all the tangible and intangible resources, generating a powerful urban bootstrapping that is capable of initiating a self-sustainable recursive process.

The PMO/Re-verse Workshop was an urban planning and social innovation initiative created within the scope of the National Interest Re- Palermo. South Coast. (Photo by Jessica Smeralda Oliva) search Project *"Re-cycle Italy"*, coordinated by Renato Bocchi (IUAV), and supported by the research unit of Palermo, together with the Municipality of Palermo, ANCE Palermo, and the Order of Architects, Territorial planners, Landscape architect, and Heritage conservationists of the Province of Palermo, with valuable institutional partners, such as the Chamber of Commerce, the National Association of Builders of Palermo, the local Gas Company, and the Second District of the Municipality of Palermo.

Added to these was a valuable and fertile network of changemakers bearing witness to the institutional and concrete interest in the results of the initiative.

Our thanks go out to all of them, also for the follow-up of the workshop. I thank my colleagues on the scientific committee and particularly Vincenzo Melluso, with whom I shared the scientific ref lections that characterized the initiative, the lecturers, mentors, and tutors who enriched the work with their experience. Special thanks are owed to the organizing committee and administrative office, without whose constant activities, passion, and smiles, the workshop would have remained an intention. It was a valuable occasion, as the area is the subject of tension, transformation, attention, and infrastructure, and could serve as a pilot project for the entire city.

The tram, the urban duty-free zone, the new general urban plan, the plan for the use of the state maritime property and the urban beach, pedestrianisation, the UNESCO World Heritage Listing, social housing, the reuse of abandoned areas, and new metropolitan relations with the other municipalities are themes that are concentrated here, but are equally paradigmatic of Greater Palermo overall.

The new metabolisms that will emerge from the coast of Palermo from Sant'Erasmo to Acqua dei Corsari will not only be functional, infrastructural or related to urban planning, but will concern lifestyles, ways of using the territory, community contributions and, above all, the improved horizon we will all see as we once again turn our gaze southward.

Porosity as a planning value.
Densifying without consuming.

Vegetation.
Capillarity and non-erosive densification.

Solids and voids.
Settlement system with varying density and porosity of open spaces:
temporary social functions.

The South Coast of Palermo.
This is a territory whose fragile physical and social identity manifests itself in a haphazard series of public housing settlements, terraced buildings, discontinued or abandoned production areas, voids, and fragments of landscape untidily coexisting beyond the Oreto River. From a planning perspective, a reversal of view rediscovers porosity as a project value and uses the voids to densify without consuming land.

(Graphics by Barbara Lino and Jessica Smeralda Oliva).

Coast and settlement.
Intervening on the transversal nature and on the waterfront-city connections.

Brownfields.
Functional densification without soil erosion.

PALERMO LIVING LAB

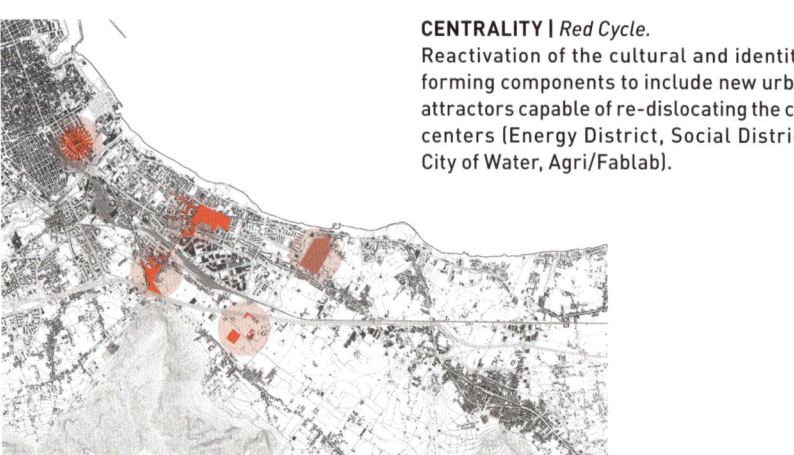

CENTRALITY | *Red Cycle*.
Reactivation of the cultural and identity-forming components to include new urban attractors capable of re-dislocating the city centers (Energy District, Social District, City of Water, Agri/Fablab).

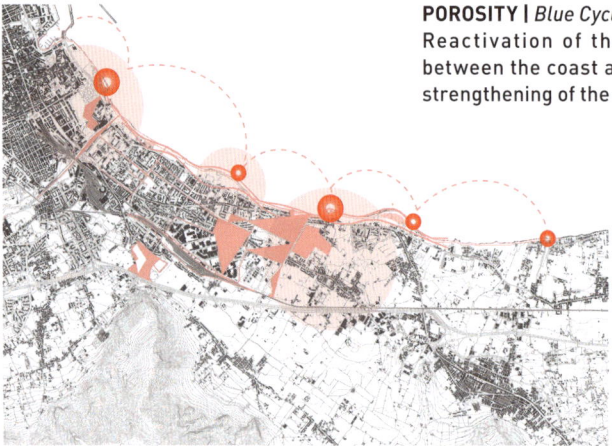

POROSITY | *Blue Cycle*.
Reactivation of the fluid connections between the coast and urban fabrics and strengthening of the porosity.

Representation by cycle of the project visions developed during the workshop: sequence of systemic actions aimed at activating the new metabolic function of the South Coast by means of a hyper-cycling action.

(Graphics by Barbara Lino and Mattia Cozzo).

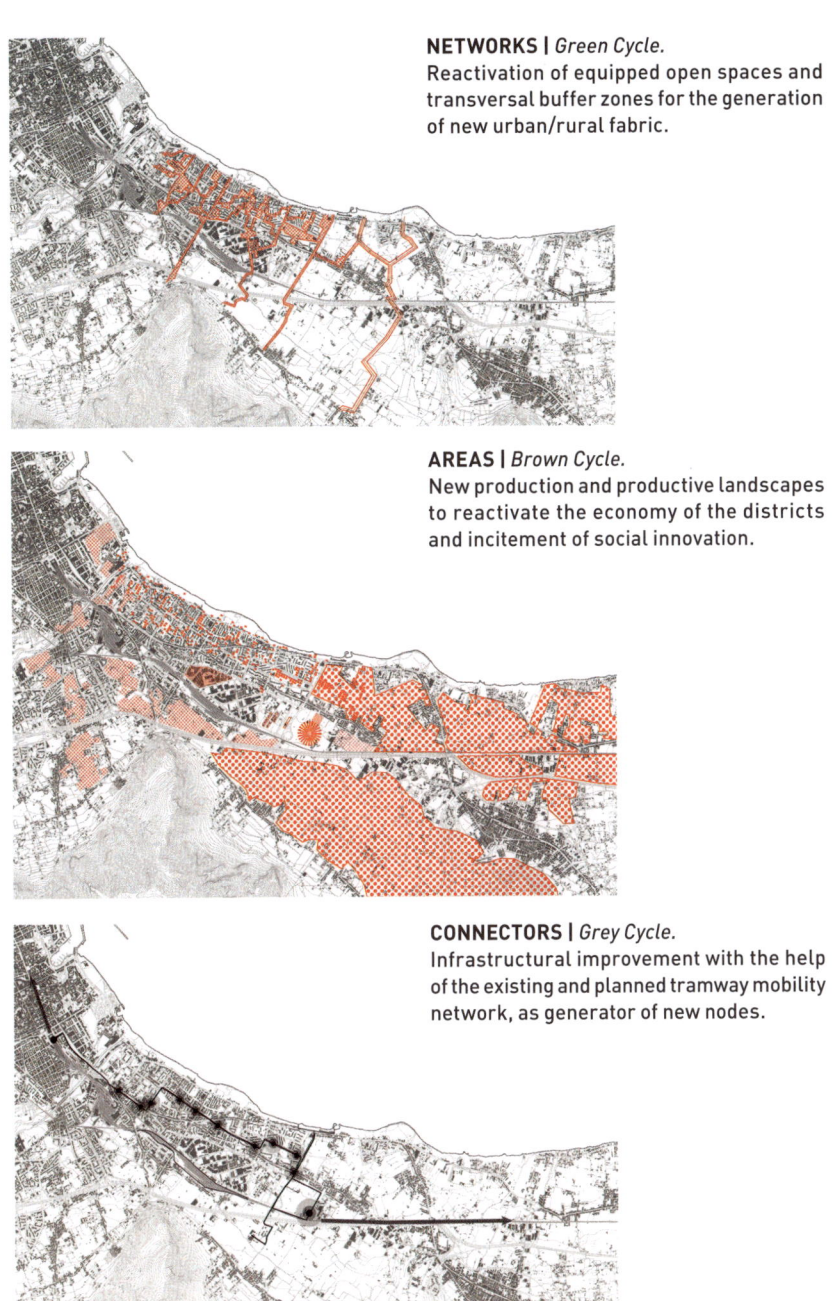

NETWORKS | *Green Cycle.*
Reactivation of equipped open spaces and transversal buffer zones for the generation of new urban/rural fabric.

AREAS | *Brown Cycle.*
New production and productive landscapes to reactivate the economy of the districts and incitement of social innovation.

CONNECTORS | *Grey Cycle.*
Infrastructural improvement with the help of the existing and planned tramway mobility network, as generator of new nodes.

PALERMO LIVING LAB

Colonising actions with low transformation intensity and high regenerative capacity, capable of triggering virtuous chain reaction effects and enabling tactics.
(Graphics by Maurizio Carta and Barbara Lino).

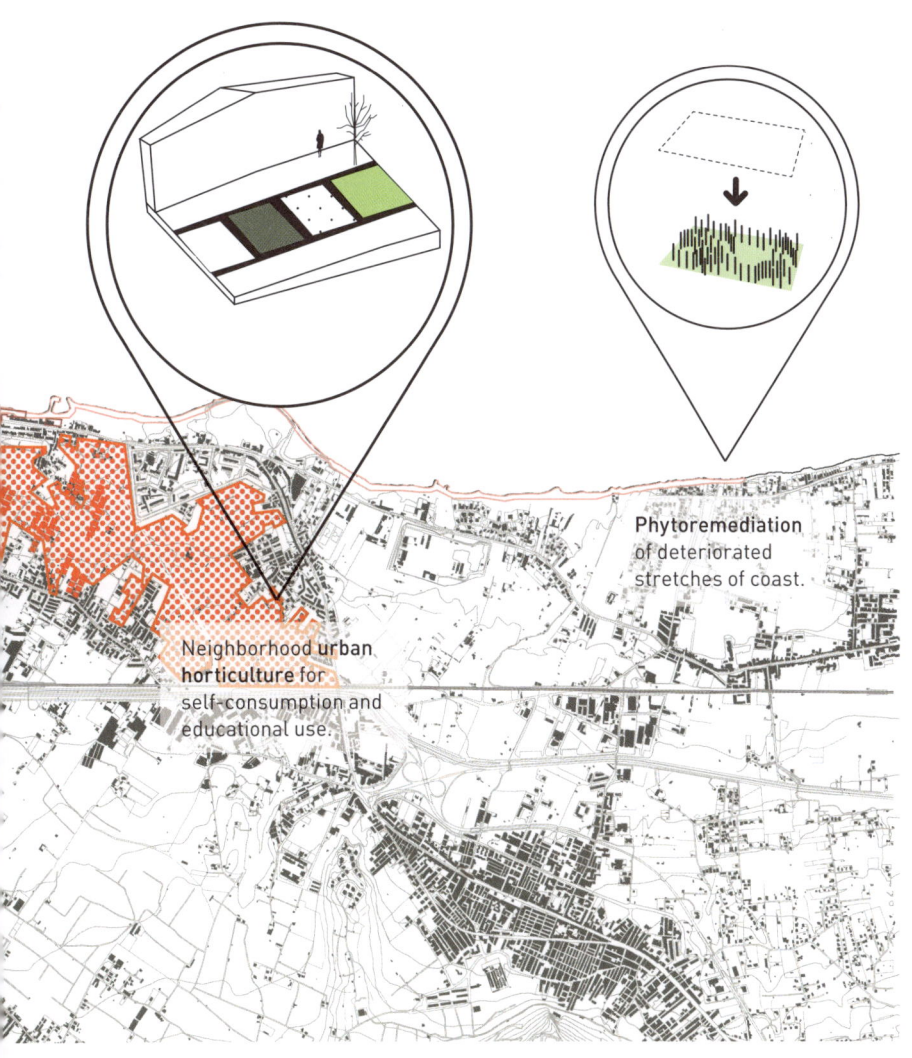

Neighborhood urban horticulture for self-consumption and educational use.

Phytoremediation of deteriorated stretches of coast.

PALERMO LIVING LAB

Consolidation actions of greater transformational intensity that act on entrenching the processes begun in the colonisation phase and in support of the new metabolic functioning of the area through the activation of multiple functions (hyper-cycling approach).
(Graphics by Maurizio Carta and Barbara Lino).

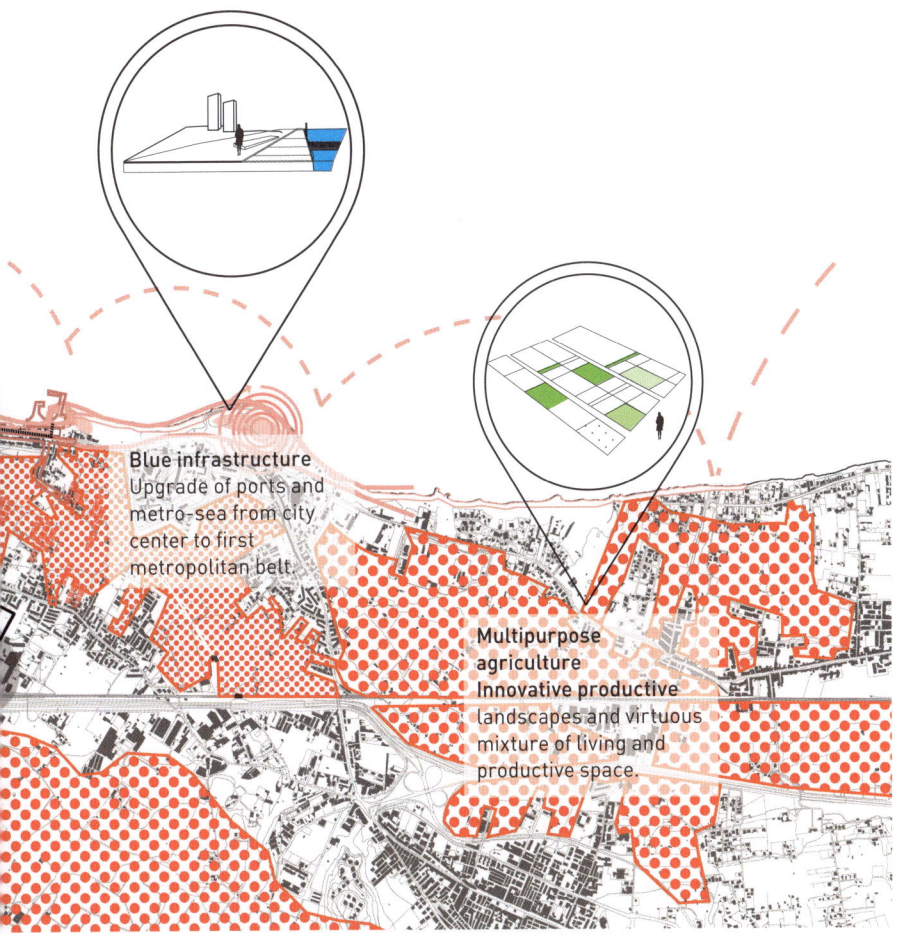

Blue infrastructure
Upgrade of ports and metro-sea from city center to first metropolitan belt.

Multipurpose agriculture
Innovative productive landscapes and virtuous mixture of living and productive space.

PALERMO LIVING LAB

THE NEW METROPOLITAN CITY AND THE SOUTHERN SUBURBS.
XL REVERSE PALERMO

BARBARA LINO

The new metropolitan city and the southern suburbs.
XL Reverse Palermo

Consistent with legislative innovations affecting the national territory, whereby metropolitan cities supplanted the provinces of the same name from the 1st January 2015, in Sicily, Law no. 15 of 4th August 2015, entitled "Provisions concerning Free Municipal Consortia and Metropolitan Cities", established the breakdown of Sicilian metropolitan cities, making them coincide with the territorial extent of the corresponding regional provinces.

The Law was challenged on the 5th November 2015 by the Cabinet which, however, saved the general structure, raising its constitutional illegitimacy limited to issues of the representativeness of the territories and of the indirect election of the governing bodies of both the metropolitan cities and the municipal consortia[1].

The contents of Article 28 of Law no. 15 specify the functions of the metropolitan city which, as a vast area authority, is appointed with the adoption and annual updating of a three-year strategic plan for the metropolitan territory, the functions of general and urban territorial planning, and the identification of areas for affiliated and subsidized public housing. Among the other functions accredited to metropolitan cities by Law no. 15 are the structuring of coordinated management systems for local public services of the metropolitan territory, mobility and road access, and support and development of university consortiums in the territorial jurisdiction. The updated regulatory framework will thus open an intense season of testing and planning, in which the new Sicilian metropolitan model will be formulated and the futures of the three metropolitan cities of Palermo, Catania, and Messina will be defined. In addition to being the capital of the Sicilian Region, with approximately 656,000 inhabitants (ISTAT, 2011) and a municipal area of 160 km^2, Palermo is the city with the greatest concentration of inhabitants. Indeed, the city has a population density of 4,278 people per km^2, while Catania has a density of 1,731 people per km^2 and Messina 1,193 people per km^2.

The Palermo territory corresponds to the province of the same name, on whose perimeter the metropolitan city is based. It has a population of about 1,300,000, extends over a surface of around 5,000 km^2, and includes 82 metropolitan municipalities. Based on these data, Palermo is the fifth largest Italian metropolitan city in terms of population and the third largest in size. Of the metropolitan city's 82 municipalities, 26 used to form the metropolitan area of the same name established by Regional Law no. 9 of 1986, whose extension was decided by the Decree of the President of the Region of 10th August 1995. The municipalities of the old metropolitan area have a population of 1,069,754 (ISTAT, 2011), of which over 60% belong to the municipality of Palermo.

An analysis of the demographic trend highlights the attractive role of the provincial territory. While the City of Palermo hasn't grown since 1981, the Province of Palermo grew by over 10% between 1971 and 2011 and the former Metropolitan Area grew by over 17%. If we exclude the City of Palermo from the former Metropolitan Area, the percentage of population growth of the other municipalities is 57%. The municipalities that grew the most were those of the first belt: first of all, Isola delle Femmine, which has grown in percentage terms by 176.5% in 40 years; Carini has grown by 138.7%; Ficarazzi by 110.9%; and Capaci by 101.7%. While in 1971 Bagheria was the only municipality exceeding 30,000 inhabitants, in 2011 this threshold was also exceeded by Monreale, Carini, and Partinico (D'Anneo, 2013).

If we observe the ways in which the urbanized land has grown from a qualitative viewpoint, urbanization has originated mainly from the welding of adjacent centers and the inclusion of pre-existing urbanized fabrics[2]. Between 1987 and 2000, with an increase in urbanized surface of just 1,156 hectares, 42% grew by infill, 26% by extension, and 32% by inclusion (especially towards Giacalone); between 2000 and 2013, on the other hand, the built-up area increased by 6,318 hectares, 30% by infill of the pre-existing fabric, 20% by extension, and the remaining 50% by inclusion of pre-existing urban centers (Carini, Capaci, Terrasini, and Bagheria) (Angel *et alii*, 2016).

The result of this process is an urbanized system of first-belt municipalities characterized by a strong settlement continuity along the coastal axis, both towards the east, where the system that goes from Bagheria to Trabia represents the element of continuity with Cefalù, and towards the west, where the Capaci-Isola delle Femmine system acts as a "bridge" to the airport and to Trapani. The main infrastructure is concentrated along the coastal axis, forming a multimodal transport "corridor" (highway, motorway, and railway) that serves the most populated municipalities gravitating to the capital, and connects the east and west parts of the Region.

The metropolitan configuration delineates a settlement layout we could define as "linear polycentrism", in which the coastal axis unfolds linearly through polarized aggregations while, towards the inland, the densification forces are oriented by the urban center of Monreale, the inter-provincial connection Palermo-Agrigento, and the Belice corridor (marked by the fast-flowing Palermo- Sciacca highway).

The presence of metropolitan-scale services in the Municipality of Palermo, such as the University and the hospitals, assigns to the capital a strong attractive role: in the 2015/16 academic year, the University of Palermo had over 42,000 enrolled students, 64% of whom came from the territory of the former Province of Palermo, while the rest came from other areas of Sicily or from other regions. Of the 4,000 beds provided by the facilities of the National Health Service in the Province (ISTAT, 2011), most are located in the Capital City. Other important relations of a functional nature are also generated by the positioning of productive and logistical centers (harbors and airports): the airport is located in Cinisi, logistics and large-scale retailing services are located in Carini, while the harbor and Fiumetorto station are found in the Municipality of Termini Imerese.

At a municipal level, the centrifugal forces of urbanization have infl uenced the geography of commercial spaces, which have settled in suburban areas both to the west and to the east, close to the motorway and to the axis of the ring road, in hub positions from a metropolitan influence perspective: the outermost districts of the city, such as the areas of Sperone-Costa Sud (District II) or ZEN (District VII) and Borgo Nuovo (District VI) have been affected by the emergence of large facilities for organized trade.

Although simple and partial, the data relating to emerging dynamics, both on the metropolitan scale and on the scale of suburban areas, show the extent of the flows and relations that the arising metropolitan city must be able to steer and govern. The definition of a metropolitan territorial agenda will require us, on the one hand, to consider phenomena already in place and pre-existing areas with high functional interdependence, and on the other, to radically redefine the system of planning and local authorities in favor of greater coordination, solidarity, and collaboration between neighboring players, also beginning from solutions that can find greater localization opportunities in the outskirts of the core city as a result of a new spatial centrality and their potential role as toothing joints between neighboring areas.

In Palermo, the greatest concentrations of marginality have been caused by settlement processes that, over time, have pinpointed the southern suburbs with two clear dividing lines — the Oreto River to the south of the city and the ring road to the west; here, "Oltre-Oreto" (Orlando, 2015) is an area which can, more than others, exemplify the potential strategic role defined by the new geography of the metropolitan city. Today, the South Coast, in particular, is the result of haphazard and random additions and substitutions, rather than accomplished planning visions. Ordering elements of the settlement principle were the coast and the railway — components with powerful inertia —, which generated separation and defined boundaries in a longitudinal direction, repudiating transversal capillary connections. While the so-called Bonci Plan had directed the development of the city towards the south in an ordered vision inspired by a clear relationship with the coast, following the war, a massive and dense expansion driven by specific speculative interests, the so-called "Sack of Palermo", reversed the expansion trajectory in the direction of the countryside to the north of the consolidated city (Lino, 2015). Coordinated action to reorganize mo

bility to serve the entry system into the city — currently underway and at an advanced stage with the so-called Punta Raisi/Cefalù Railroad Link — and to reorganize the urban level connections — by means of the tramway, connections, and the so-called Rail Circuit — is radically redefining the role this area can play as an urban gateway from the south.

Various redevelopment initiatives have already begun in the area: an Urban Duty-Free Zone has been established, which could give economic activities a significant boost; the hypothesis of localizing an Aquarium through a project financing intervention has been put forward; reconversion of the San Paolo Palace Hotel — confiscated from organized crime — into a residence for university students has begun; a huge investment of 130 million euros has been allocated for projects, all already compliant with the estimates approved by the Municipal Council, inserted by the National Funds for Metropolitan Cities (European Programme 2014/2020), approximately half of which relating to the technological innovation of existing buildings and urbanisation, and the other half to social inclusion.

From a metropolitan city perspective, the redevelopment of the South Coast could be accelerated by the integrated management of collective mobility services and by integration between urban and extra-urban mobility, also in terms of fares: let's imagine transforming the railway service from Termini Imerese to Capaci into a service with metropolitan frequency and fares. The South Coast is close to Ficarazzi, Villabate, and Bagheria: overcoming the view of competition, building networks, agreements, and pacts, and coordinating planning tools could favor the exchange of opportunities and intra-territorial interventions to create consistent and complementary common services. The reclamation of abandoned buildings, the issue of urban agriculture, through which to promote the agricultural production already present (the citrus cultivation of Ciaculli and the agricultural areas of Ficarazzi and Bagheria), and the issue of housing access support, though the redevelopment of districts and existing villages and support of a new experimental housing offer (residences for university students or young couples) are becoming particularly relevant topics.

XL Reverse Palermo

In adopting an extra large metropolitan scenario, the "Feasibility Study for the Action Plan of the Palermo Capital of the Mediterranean Strategic Plan" proposes a "Vision for Palermo Metropolis 2025"[3], which does not settle for sharing the highest-ranking services in the territorial context, but intends to take on the role of orientation, guidance, and coherence of territorial transformations, within a 2025 vision of the future governance of the metropolitan city.

One of the developments at the foundation of the new XL metropolitan vision of the city of Palermo is the map of "Reverse Palermo" (Carta, 2015), which gives, as a contrasting agent, an unprecedented geography of the city made up of recurring exceptions, "differences that make the difference": "suspended" places, temporarily "empty", abandoned, or underused. The title of the map cites the "Reverse City" (Viganò, 1999; 2012) — a fractal city, built of fragments (Secchi, 1999), which centers on the void and not the solid, is structured beginning from large open spaces, and interprets the "void" not in a physical sense, but rather, in a functional and relational tone.

The mapping is planning in itself.

Selective and summarizing, rather than imitative and itemizing, mapping is the act of thinking in images to communicate. Conceptualizing by maps and diagrams provides a useful tool to interpret the complexity of the city and territorial phenomena, to represent the structure that can be inferred from the complexity of reality, compressing information, organizing, selecting, and classifying it. Referring to the diagram as a synthetic form of mapping, Gilles Deleuze states that a diagram is a thinking machine (De Landa, 1998), a proliferative machine: by mapping and by creating diagrams even more so, we attempt to gather, extract, and communicate the existing or potential, functional, symbolic, or spatial relations of territorial phenomena. The act of mapping works like a resizing machine, which compresses information, but, at the same time, selects and thus emphases it.

By recombining territorial complexity, a map works as a matrix capable of reactivating a new meaning. In his 1748 Map of Rome, Giambattista Nolli revolutionized the way the city was represented, placing emphasis on the binary opposition between public and private, representing, as a blueprint, spaces that have continuity of public use with roads and plazas and which are in some way an extension of them. In The Image of the City (1960), by mapping its five elements, Kevin Lynch summarizes the way in which people experience space, making sense of the complexity of movement and perception in space and over time. In Envisioning Information Graphics (1991), Edward Tufte indicates "graphic integrity" among the effective criteria of representation, meaning the ability to not distort information and an expression of the intellectual honesty of the creator.

Mapping "voids", therefore, is an act that implies their value, at the same time attributing to them a new meaning. The "voids" outline an armature of possibilities — they are an opportunity to re-aggregate fragments, through tangible and intangible re-composition actions capable of defining new propellant vital components.

The mapping of abandoned or underused places is the basis of recent temporary recycling operations, which work in the "time gap" between one preceding use and a future one, and which respond, by providing spaces, to forms of social innovation and new practices of using the contemporary city. The institutional

Reverse Palermo.

The recycling areas with which to reactivate the metabolism of the city.

The territorial dimension of the ecological footprint of the recycling areas in Palermo broken down into the various disrupted cycles generated by discontinued production (brown), functional mutation (red), infrastructural change (gray), agricultural decline (green), and water transformation (blue).

The surface or linear dimensions of the individual cycles are compared with the municipal size of Palermo.

(Carta, Lino, 2015).

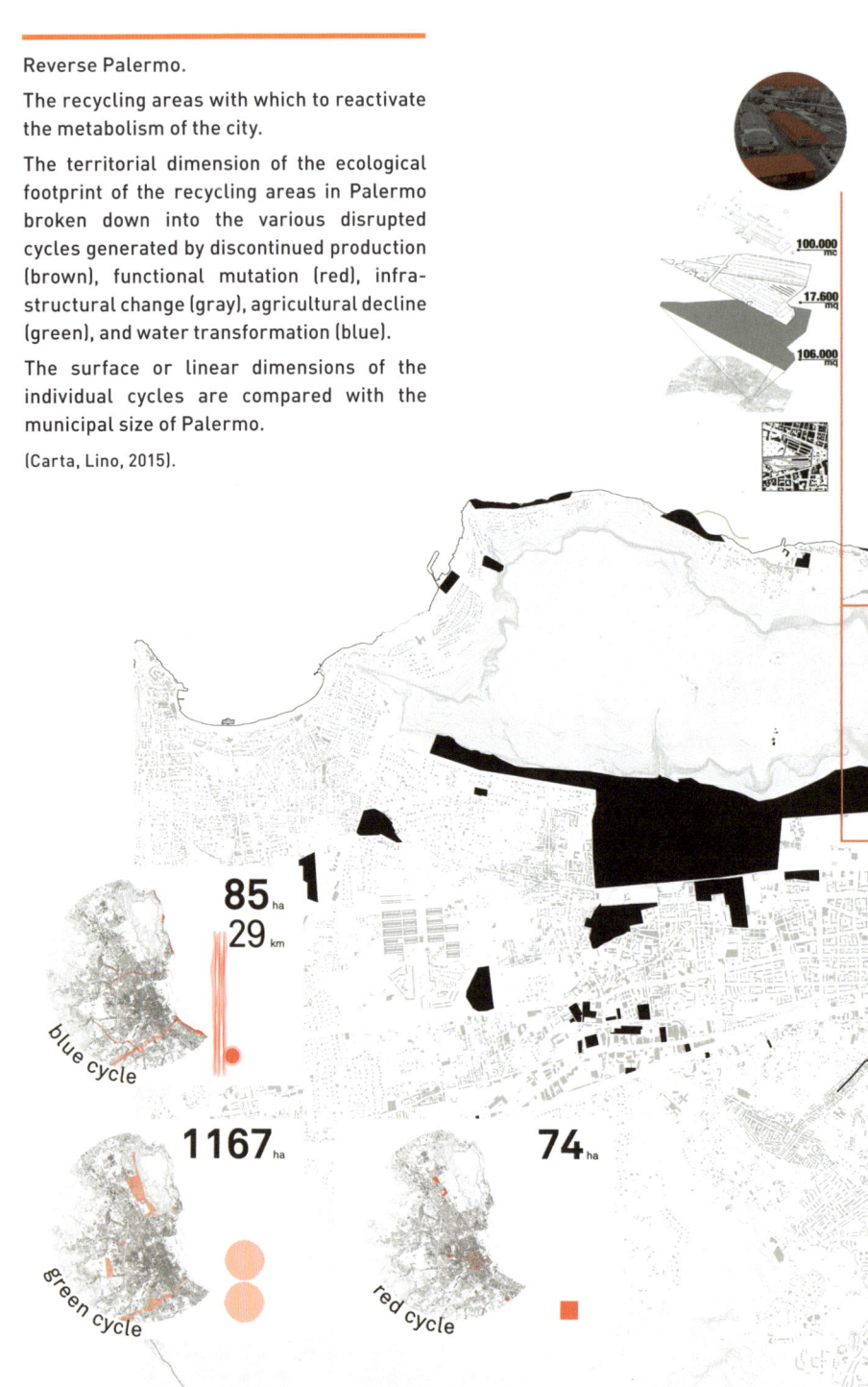

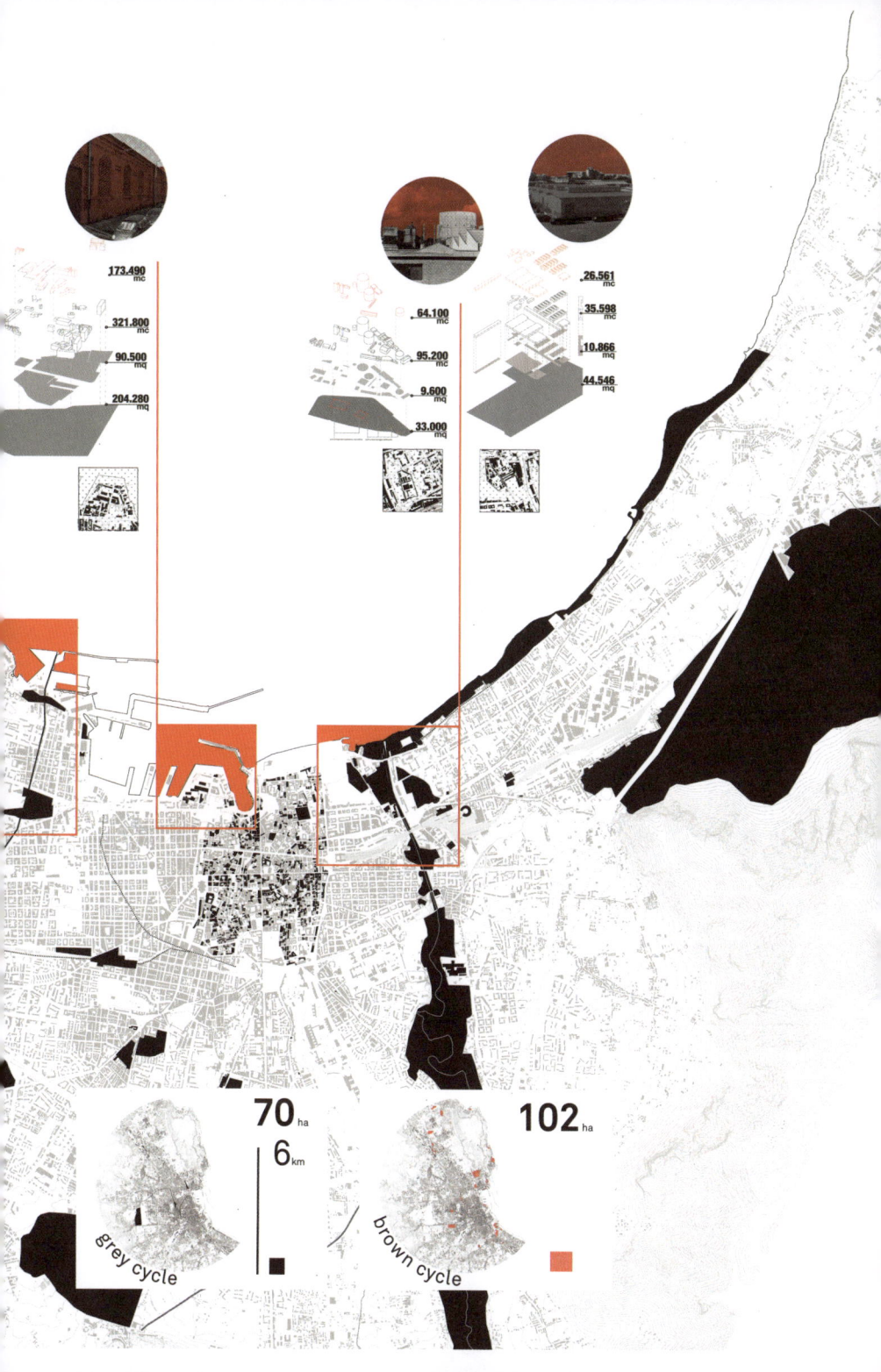

culture's new focus on issues of temporary recycling is emerging through tender notices, calls for ideas, and regulations of use in initiatives such as "Reinventer Paris", a public call for the innovative urban planning of 23 abandoned sites of the city or the "Temporiuso" initiative in Milan, in which mapping of the potential proposal and the definition of the taxonomy of the spaces to be reconverted is accompanied by the formulation of rules for the sharing of spaces and of potential public policies to be activated to consolidate and renew practices of reuse (Inti *et alii*, 2014).

With this meaning, the map of Reverse Palermo — developed in its beta version for the municipal territory but currently being drafted for the territory of the entire metropolitan city — shows the geography of urban life cycles disrupted by ablations and caesuras, fragmented water and vegetation cycles, infrastructural and productive cycles abandoned in hasty flight from development trajectories too fragile to consolidate. Drosscapes and brownfields, the palimpsest of blue & green cycles, and buildings confiscated from the mafia provide reserves of resilience and transformation. The small and numerous recycling areas and the larger pilot hyper-cycling areas of the Fruit and Vegetable Market, the Trapezoidal Quay, the Gasometer, and the Slaughterhouse can contribute in a more creative and less erosive manner to redesigning the way we experience and produce the new metropolitancity in new shared forms.

They are the essential connectors to close the energy cycles and reweave creative relationships with the environment, looking at the city as a complex ecosystem, capable of transforming itself by reorganizing its functions and offering a different model for the selection and use of its active and latent resources. Intentionally, the map does not point out the difference between public and private, being based on the idea that while these sectors once acted within separate and well-defined boundaries, today there are many more interaction spaces in which to build innovation.

The elements that make up "Reverse Palermo" are thus considered to be essential materials for planning the new landscape at a metropolitan scale. They are features capable of fuelling new settlement cultures, activating new urban metabolisms, and facilitating social innovation practices based on new forms of citizenship, co-production, and co-management that are the new protagonists of XL communities..

Bibliography

Angel, S., Blei, M., Parent, A.J., Lamson-Hall, P., Galarza Sánchez, N. (2016), *Atlas of Urban Expansion*. The NYU Urban Expansion Program at New York University, UN-Habitat and the Lincoln Institute of Land Policy. Available at: http://atlasofurbanexpansion.org.

Carta, M. (2015), "Urban Hyper-Metabolism: un paradigma dirompente", in Carta, M., Lino, B., editors, *Urban Hyper-Metabolism*. Rome: Aracne Int.le, pp. 11-13.

D'Anneo, G. (2013), "Fuga dalla città. I trasferimenti dalla città di Palermo ai comuni dell'area metropolitana", *StrumentiRes*, *online magazine of Fondazione Res*. Year V, no. 2, March. Available at: http://www.strument ires.com/index.php?option=com_content&view=article&id=422:fuga-dalla-citta-i-trasferimenti-dalla-citta-di-palermo-ai-comuni-dellarea-metropolitana&catid=3:cultura-a-societa&Itemid=110

De Landa, M. (1998), "Deleuze, Diagrams and the Genesis of Form", *ANY: Architecture New York 23: Diagram Work: Data Mechanics for a Topological Age*, pp. 30-34. Available at: https://seansturm.wordpress.com/2011/06/09/morphogenesis- diagrams-a-la-deleuze-and-delanda/

Insolera, I. (1980), *Roma. Immagini e realtà dal X al XX secolo* [English: *Rome. Images and Reality from 10th to 20th Centuries*] Rome-Bari: Laterza.

Inti, I., Cantaluppi, G., Perischino, M. (2014), *Temporiuso. Manuale per il riuso temporaneo di spazi in abbandono in Italia*. Milan. Altreconomia.

Lino, B. (2015), "Vecchie e nuove visioni per Palermo. uno sguardo rivolto a Sud", in Carta, M., Lino, B., editors, *Urban Hyper-Metabolism*. Rome: Aracne Int.le, pp. 170-179.

Lynch, K. (1960), *The Image of the City*. Cambridge (MA): MIT Press.

Orlando, L. (2015), "Oltre Oreto", in Carta, M., Lino, B., editors, *Urban Hyper-Metabolism*. Rome: Aracne Int.le, pp. 15-17.

Secchi, B. (1999), "Città moderna, città contemporanea e loro futuri", in De Matteis, G., Indovina, F., Magnaghi, A., Piroddi, E., Secchi, B., Scandurra, E., editors, *I futuri della città. Tesi a confronto*. Milan: FrancoAngeli, pp. 41-70.

Tufte, E.R. (1991), *Envisioning Information*. Cheshire (CT): Graphics Press.

Viganò, P. (1999), *La città elementare*. [English: Elementary City] Milan: Skira. Viganò, P. (2012), "The contemporary European Urban Project: Archipelago City, Diffuse City and Reverse City", in Crysler, C.G., Cairns, S., Heynen, H., eds., *The SAGE Handbook of Architectural Theory*. London: SAGE.

1. The illegitimacy of the Regional Law was raised to ensure the representativeness of the territories for the indirect election of the governing bodies of both the metropolitan cities and the municipal consortia, as well as, "for the conferment to municipal consortia of administrative functions subsidiary to those of the Authority area for the management of integrated services regarding water and waste, and general authority to the Region regarding the environment » (see what is said by M. Greco in the article «Parzialmente impugnata la riforma siciliana dell'ente intermedio" available at: http://www.leggioggi.it/2015/11/23/parzialmente-impugnata-riforma-siciliana- dellente-intermedio). The Cabinet resolution of 05/10/2015 is available on the website of the Department of Regional Affairs, Autonomy and Sport: http://www.affariregionali.it/banche-dati/dettaglio-leggeregionale/? id=10264.

2. The *Atlas of Urban Expansion investigates* the current and emerging conditions of urbanization phenomena in cities throughout the world, revealing how the contemporary model of urbanization is becoming highly unsustainable. Urban expansion, according to the classification proposed by the Atlas, occurs by "infill" of the urbanized open space within the previously urbanized fabric; contiguous outward "extension"; "leapfrog" of rural open spaces urbanizing new areas in a non-contiguous manner, and "inclusion" by annexing former urban and rural settlements already previously inhabited. See Angel, S. *et alii* (2016).

3. The "Feasibility Study for the Action Plan of the Palermo Capital of the Mediterranean Strategic Plan" of the Municipality of Palermo was drafted with the external consortium advice of prof. arch. S. Stanghellini, prof. arch. M. Carta and Creta srl.

"Porta del Parco" is a set of gateways.
(Graphics and planning by Giulia Bortolotto, Federico Calcara, Simona Di Pasquale, Giuseppe Rago, Silvia Tagliazucchi, with the mentoring of Antonio Biancucci).

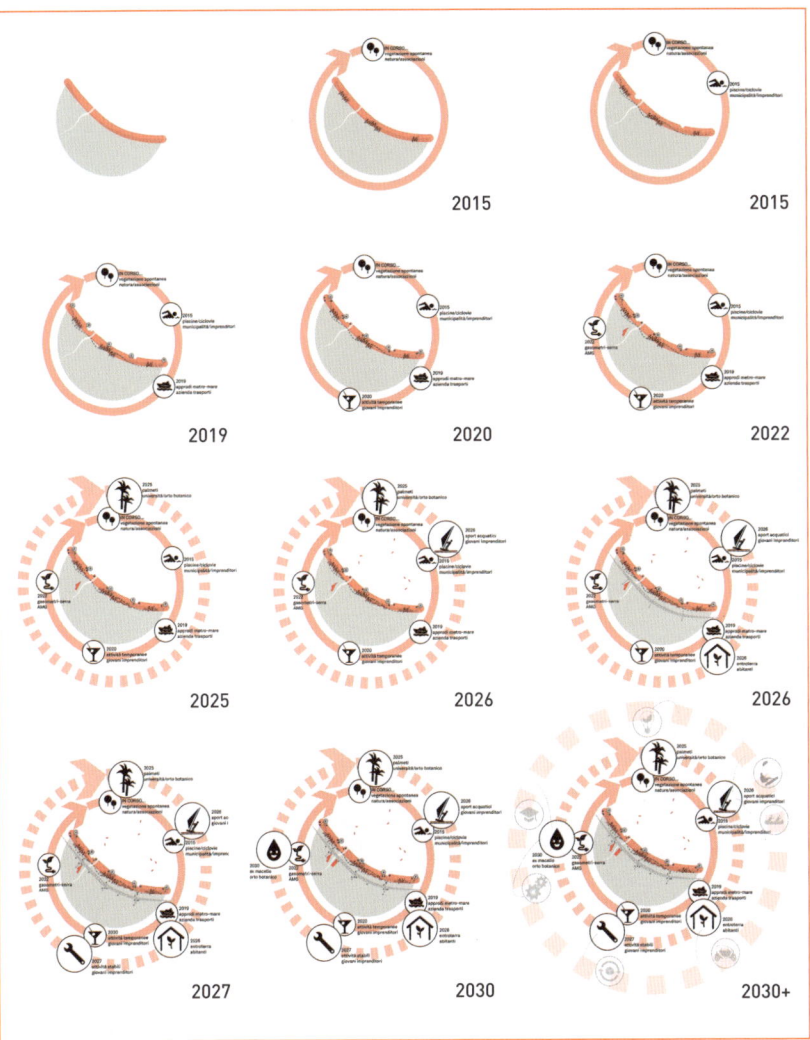

Time lapse of planning actions.
(Graphics and planning by Chiara Bonardi, Marika Fiore, Sandra Maglio, Marcello Modica, Elisabetta M. Caruso, with the mentoring of Sebastiano Provenzano).

PALERMO LIVING LAB

THE SOUTH COAST OF PALERMO

PLANNING THE RESILIENT CITY

DANIELE RONSIVALLE

RE-CYCLICAL URBANISM

The South Coast of Palermo is a territory with strong identity resilience but its current fragile physical and social dimension can be seen in a haphazard mosaic of public housing, factories, voids, fragments of landscape, and large abandoned or discontinued areas such as the former Slaughterhouse and the former Gasometer, bunched together with other now inactive productive areas, just before the mouth of the Oreto River. It is a glorious mosaic for the history of the city, with recognizable tiles but a frame that can no longer be perceived and, above all, an overall image that remains unknown. The stretch of the river near the delta features a regimented riverbed and lies in an area of high hydrogeological risk.

The processes of stratification and accumulation along the coastline have created a marginal landscape in which the existence of a now "disrupted" productive past, together with old and new layouts, can still be recognized, and in which village areas, public districts, and new commercial districts coexist in a disorderly fashion.

Recycling strategies and regeneration tactics will have to contribute to generating new life cycles for the area, capable of activating a new metabolism and defining a renewed role in the urban and metropolitan settlement system, in relation to the coastal functions located from Palermo to Aspra. Within the scope of the "PMO/Reverse: Hyper-cycling Costa Sud. New Urban Metabolism" workshop, the area is an open-source and crowdsourcing project laboratory, in which, thanks to the shared work of institutions, the private sector, associations, groups, designers, and makers, it is possible to develop integrated intervention strategies, conversion and recycling practices, and practices of urban making.

The project for the South Coast is thus a public opportunity for reflection at a time when the General Regulatory Plan is being reelaborated. It proposes projects and change scenarios compatible with the new requirements and sensitivity towards an urban redevelopment capable of integrating the dimension of economic sustainability and public/private partnership with the challenges of a more creative, ecological, and intelligent city.

From the Gasometer to the Mouth of the Oreto River

The area is characterized by the final stretch of the Oreto River and its fragmented delta. Here the river disappears, becoming a canal system; the water becomes stagnant and polluted, and the city ignores its presence. The surrounding territory, where productive activities once took place, is packed with abandoned or underused areas: the former Gasometer and the Coalma plant are the largest.

The forgotten river mouth is occupied by constructions and the partly abandoned warehouses of the building tile company Fogazza. While some elements have the characteristics of industrial archaeology, as in the case of the Gasometer site, others instead contribute to raising the area's level of degradation due to their state of disrepair or contradictory location. Other culturally and environmental-

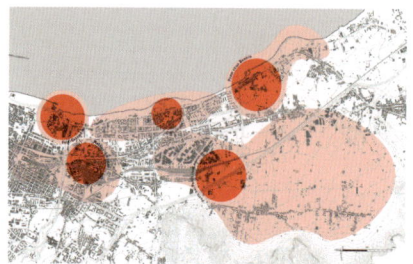

ly prestigious entities coexist in the same area: the invaluable historical garden of Villa Giulia, the splendid Botanic Garden, and the Scientific Departments of the University. The recycled former Railway Depot of Sant'Erasmo is today the home of the Diffused Ecomuseum *"Mare Memoria Viva"*. Not far off, the Admiral's Bridge bears witness to the ancient course of the river — silent protagonist of a historic and geographical past.

From the former Slaughterhouse to Palermo Centrale Railway Station

To the south of the city's historic center and structurally connected to it, the area stretches from the main railway station to the former facility of the municipal slaughterhouse. The area contains several important historic architectural discoveries: San Giovanni dei Lebbrosi church, the leprosarium, and the Admiral's Bridge (belonging to the UNESCO WHL "Arab-Norman Palermo and the cathedrals of Cefalù and Monreale"). In addition to the large railway site of Palermo Centrale Station, the area is characterized by the presence of the now abandoned municipal Slaughterhouse: a horizontal distribution of pavilions and facilities, characterized by the adjacent arrangement of various pavilions, like blocks of a small town. The area contains numerous abandoned buildings and can be seen as a drosscape expanse of urban connecting joints, to be rethought and redesigned.

The Fluid City

The study area includes the stretch of coast extending beyond the Mouth of the Oreto River to the border with the historical village of Bandita and its namesake harbor. The haphazard process of urbanization has superimposed disrupted life cycles or life cycles being depleted. These have left traces and scraps that produce a layered landscape composed not only of village and building fabric of the 1970s and 1980s, but also of the Buccheri La Ferla hospital facility, several monumental buildings, such as the Stand Florio, designed by Ernesto Basile, and abandoned constructions, such as the *Istituto Solarium* (former center for aero-helium treatment therapies) and the former San Paolo Hotel, a confiscated property assigned to the university and intended to house residences or university services. A large part of the state-owned area is devoid of specific functions and, despite the morphological characteristics being favorable to coastal use, the conditions of neglect — although currently being reduced with specific maintenance interventions — still discourage activities related to use of the sea for bathing, sport, or recreational purposes.

Porto della Bandita

Situated in the south-eastern suburbs of the city, Porto della Bandita is the ancient port of the seaside village of the same name. It is located in one of the stretches of coast most affected by physical and, above all, cultural degradation. A coastal strip improperly used as a dumping ground to the point of compromising bathing, today it is also strongly disadvantaged by the loss of its fishing activities as a result of the continuous siltation of the port. It suffers above all, however, from a loss of identity.

Morphologically and strategically, Porto della Bandita configures as a connecting joint between the various urban identities surrounding it: there's the urban territory at its rear, characterized by strong economic and social hardship and the coastal strip continuing to the north-east; to the south-east, on the other hand, is the so-called "mamelon", an artificial hill created with backfill overlooking the sea — the subject of uncompleted attempts at urban regeneration.

The Ciaculli Agricultural Park gateway: Maredolce and Forum

Porta dal Parco is an area strongly marked by a wide diversity and discrepancy of often contrasting uses. Juxtaposed in the location, these uses create situations of friction. The large distinctive agricultural area of Ciaculli — which gives its name to the late mandarin, the Marzolo of Ciaculli — has become indifferent to what happens around it: iron scrap deposits, road and railway infrastructure, and skeletons of never-finished buildings dot the walled mandarin gardens, jeopardizing any chance of their recognition as a place, product, and production process. In the strip between the motorway and the former site of the Consortium for Industrial Development of Brancaccio, new urban designs conceived for higher density living and the underused commercial railway park are becoming places to abrade with the recycling style in order to rediscover the historical development sites of this area. The most vital area from a transformational point of view is that occupied by the Forum shopping center, situated near the terminal of the no. 1 tram line, the new, still incomplete motorway junction, and the "Roccella" railway station. Vain and senseless landfill attempts cannot manage to make the weir of Arab-Norman solace in Maredolce disappear, which lives a life cycle parallel to the setting: while the recent, violently installed system tends inexorably to unravel, the permanent traces of history offer themselves as identity-forming features to be promoted.

The project theme, therefore, is the reconnection of fabrics by means of the rebalancing of vegetation, water, and historic cycles. The definition of an area of access from the city to the future agricultural park of Ciaculli, and vice-versa, consists of functions that can give new weight to the agricultural activities integrated into productive (no longer industrial) functions, and into the stratif ied and never sufficiently erased local identities.

FORM WHICH IS TRANSFORMED

VINCENZO MELLUSO

In a paper I recently published in issue 15 of the *Re-cycle*[1] periodical series, in reference to a paper written by Anna Li Vigni, *"Non c'è forma che non si trasformi"*[2] (There is no form that isn't transformed), I cited the concept of "metamorphosis" as a strategic condition to represent the approach for a significant research project on the contemporary city — a project attentive to the requests of modernity and interpreter of its criticality and potential.

The reference to "metamorphosis", even in its literary variation made by Ovid two millennia ago, is fundamental in bringing into focus the method with which, through planning, we look at the dynamics of urban evolution, like a continuously transforming organism that develops and grows, changing the shape and functions even of some of its major parts.

One of these significant transformations is that which is prefigured by the Re-cycle Italy research project carried out on Palermo, developed according to various approaches within the South Coast system, from Sant'Erasmo to the seaside village of Aspra.

The seafront is a paradigmatic place in the large Sicilian metropolis, where the potential and contradictions of its recent settlement development can be seized.

This is a part of the urban territory that highlights the overall lack of a strategic vision to organize the city's development, so providing an equally significant place — like its rich historic center — to create a new polarity in the metropolitan area.

With the "PMO/Re-verse Hyper-cycling Costa Sud" Workshop, Palermo has once again become a "city experiment", a modern Phoenix rising from its ashes, subject to the investigation of scholars, architects, and researchers who, seizing an ambitious challenge, have attempted to resituate it within a 21st-century city dimension. The Re-cycle Italy study, in fact, assigned itself the prerogative of renewing some methods of approaching urban transformation issues, inputting new motions that view the regeneration issue as an important moment for the development of the contemporary city.

Starting from issues related to the application of "creative and proactive recycling" mechanisms, it was possible to verify which mechanisms permit the regeneration of even extended systems of landscape, urban districts, and architectural artifacts. Within the scope of a general strategic vision, I also like to recall a 1988 initiative led by Pasquale Culotta[3] regarding a research project that would have projected Palermo towards 1991, the centenary year of the 1891 National Exhibition held in the Sicilian capital. On that occasion, Italian and foreign architects were involved in the drafting of nine projects, positioned in nine crucial points along the city coastline. Even then, the goal of the initiative was to create an urban system of correspondence between the coast, the settlement fabric, and the hills of the Conca d'Oro by means of a single but well-structured design. They wanted to envision the possibility of

The Oreto River delta area, with the Botanic Garden, Villa Giulia, and the Gasometer. Recently, the agricultural area on the left bank of the river was transferred by the Unicredit Property Fund to the University of Palermo.

Below. Aerial views of Acqua dei Corsari (left) and the mouth of the Oreto River (right).

(Photos by G. Cappellani, 1987).

once again assigning to the city the centrality of the relationship between the settlement system and the geographic characteristics of its territory through a preliminary definition of a settlement principle capable of providing the best possible transformation guidelines for the city. Remaining in the wake of these experiments, an additional variation of the research opportunity took place within the scope of the Planning Laboratory run by me during the 2013/2014 academic year in Palermo. Once again, the study used the probe of architectural design to verify the criticalities and potential of the places, so as to define transformation hypotheses through a real projection and testing of human housing in the physical environment from a thematic, theoretical, and applied point of view. Having as a reference scenario the research connected to the reclamation of parts of cities and modification of urban layouts — with a special focus on the experience gained in European contexts — we devoted ourselves to a complex of discontinued areas or areas whose original identity has been weakened, which today require a new architectural and organizational connotation. A large part of the city between the coast and Corso dei Mille, from Villa Giulia to the edges of the Oreto River delta, made up of a heterogeneous set of abandoned places, uncertain landscapes, and derelict buildings that have thus been proposed again as part of a program whose buzzword is "reconversion".

This area, like the whole system of the South Coast of Palermo, shows how the value of the different systems present — from the productive and commercial system to the historic and cultural one — is today transfigured and fazed.

The importance and extent of the phenomenon are driving a comparison between different planning strategies, aimed at signif icantly recomposing the places, through signs capable of forming an idea of city, and clarifying and reordering a present situation of increasingly rapid transformation.

In the complex issue of urban disposal, we can trace out a very clear sign of the fragility of the contemporary city, marked by a continuous dynamic development of changes at different levels and also in its most defined and solid parts. Today, the criticalities of the city are traced in the loss of identity and in the fragility of large urban areas which, due to the mutation of uses and advancement of the technological building process, create unresolved spaces, deprived of their original design and thus open to subsequent modification.

This change of direction is often sudden and profound and breaks up the urban material we have before us into forms difficult to decipher. The plan to reactivate these parts of the city must therefore guarantee, in addition to the required level of integration of different disciplines, continuous interaction between all the system variables at an urban and architectural scale. Rem Koolhaas's drawing, which appears in his book S,M,L,XL[4], is emblematic in this sense. With an extremely effective summary, he highlights that a regenerative action must be launched through an essential reformulation of the relational spaces and system of flows, within a new strategic urban design.

Among the fundamental aspects in reassessing the building blocks of a possible planning procedure, a central place is occupied by a reappropriation of the concept of "place", or better, of what is quality in a context and thus necessary to orient the choices to implement change. The term "context" is used in the sense attributed to its original etymology, *contexere*, to be acquainted with and thus weave together and intertwine the series and chain of ideas and events that have established the configuration of the artifacts[5]. With this interpretation of the context, the subsequent intervention actions, as planning hypotheses, have the goal of challenging themselves as an architectural response to the reconfiguration of a part of the city, adopting Palermo as a field of investigation. For this purpose, a description of the city design along the South Coast was crafted, using two main reading systems. The first, defined as "horizontal", dwelt on the description of several fundamental components of the urban structure of this area: dense city, building sprawl, small villages, and productive areas (active and abandoned).

A second reading, defined as "ver-

Planning outlines for the definition of the planimetric and volumetric configuration, particularly regarding the ground structure for the study areas of the former Gasometer and the former Unicredit Property Fund site.

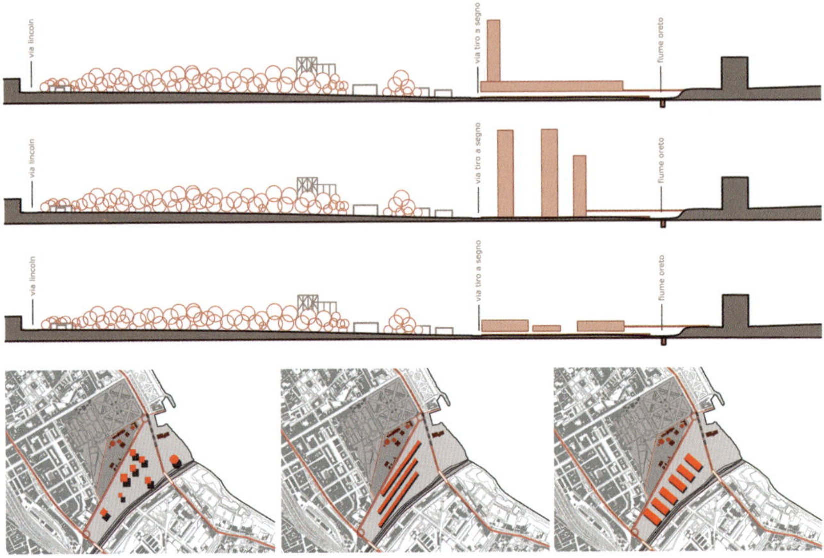

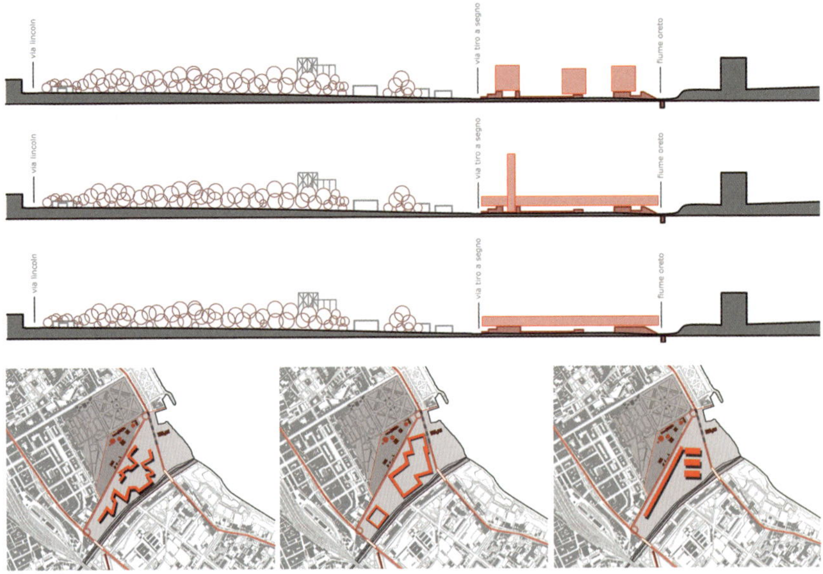

tical", identified several of the main systems that characterize this area and establish relations with the entire city: mobility circuit system; system of open spaces; and margin system (coastline).

A reading of the context, the relationships between typology and morphology, the settlement principle concept, and a study of the morphology of the territory and its history formed the bases, setting the "place" as the foundation of the project[6]. A place which, in the case of the South Coast of Palermo, appears to be a complex system. For this reason, in order to find its bearings and achieve a valid compatible result, the project must establish a precise identification of hierarchies through a selective transcription of the outlines derived from reading the context.

In my view, the challenge of our research, even today, is still to define scenarios that can test suitable transformation strategies, in which the technical and architectural solutions are able to adapt to the sustainability criteria of architecture in the existing context. The goal, in any case, is still to identify the layouts capable of enhancing the living space by combining the private and public building system with the system of open, closed, private, and public relational spaces, in order to overcome the condition of marginality that is often generated by the inadequacy and poor livability of large recent parts of our cities.

Thus demolishing the very concept of "outskirts".

1. Carta, M., Lino, B. (editors), *Urban Hyper-Metabolism*. Rome: Aracne Int.le, 2015.
2. Li Vigni, A., "Non c'è forma che non si trasformi", *Il Sole 24 Ore*, "Domenica" supplement, 24th July 2011.
3. Various authors, *Palermo 1991. Nove approdi per l'Esposizione Nazionale*. Palermo: Christian Democracy, 1988.
4. Koolhaas, R., Mau, B., *S,M,L,XL*. New York: Monacelli Press, 1995, pp.992-993.
5. "Contesto" [context] entry, in Cortellazzo, M., Zolli, P., *Il nuovo etimologico. Dizionario etimologico della lingua italiana*. Bologna: Zanichelli, 1999.
6. "[...] *The notion of belonging expresses interest in the history of the discipline in its continuity, in the idea of place as identity but also as impure material. It develops crosscutting relationships for which the planning process is in the foreground, a modification process that attracts and organizes the rubble contained in the environment, which builds its asymmetry, its different density, and its diversification values*" (Gregotti, V., *Dentro l'architettura*. [English: *Inside Architecture*] Turin: Bollati Boringhieri, 1995, p.71).

Three project hypotheses for land use on the left bank of the Oreto River, with interventions on the former Gasometer and on the former Unicredit area.

From the top left of this page, projects by the architecture students: Giovanna Bonica, Alessandra Gullo and Marta Gambino; Alba Fiduccia, Vittoria Lo Dico and Ilenia Zunino.

Opposite page: Giorgio La Leta, Gaspare Lipari and Salvatore Oddo.

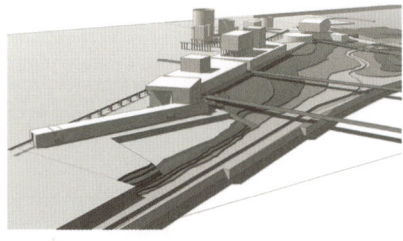
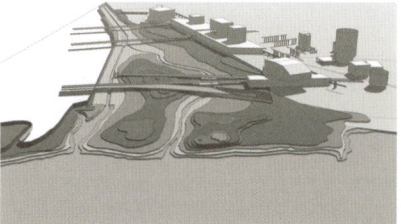

PALERMO LIVING LAB

P4

NOT CONVENTIONAL MAPS

4.1 **FROM FABLAB TO FABCITY**
THE PALERMO MAP OF TALENTS
Maurizio Carta

4.2 **ADAPTIVE CITIES, COMMUNITIES, AND TECHNOLOGY**
Carta, Ronsivalle, Schifani, Tumminello, Galati Tardanico, Lucido, Giambalvo

4.3 **PALERMO LIVING LAB ON THE ROAD**
Annalisa Contato

4.4 **RE-POSTCARDS**

FROM FABLAB TO FABCITY

THE PALERMO MAP OF TALENTS

MAURIZIO CARTA

Makers, fablabers, urban farmers, startuppers, smart citizens, and co-workers are terms that more and more often emerge from the technological vocabulary in which they arose to become leading figures of the contemporary city — players in urban planning, politics, and society, but, above all, new producers in the third industrial revolution we have entered.

Indeed, urban policies fuelled by the DIY (Do It Yourself) paradigm are increasing in number, turning the city into a place composed not only of citizens who make requests, but more and more often, citizens who respond, act, and produce. In contemporary cities, putting together digital and real, bits and atoms (as the MIT laboratory from which the FabLab revolution began is called), citizens once again become producers. Not just producers of goods and services for the market, but farmers, who once again enliven abandoned parts of cities by means of urban agriculture, or knowledge workers through workshops or creative incubators. Or they create cultural events through crowdfunding or manage occupied theaters, running them as an institution and not just as a reaction to the abandonment. Or they are the new artisans of the digital revolution: producers of 3D-printed objects, manufacturers of sensors, or repairers, at a time when repairing is becoming more impor tant than throwing away, when recycling is becoming more important than scraping or producing from scratch. Moreover, these new citizen-artisans are a community response to the needs of the elderly, or of those who cannot afford to access the market or services. Citizen-makers are becoming amplifiers of a new sensitivity towards the quality of the landscape, the environment, and energy conservation, renewing the traditional role of associations and no longer limiting themselves to pointing out the problem, but instead becoming part of the solution — taking charge in an active and responsible way. Nowadays, urban makers don't just adopt parts of cities but are becoming generators of new public spaces, adopting more adaptive lifestyles and fairer and more ethical consumption patterns. They are smart citizens, constantly connected to the web with their devices, becoming thousands of city sensors, boosting knowledge where it otherwise would not have arrived, reporting inefficiencies before they turn into emergencies. They are those who become aware of a problem and, using geoblogging, convey its existence to the public administration, which is often subject to greater cognitive inertia, distracted as it is by too many emergencies. Finally, they are the people who reactivate unused spaces that administrations are unable to reconsider and reuse, restoring them, recycling them, reusing them, and opening them up to creative urban communities. They are the bricoleurs of a city, which more and more often accompanies development strategies with maintenance, repair, and recycling tactics. By reactivating industrial buildings, old stations or abandoned barracks to allow them to once again be places of production, they reanimate public spaces, restoring their value as community locations.

In the recent international FabLab conference "Fab10", the city of Barcelona launched the ambitious project "Fab Cities", with which it aims to create a network of district FabLabs. Its goal is to have, within 6 years, an active laboratory for each district, integrated with the local communities and urban policies. The idea of creating a city network of FabLabs arose out of the desire to bring production back to the metropolitan area and, in particular, towards citizen-producers, attempting to recreate a modern version of the medieval corporations that once characterized and identified the cities.

Heading in the same cultural direction, the Smart Planning Lab of the University of Palermo has begun to develop a Map of Talents, identifying all the places dedicated to creativity and innovation, in order to understand the logic of the now spontaneous settlements of new urban makers, but above all to orient future planning decisions towards the establishment of a creative ecosystem that facilitates the birth, development, and profitability of the city of innovative production. The first edition of the map identifies and locates more than 200 places of talent, divided into the two macro-sectors of creativity and innovation. The first category has been expressed as places of culture (museums, theaters, etc), communication activities (publishing, open gov, digital services, etc.), and cooperation spaces (social streets, co-working, etc.). Innovation has been divided into places related to digital production, sustainable mobility, and renewable energies. Among the various fields of activities, any relationships among sites or subjects have been identified, in order to understand the network of connections and flows that make up the ecosystem. Finally, the analysis has been conducted on three spatial levels: the core city, the sprawled city, and the metropolitan city, in order to diversify the diagnosis and the subsequent actions.

The Palermo Map of Talents is beginning to provide an interesting clustering of the city and offers a glimpse of forms of spontaneous aggregation that should be encouraged, facilitated, or re-oriented for greater efficacy.

It thus aims to be a first contribution to building the Fab City network, which will be able to act on urban policy following the principles of the circular economy, which not only fuel the Third Industrial Revolution of producers but also the social — and hence urban — revolution based on recycling. The new recycling philosophy, in fact, shows how marginal economies are producing new collective projects and new forms of sociality to counteract the local and global decline.

All of this is once again becoming the city: a city made up, not only of citizens who make requests, but more and more often, citizens who respond. A city not only made up of consumers of products built elsewhere but also made up of producers for self-consumption or for the consumption of other cities from a metropolitan or global perspective.

A city made up not only of censors but sensors, not of reactive citizens but proactive players.

Shakespeare said, "What is the city but the people?", "True, the people are the city", makers, we can add!

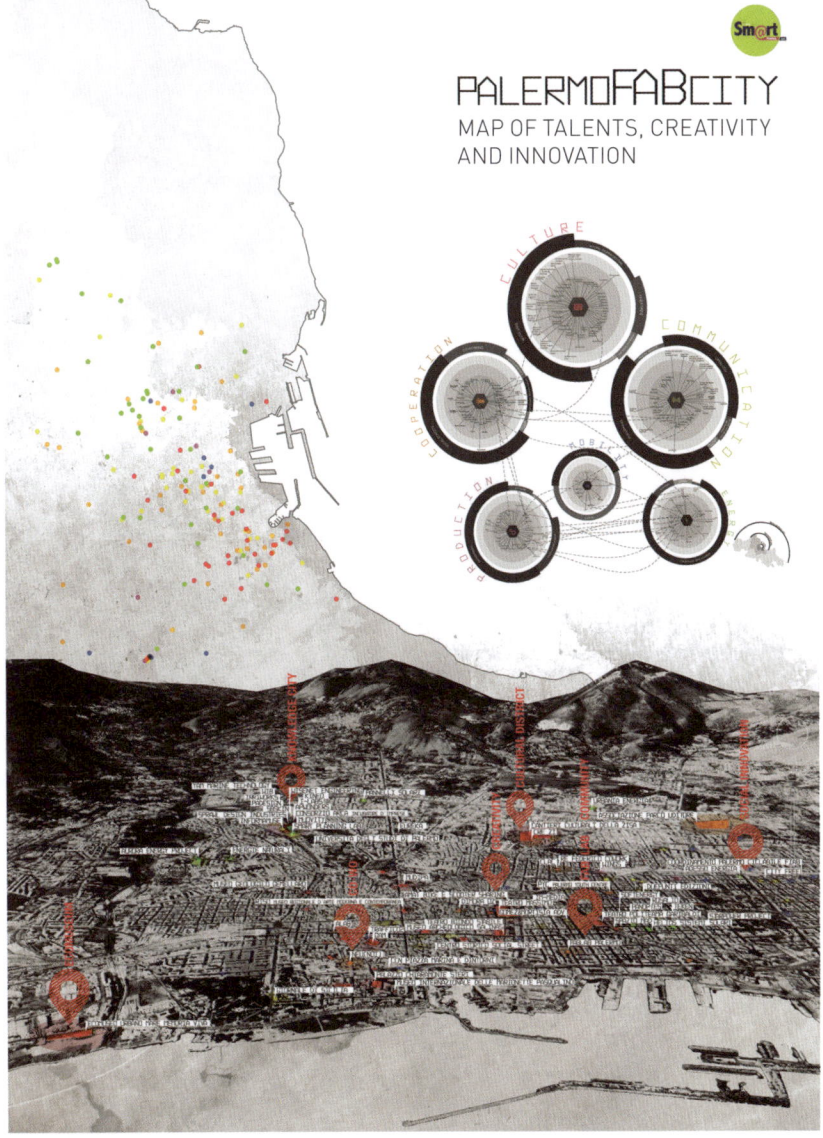

PALERMOFABCITY
MAP OF TALENTS, CREATIVITY AND INNOVATION

NOT CONVENTIONAL MAPS

> **CLAC: "cultural enterprise", resilient organization!**
> Working on new forms of design, production, and promotion of services, products, and cultural projects.

RE FEDERICO
COWORK

❸ MARE MEMORIA VIVA

CONNESSIONE, RELAZIONI, NETWORKING, PROGETTAZIONE E IMPRENDITORIA CULTURALE

FORMAZIONE PERMANENTE, ARRICCHIRE CONOSCENZE, AGGIORNARSI, STARE AL PASSO

FRUIZIONE CULTURALE, ARTI CONTEMPORANEE, INNOVAZIONE

RISPARMIO, SHARING, CONSUMO CRITICO, GRUPPI D'ACQUISTO

SOCIALITÀ EFFICIENZA IMPRENDITORIALITÀ

The urban ecomuseum *Mare Memoria Viva* arose from a research and community project on the memory and present relationship between the city of Palermo and the sea.
For *Mare Memoria Viva*, CLAC worked in the districts of the city's coastal strip to outline a map of the waterfront community of Palermo, meeting with and interviewing the inhabitants and seafaring people, mapping the territory's significant places, gathering stories, photographs, videos, and recipes, and organizing activities and encounters in public spaces and places of aggregation.
The ecomuseum space is open to the proposals of the territory, a place of strictly plural cultures and aggregation for all generations. It promotes shared social responsibility, participatory care of the territory, and community tourism; it proposes cultural, tourism, educational, alternative economy, and active citizenship activities.
The ecomuseum at the former railway depot of Sant'Erasmo is a public space, available for varied activities serving the city beyond the Oreto river primarily, as well as all cultural and social organizations that want to use it. The space is managed by the Municipality, through a coordinating agency in which the CLAC association, which is responsible for its setup and guided tours, also takes part. This mixed working group is the point of reference for planning activities; its goal is to test new forms of collective use of a space that remains public.

❶ **CLAC - Centro Laboratorio Arti Contemporanee**
Cristina Alga, Filippo Pistoia

Via Re Federico, 23
Palermo (ITALY)
C/O COWORKING RE FEDERICO
info@clac-lab.org
(+39) 328 62 80 306 - Filippo
(+39) 335 84 17 307 - Cristina

www.clac-lab.org

❷ **Cowork Re Federico**

Via Re Federico, 23
Palermo (ITALY)

info@coworkingpalermo.net
091 8430492

www.coworkingpalermo.net

❸ **Mare Memoria Viva**
Ecomuseo Urbano, geoblog

Via Messina Marine, 27
Palermo (ITALY)
C/O EX DEPOSITO LOCOMOTIVE SANT'ERASMO

Via dell'Arsenale, 140-148

info@marememoriaviva.it

www.marememoriavia.it

CHANGEMAKERS

> neu [nòi] spazio al lavoro is an association for social development, created for the purpose of proposing an innovative and participatory working model in the context of Palermo: coworking

ROSALIO

neu [nòi]
spazio al lavoro

> FabLab Palermo is a creative hub of makers. Creativity, accessibility, sharing, and innovation are the four axes on which the activities turn and with which the maker community of reference interfaces: artists, designers, architects, students, craftspeople, creative individuals, and common people with creative ideas that require support to fulfill them.

Associazione Culturale PALAB

 FABLAB PALERMO

nautoscopio

LONDRA
MILANO
ROMA
MONDELLO (PA)

 MOSAICOON

SOCIAL MEDIA & INTERACTIVE Viral
VIRAL Seeding & Tracking
VIRAL VIRAL VIRAL VIRAL SEEDING
Social Media & Interactive & TRACKING
VIRAL

---

④ neu [nòi] spazio al lavoro
Michelangelo Pavia,
Giuseppe Castellucci

Palazzo Castrofilippo
Via Alloro 64
Palermo (ITALY)

info@neunoi.it
091 783 21 07

www.neunoi.it

⑤ FabLab Palermo
Demetrio Siragusa,
Michele Ivan Pizzuto,
Marcella Pizzuto

Via Mariano Stabile, 52
Palermo (ITALY)

palermomakers@mosaicoon.com
091 784 60 77

www.fablabpalermo.org

⑥ Rosalio
Tony Siino

info@rosalio.it

www.rosalio.it

⑦ Mosaicoon
Ugo Parodi Giusino

Via Venere, 35
Palermo (ITALY)

info@mosaicoon.com
091 748 72 39

mosaicoon.com

⑧ PALAB
Nautoscopio
Tiziano Di Cara,
Giuseppe Romano

Piazzetta del Fondaco
Palermo (ITALY)

info@palab.it
091 6515527

www.palab.it

 places in which talent, creativity, and innovation produce enterprise and activate sharing

350

 # 42.000
university students

7.600
graduates per year

3 business incubators

2 proto-clusters of innovation

3 proto-districts of creativity

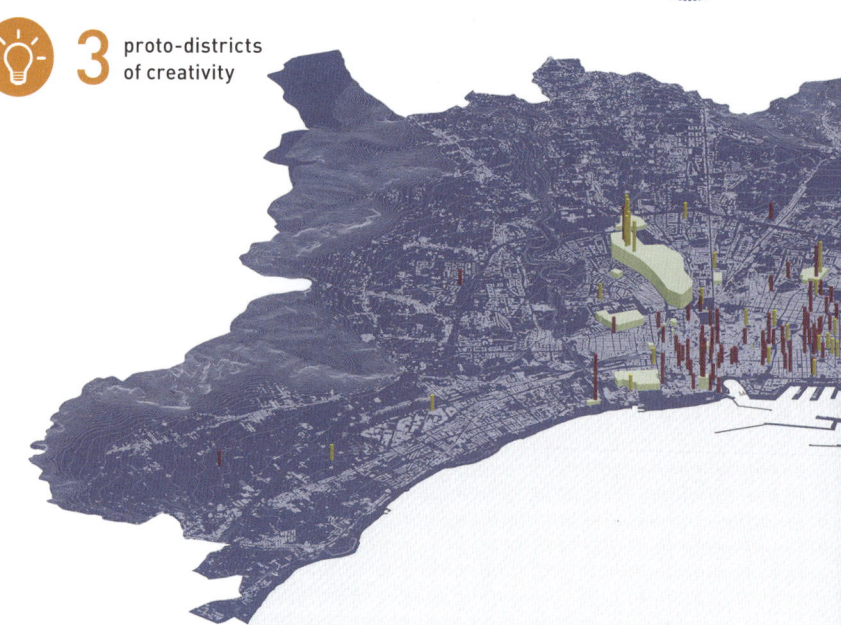

RE-CYCLICAL URBANISM

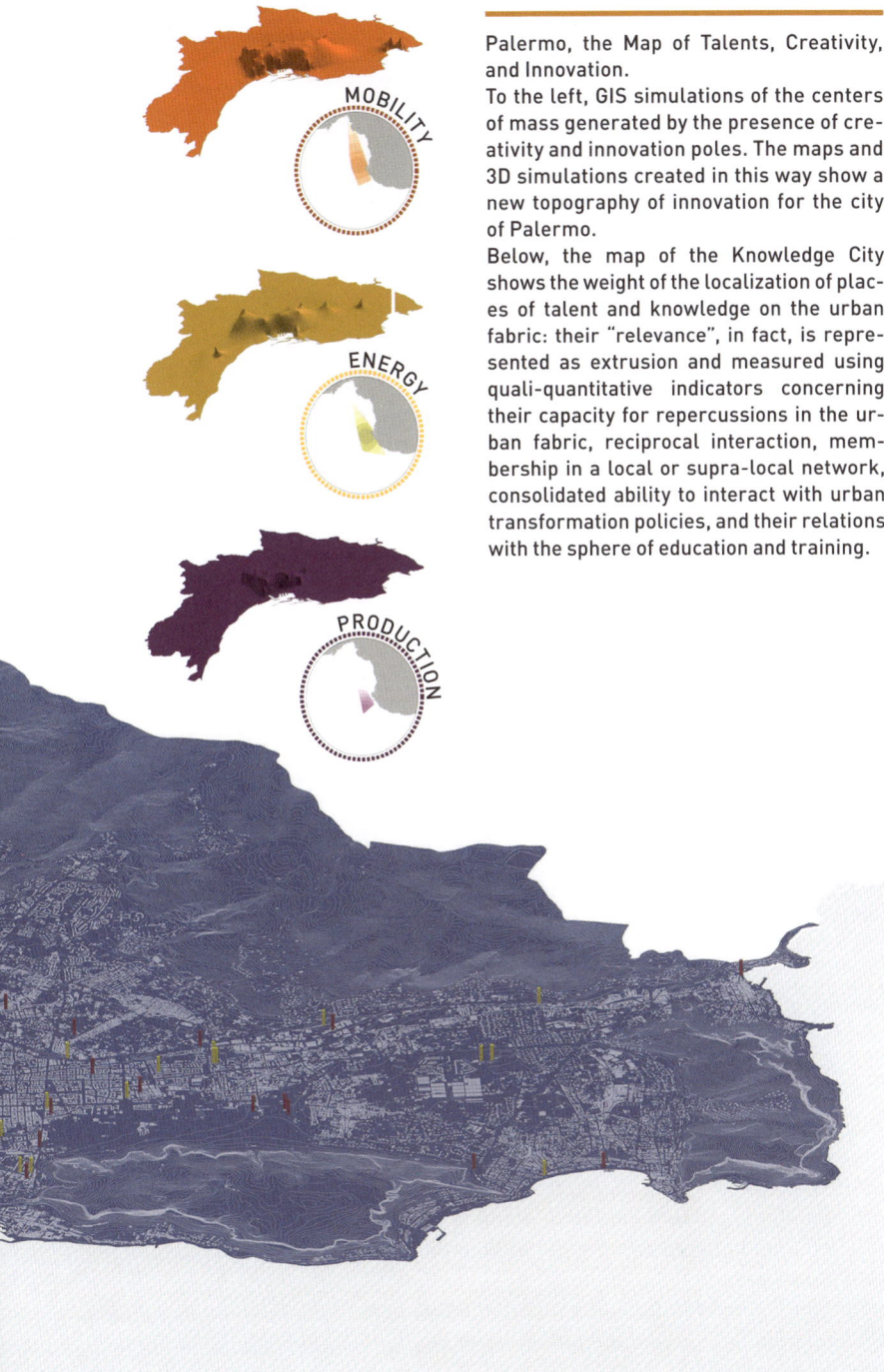

Palermo, the Map of Talents, Creativity, and Innovation.

To the left, GIS simulations of the centers of mass generated by the presence of creativity and innovation poles. The maps and 3D simulations created in this way show a new topography of innovation for the city of Palermo.

Below, the map of the Knowledge City shows the weight of the localization of places of talent and knowledge on the urban fabric: their "relevance", in fact, is represented as extrusion and measured using quali-quantitative indicators concerning their capacity for repercussions in the urban fabric, reciprocal interaction, membership in a local or supra-local network, consolidated ability to interact with urban transformation policies, and their relations with the sphere of education and training.

NOT CONVENTIONAL MAPS

ADAPTIVE CITIES, COMMUNITIES, AND TECHNOLOGY

MAURIZIO CARTA

CARMELO GALATI TARDANICO

DANIELE RONSIVALLE

SIMONE LUCIDO

CLAUDIO SCHIFANI

MAURIZIO GIAMBALVO

CARLA TUMMINELLO

Data survey (the Urban Cloud)
Analyzing and monitoring the city of the future from a smart perspective requires a careful analysis of the data and information that pass through it directly and indirectly. In the first instance, we will have information whose main subject is the emerging aspects of the city itself (e.g. waste, energy consumption of public buildings, data from control units, etc.); in the second instance, we will be faced with information concerning the city indirectly or in which the origin of the information is not the city itself, but a more extensive and widespread spatial area (e.g. Google traffic data, social networks, etc.). To properly observe the evolving city, it is necessary to codify such data, identifying its origin, type, and repercussions. This investigation has led to the drafting of an initial catalog of data. The phase of collecting, codifying, and filing the available data sets is necessary and preparatory to the subsequent phase of processing and returning information.

Database
Starting from a survey of the available data, provided directly or using data mining operations, it's possible and indispensable to organize a solid database in which the large amounts of data can be filed, but also processed and organized, and from which all information useful to urban phenomena interpretation processes can be extracted. From an IT perspective, technology now provides numerous commercial and free tools. The latter are preferable, both in accordance with recent legislation regarding spending reviews and because of their ability to be manipulated from the inside.
The iNext database is an open source and multiplatform database, which can, therefore, run on Windows, MacOS, and Linux platforms. SQLite meets these requirements, in addition to being a personal database, and therefore able to be easily "transported physically" from one workspace to another. SQLite, with its SpatialLite extension, can handle alphanumeric information, as well as the geographic component contained in it, both directly and indirectly. That said, the logical schema defining the database starting from raw data is shown below.
All the information filed in the SQLite Database can also be integrated into and analyzed with the free and multiplatform geographic interface QGis. The management of both spatial and tabular information using a database allows rapid analyses and screening of data to be carried out as a pre-processing phase.

Visualization methods and communication language
Urban phenomena, together with their complexity, arise from the increasing appearance of joint causes. The development and capillary dissemination of new information and communication technologies are establishing a new potential knowledge framework spread throughout the territory which, however, in order to be read and interpreted, requires new tools and new filters. The integration

Human data.
The social pattern of the city of Palermo derived from social network activity between September 2014 and March 2015. The data shows the greater or lesser social relevance of individual places in relation to the geolocation of activities "posted" by the users. The city takes on a new configuration when viewed through this non-physical centrality and with a network sentiment

(Data source: Twitter Inc. - API; Facebook Inc. - API; Foursquare Inc. - API)

RE-CYCLICAL URBANISM

of this information on a geographical basis alone is not representative of the urban phenomenology. On the one hand, these new types of data from mobile phones, social networks, diffused sensors, etc. require new and more daring methods of analysis and processing (e.g. through solid databases). On the other, they call for new forms of communication and language in order to be comprehensible, not just to experts (specialists, decision makers, investors, etc.), but also to the community that also often produces this bulk of data.

With a group of researchers led by Carlo Ratti, the SENSEable City Lab at MIT in Boston has for years been working on projects related to both the pervasiveness of city surveying technologies and to their new communicative multimedia and three-dimensional forms, representative of the complexity of urban phenomena. Many of these SENSEable City Lab projects deal with an "ocean of information", as in the case of the Real Time Rome project, and the "emotional signature", that is, the type of phenomenon that is the subject of the analysis and communicative potential of a three-dimensional visualization oriented to even non-expert users (Borga, 2013). We are talking, therefore, about the dissemination of information by means of its visualization on a territorial and even unconventional basis.

In the specific case of Real Time Rome, the "Ocean of Information" produces multimedia dynamic representations of data collected in real time from mobile phones and returned using data mining operations carried out on the city of Rome. The result is the dynamic representa-

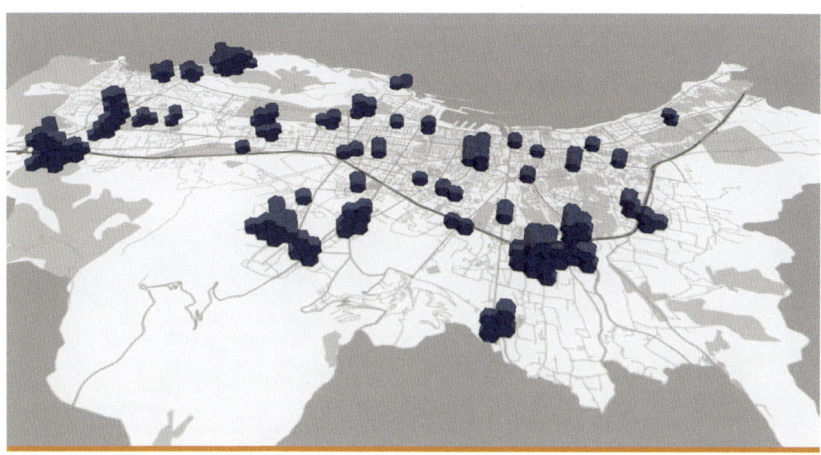

Energy.
Forecast hypotheses on a hex grid of the consumption of municipal utilities (above 10,000 kWh per year) following the localization of new large urban centers.
(Data source: AMG Palermo - Electric power delivery points of municipal consumption)

Mobility and tertiary industries.
The main tertiary sector and commercial services (in red) and quaternary sector services (in black) and the intensity of pauses in the time unit for each stop on the AMAT network (December 2014) during the 5.00 - 5.30 pm time slot.

Mobility and tourism.
The main tourist sites (in yellow) and the intensity of pauses in the time unit for each stop on the AMAT network (December 2014) during the 11.00 - 11.30 am time slot.

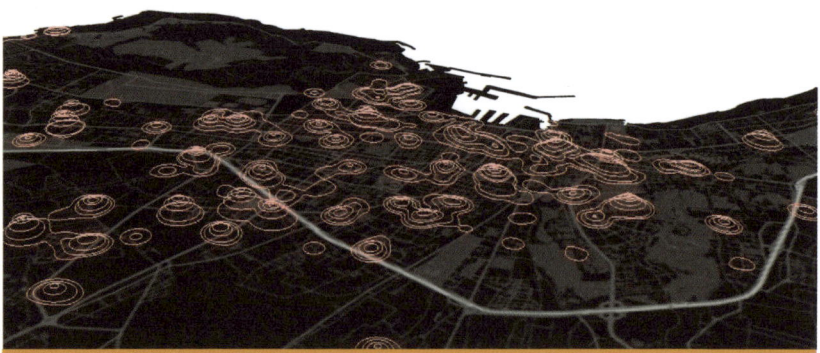

Human Data.
Potential urban centrality filtered using the density and concentration of social activity. Survey campaign between September 2014 and March 2015.

(Data source: Twitter Inc. - API; Facebook Inc. - API; Foursquare Inc. - API).

Mobility and schools.
The school services (in black) and the intensity of pauses in the time unit for each stop on the AMAT network (December 2014) during the times of school entrance (left) and exit (right).

Human Data.
Polarization of urban users in some places of the city in relation to the events of 15.03.2015: sport and tourism polarize the position of potential users of urban services.

(Data source: Twitter Inc. - API; Facebook Inc. - API; Foursquare Inc. - API).

tion of urban patterns during the various hours of the day and night, based on specific events more or less spread throughout the city. Similarly, we also talk about "cognitive maps" (Wakamiya et al., 2012) based on crowd movements, which are able to show the "urban signature" throughout the various moments of daily life of a city.

These innovative approaches to observing urban phenomena based on crowds and their movements throughout the day, extracted from social networks (Twitter, Foursquare, Facebook, etc.) and mobile phones, can be crossed with the locations of structures, buildings, events, and phenomena. This gives structure to an integrated knowledge base of real-time tangible and intangible information and ancillary sources, providing new visions, scenarios, and starting points for the programming and planning of the future city.

In this new urban planning, the city project is an adaptive, intelligent process in continuous flux, thus also able to respond reactively to the urban problems of "mobility" and "energy". Beginning with these premises, the analysis of data on the themes of mobility and energy of the Smart Planning Lab aimed to integrate various sources of information, which are often widespread and not always easy to find, also integrating new forms of communication and keeping a constant information base: the physical urban territory.

Potential urban scenarios

Following the survey of existing processed and raw data and potential new sources of information in accordance with the new methods and approaches described in the previous paragraph, we proceeded to classify the data and their aggregation based on their possible informative value to urban planning and programming processes. The analysis procedures and the relative data mining operations will be described in the following paragraphs in relation to the issues of "energy" and "mobility".

On the issue of "energy", a list of the main descriptive analyses of urban phenomena and their cognitive return is given below:

- widespread analysis by time intervals (months) of urban energy consumption. This approach allows us to become familiar with and describe the "urban energy signature", identifying opportunities and critical issues;

- widespread analysis (by interpolation) by time intervals (months) of urban energy consumption crossed with the main existing and project sources of energy consumption (e.g. car-sharing project with electric vehicles);

- ISTAT-based synthetic analysis by area average of urban energy consumption. These analyses allow us to monitor the average annual consumption of the city, organized by individual census units, in order to identify high consumption "cells" and virtuous "cells";

- analysis of the average energy consumption of public consumption sources (e.g. public services, traffic light systems, public lighting, and trams). This information allows us to monitor the level of public lighting within monitoring activities in relation to urban safety and consumption from public sources.

The energy consumption data, analyzed in accordance with the approaches described above, not only allow us to produce new cognitive maps of the urban "energy footprint", but if made operative with periodic scans in batch mode, also allow us to monitor any urban energy anomalies, albeit with a monthly delay, and to orient any future investments, such as the localization of new commercial and/ or productive settlements (potential large consumers of energy).

For the mobility issue, we used additional information sources together with the canonical traffic data (e.g. Urban Mobility Plan), innovating the approach. Today, in fact, while urban mobility can be directly identified from the number of vehicles passing two given points on the road network graph in a time interval (e.g. hourly), it is also possible to analyze the additional flows of mobility and urban vitality provided by social networks. In fact, using Twitter, Foursquare, and Facebook — to name the main protagonists —, we can visualize new "urban signatures" calculated from the crowd in movement, whether on foot, public transport, or using private vehicles.

The vision of a sustainable and intelligent city cannot exempt itself from constantly monitoring its "urban signature" during the various hours of the day, month, and year as a function of the existing and planned evolving urban-scale mobility scenario. The need thus arises to test cognitive models that are able to cross data extracted from traffic flows with data calculated from the geolocation of the crowd from social networks. Details about these calculations and data mining operations will be described in the paragraph dedicated to the issue of "mobility". Below is a summary of the main descriptive analyses of urban phenomena and their cognitive return.

Crowd mobility

- Crowd movement analysis based on Twitter geolocation data by time slots. This analysis allows us to monitor the "urban signature" by time slots, from the early morning to the late evening, permitting us to identify attractor places and/or critical issues regarding mobility at an urban level;

- Crowd trajectories analysis based on Twitter geolocation data by time slots. This allows us to identify the trajectories of mobility at a large and small scale (e.g. home – work). The critical issue lies in the need to have a large amount of data available in order to limit errors caused by the sedentary nature of most tweets. Integration with data from mobile phone networks (e.g. Telecom) is thus also desirable;

- Crossover analyses between crowd mobility and mass public transport. This calculation allows us to verify the degree of accessibility of the most active places from a social point of view, steering and/or confirming policies to renew the public transport system;

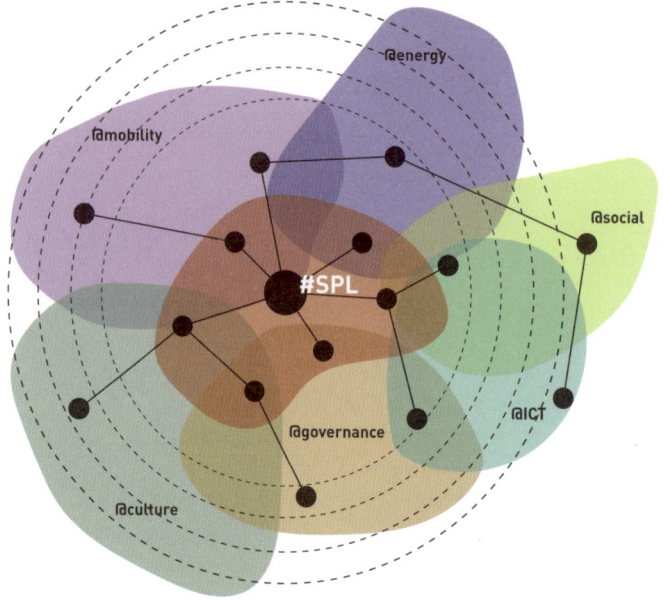

With the activities of the Smart Planning Lab (SPL), the classic Smart City model has taken on a new structure. It has become a cloud of interactions, within which it is possible to retrace the routing function of the laboratory and the interlacing of research functions and applicative goals. The nodes in the gravitational field of the Smart Planning Lab are connected on the issues of the smart city framework, but the SPL uncovers new interactions, with the help of new technologies and the support of the Collaborative Arena (CA) and social innovation.

- Crossover analyses between crowd mobility and alternative mobility (car sharing and bike sharing). This calculation allows us to verify the degree of accessibility of the most active places from a social point of view, steering and/or confirming policies to activate sustainable mobility.

Place Detection
- Place Detection analysis from Facebook and Foursquare sources. By crossing the semantic value of geotags originating from Facebook and Foursquare, we can map the places with the most urban activity. This analysis allows us to classify parts of cities in relation to their social vitality, making information available for decentralization or incentive actions and the strengthening of places that have launched gravitation processes at an urban scale;

- Urban cluster analysis based on crowdsourcing. This analysis allows us to identify clusters of greater concentration and urban attraction according to parameters such as type of attractors, moments of daily life, etc. As with the "energy" issue, for the "mobility" issue it is also possible to sub-articulate each of the above analyses into specific additional calculations, not only based on the amount and level of detail of the data possessed but also defining new intersections according to the availability of new data — both geolocalized data and data to be localized using similar procedures to those described in the following paragraphs.

Communication and digital participation for smart circular planning

The representation of the digital city and its connections is missing the social components that contribute to the formulation of the Human Smart City hypothesis if these social components are not integrated into the processes of active participation, the identification of problems, and the choice of potential solutions. The participatory frameworks we are accustomed to often respond to a social washing criterion, in which no subject really takes part in the decision-making processes, if not to simply provide the planning processes with a fashionable quality. The Smart Collaborative Arena described below responds to the intention to proactively revise participation, dividing and articulating mainstream participation and expert participation in the best way possible.

Executive planning of the activities began on the 3rd December 2014 with an executive meeting attended by both the staff members of the Smart Planning Lab and the team of Next-Nuove Energie Per il territorio. The meeting allowed us to share updates on the status of the project, agree upon the details of the specific objectives of Collaborative Arena interventions, and to launch a reflection on the subjects to be involved (city users, opinion makers, gatekeepers), as well as timeframes for the various actions to be taken.

Firstly, the structure of the interventions was shared. These interventions were conceived as participatory governance action, in which the developed contents — already clustered into planning forms — merge into the smart planning logic.

To achieve this purpose, the Collaborative Arena methodology consists of a digital/physical hybrid and interactive territorial intervention model, in which face-to-face meetings are prepared and designed with the help of a large set of communication, participation, and online collaboration tools. Thus, between December 2014 and January 2015, the Next and Smart Planning Lab teams agreed upon and subsequently implemented the construction of a multi-platform digital forum capable of facilitating discussions, in-depth analysis, and the construction of visions, maps, images, text, and infographics in a co-design logic.

The multi-platform for this interaction is based on the integration of the following tools:
- The Smart Planning Lab blog hosted on University of Palermo servers (http://smartplanninglab.unipa.it/);
- A dedicated blog on the social network Renurban, specifically conceived to favor discussions and interaction on urban change issues

(http://www.sicilia.renurban.com/smart-planning-lab);
- An account on the social network Twitter (https://twitter.com/smartplanningpa);
- An account on the social network Facebook (https://www.facebook.com/SmartPlanningLab).

The choice to build a digital interaction platform on multiple channels was required to articulate communication about the project according to an architecture in which the contents and results of I-Next were disseminated, taking into account the different representatives and distribution specificity of the information provided by the individual channels. Once published on the Smart Planning Lab blog, the I-Next contents and results were subsequently relaunched and discussed on Renurban and on the other channels, with a stakeholder-activating mechanism that allowed new contents to be produced, redeveloped as a result of comments and notes made by the participants of the online debate. During the first quarter of 2015, these online activities played a role in consolidating and expanding the number of I-Next participants, suggesting topics for reflection and research on the project, and introducing the physical Forum, which consisted of thematic focus groups involving players (institutions, enterprises, and research centers) who already act as components of the smart city. This type of player was actively involved in the Collaborative Arena process through the integration of the two modes of analysis: digital forum and physical forum. Four thematic focus groups were promoted against this backdrop.

The thematic focus groups were prepared in collaboration with the I-Next team (through specific encounters with the executive meeting setting, at twice-weekly intervals on average). Institutional representatives, experts, entrepreneurs, members of nonprofit organizations, committees, and movements were sent there, and the results and scenarios produced during the I-Next activities were discussed with them, aided by computer support, infographics, and visualizations. At the same time, the data, findings, and visions emerging from the discussions were relaunched by the team of researchers and facilitators on the digital platform through dedicated posts on the Smart Planning Lab blog, Renurban, and the other social networks, thus allowing the online debate to continue. The thematic focus groups concerning key issues of urban interaction (how people and goods move in cities; how they produce/consume energy; where and how they generate ideas) provided stakeholders an arena in which to share representations and innovation hypotheses and permitted the catalyzation of data and physical and digital materials to kindle further processing, debates, and shared projects. At the same time, the physical forum constituted an effective tool for upgrading the maps of territorial stakeholders, by means of a capillary task of organizational administration (contact searches and personal invitations, building mailing lists, and periodic meetings). The data related to this task were shared on Google Drive so as to favor interaction within the NEXT/I-Next work group and establish a wealth of useful information for subsequent initiatives.

The results of the listening, processing, and dissemination actions carried out in the physical and digital environments during the first semester of 2015 merged into a task of developing urban metabolism scenarios, culminating on the 28th September of the same year in the Smart Collaborative Arena workshop event, aimed at presenting and discussing the results of the experimental products of the I-Next project, as well as contributing to the development and integrated regeneration of the city and its metropolitan system through multidisciplinary platforms, in which the issues of mobility, society, culture, energy, and governance were put forth to the participants from a smart planning and smart city perspective, according to the following discussion framework:
- governing the timeframes and life cycles of the city: mobility and society;
- the major urban attractors: energy footprint and information technologies for the provision of metropolitan services;
- social inclusion and the outskirts: mobility and intangible accessibility for active citizenship.

NOT CONVENTIONAL MAPS

PALERMO LIVING LAB ON THE ROAD

ANNALISA CONTATO

"Re-cycle Palermo Lab on the Road", an experience that began in 2013 and is now in its third year, is dedicated to the critical examination of places and experiences and the exchange of reflections with scholars, who contribute to delineating the paradigms and tools of a nascent Re-cycling Urbanism. The initiative involved the students of the "Creative City" Urban Planning Laboratory of the Department of Architecture of the University of Palermo, held by Professor Maurizio Carta, who participated in the National Interest Research Project "Re-Cycle Italy. New Life Cycles for Architecture and Infrastructure of the City and Landscape", testing various approach methods for creating new life cycles in discontinued, abandoned, and non-city places.

The purpose of "on the road" is to show to the future designers and urban planners a creative European city as an example of established good practice of urban regeneration tactics connected to the sustainability and quality of architectural experimentation, social innovation, advanced technological solutions, and creative reclamation of places and buildings. This need to show the various urban planning tactics adopted, the various planning approaches, and the experiments underway arises from the realization that the contemporary city is a city undergoing transformation, which contracts but also expands into neighboring territories, becoming dense in certain parts and sparse in others. This produces "urban fragments, functional shavings, and development wreckage" and only through recycling-oriented interventions is it possible to reactivate life cycles, or interventions that are useful for inputting new cycles, to generate renewed attractive and sustainable urban landscapes. We need to once again look at the territory as a generative resource and not just a space of consumption by means of a more precise analysis of existing resources that reveals the presence of valuable "resilience reserves" in cities: places of reverse geography that are indispensable in reactivating the evolving vital mechanisms required to replan cities. These resilience reserves allow processes to be activated in order to manage a greater number of interacting problems, involve a multiplicity of players and diverse social networks in decisions, and implement forms of governance capable of offsetting competition between cities. In new resilient settlements, which are dialogue-based and sensitive, the cycles of elasticity and adaptation require renewed flexibility of functions, greater permeability of spaces, and the fruitful adaptability of settlements.

These are not purely conceptual and spatial problems, but relate to the social effect of a growing demand for sharing, with the economic effect increasingly oriented by circularity, and the technological effect guided by distributed intelligence: components that become structural parts of building the city, becoming planning issues/tools/rules for a new Re-cycling Urbanism.

RE-CYCLE

Barcelona
re-loaded

Today, the city of Barcelona is increasingly crystallizing its role in urban transformation strategies, providing an open and continuously developing laboratory.
In recent decades, the city has been the site of international events that have initiated an important period of redevelopment and urban regeneration, with the launch of processes of renewal, transformation, and the creation of new centrality.
The first important event was the Olympic Games in 1992, which brought attention back to the waterfront. The waterfront became the target of not just functional but, above all, symbolic reclamation, with the demolition of industrial warehouses that hindered access to it, public reappropriation of beaches and piers, and the construction of walkways along the coast, which also contributed to restoring the city's historic role in the Mediterranean.
The planning of Vila Olímpica is particularly interesting, involving the construction of 2,000 apartments (first to accommodate 15,000 athletes and today converted into civil housing) and public utility buildings of architectural quality, also paying

attention to pedestrian areas and street furniture. Previously occupied by an abandoned railway yard and several material depots, the site was expropriated and reclaimed between 1987 and 1989. The disposal of the coastal railway track, the burial of the Glóries connection with the maintenance of Estación de França, the new wastewater purification plant, and the creation of 5 km of new beaches gave the city an important coastal recreation area just outside the center.

The Port Olímpic, created to host sailing races, was designed to become a sports and urban activity center after the closing of the Olympic Games. The facilities were conceived to give shape to an integrated system of spaces — squares, paths, terraces, and services — and a planning pluralism was created through the diversification of structures.

In addition to places directly intended for the Games, the whole Poblenou district took advantage of the event to activate processes of development, regeneration, and the reconversion of old factories (processes that began in the late 1960s following the dismantling and transfer of many industries that had caused an increase in the degradation of the urban space and the recession of the district's productivity that was beginning its period of decline), which were transformed into lofts and galleries for artists and designers bringing creativity and productivity back to the neighborhood.

Finally, the Montjuic hill was the target of transformation and reclamation interventions for the Olympics.

These interventions saw to the placement of sporting equipment inside a ring with an articulate system of public spaces at its center.

The second international event that brought important urban transformation to the south-eastern part of Barcelona was the *Fórum Universal de las Culturas 2004* (an event jointly funded by the Barcelona City Council, the Government of Catalonia, and the Spanish central government, organized with the collaboration of UNESCO).

The event provided the opportunity to transform this area into a central dynamic hub for the part of city served by the Diagonal Mar, that is, the Diagonal-Besós area, a place of concentrated facilities including the purifier, incinerator, and power stations that once occupied around 2 km of coast and gave the area a residual and degraded character.

The process of planning and designing the Fórum area — which began in 1997 — involved the construction of a large public square, the Esplanada del Fórum, an extension of the Diagonal in the shape of a hand with open fingers, which creates connections with various systems of ramps and panoramic terraces, the Parc dels Auditoris and the Parc de la Pau (containing a former incinerator converted into a power station for heating and refrigeration, which supplies the Fórum area and the neighboring districts), and the marina, which is surrounded by a variety of commercial buildings and public spaces. The project also involved the redevelopment of the

Besòs river bank (with the recent start-up of a water purification plant), new beaches, and a residential district acting as a link between the Diagonal and the Fórum. Finally, the Poblenou district is the subject of an important plan to create the Districte 22@ (which occupies 115 city blocks, with a surface area of 200 hectares), an innovation district, and an attraction center for companies dealing in technological innovation, communication, biomedical research, and energy, aimed to make the city a leader in the fields of communication and cutting-edge technologies.

Approved by the Municipal Council of Barcelona in 2000, the project responds to a need to reinstate the economic and social dynamism of the Poblenou district, creating a varied and balanced environment with production centers, social housing, services, and green areas, aimed at improving quality of life and the workplace.The new district services include modern electrical supply networks, telecomunication networks, centralized air-conditioning, and waste collection systems, energy efficiency, noise pollution control, and the reduction and responsible management of natural resources.

The project was well received by the business community: over 80 of the most important companies in the respective sectors established a site in Districte 22@ and, in terms of new buildings, the productive activity of the district increased by over 255,000 m². The *Plan Especial de Protecciòn* guarantees the conservation of industrial assets considered identity-forming, while the creation of local services and services for the settled businesses is guaranteed by a specific plan.

Districte 22@, MEDIA-TIC

Poble Sed, Parallel Sede FECSA

Poblenou,
Campus Universitat Pompeu Fabra

Poblenou,
Biblioteca Universitat Pompeu Fabra
(ex Dipòsit de les Aigües)

Passeig Marítim del Port Olímpic

Poblenou, Parc de la Nova Icària

NOT CONVENTIONAL MAPS

Port Forum

LabUrba 2013/2014

Forum, Pergola solar

RE-CY-CLE ITALY

Stockholm
re-silient

Nominated the first European Green Capital in 2010, Stockholm has been committed for many years to ambitious projects to protect the environment and its citizens' quality of life. The Swedish government has long paid special attention to environmental issues and to the sustainability of development. This can be seen in its consolidated strategy for the reduction of greenhouse gas emissions, which has involved economic control and international efforts.

The Environmental Code, which came into force in January 1999, contains the fundamental laws for environmental protection, integrating the issues in each planning document, and expanding the provisions of the Act of Management of Natural Resources of 1987 for the preservation of natural resources within regulatory plans. By 2050, total national emissions must be reduced by 50%, guaranteeing levels of less than 4.5 tons of CO_2 equivalent/year/inhabitant, to decrease further still.

The capital city's contribution to emissions reduction began in the 1990s with the approval of the Action

Programme on Climate Change, which involved the local economic system and the population, achieving a reduction of CO2 emissions from 5.4 tons per capita in 1990 to 4 tons in 2005.
The city set itself the goal of becoming climate neutral, and already today over 60% of the electricity consumed by the city and 20% of overall energy consumption comes from renewable sources.
In order to pursue the goals set, Stockholm's recent urban planning experiments are a paradigmatic and exemplary case on the European stage, centered on the reconversion plan for the industrial area of Hammarby Sjöstad, which contributed to the success of the environmental and ecological sustainability principles. The Hammarby Sjöstad district project, which got underway in 1990, responded both to an increase in housing demand and to the willingness of the administration to enhance the predominantly public-owned area, assigning it to residential use, supplemented by offices, trade, and services.
The district planning process and its current shape were influenced by the pursuit of urban quality connected to the typical forms of the compact city. An additional aspect that pushed for densification was a desire to return to an urban functional mix, both in terms of the liveability of the areas throughout the whole day and greater safety — a politically driven incentive. In the first phase (1992-97), the neighborhoods of Mjärden and Mandeln-Barnängen were created (1,200 apartments); the second phase, (which began in 2000), concerned the three centers Sickla Udde, Sickla Kaj and Sickla Kanal; the third (2004-05) Hammarby Gård, as well as Hammarbyleden; finally, the fourth phase (2007-13) saw the development of the Lugnet and Henriksdalshamen areas.
With regard to environmental issues, the main goals of the project were: reduction of land consumption by reusing and transforming the most exploited land in residential areas, equipped with large parks; focus on energy aspects, turning to renewable energy and controlling consumption; efficient water disposal systems; recycling of waste wherever possible; and a fast public transport system to discourage private vehicles as much as possible. Expansion of the alternative energy supply was one of the leading goals, and precisely for this reason, the definition of a model to integrate the different technological aspects and cooperation between the different appointed planners was fundamental, right from the early stages of the project.
The Stockholm Water Company, Stockholm Waste Management, Fortum, and the regional public transport company together developed an urban metabolism conceptual model, that is, of integrated cycles of resources, water, energy, and waste, known as the Hammarby Model. The model considers the settlement as an urban ecosystem, in which discarded materials are reinserted in a virtuous

cycle that allows almost everything to be reused for the operation of the district itself.

Another important urban development and reconversion project is the plan for the Royal Seaport (Norra Djurgårdenstaden district), an area at the north-east fringes of the city, historically denoted by the presence of the gasometers of Hjorthagen, the Värtahamen cruise terminal areas, the Frihamen commercial port at the center, and the Loudden industrial area (to the south).

The intervention is called the Royal Seaport because of the presence of touristic-cruise districts and its proximity to the Royal National City Park. The plan provides for 10,000 new homes and 30,000 new jobs. Above all, the intervention is significant in relation to the environment and sustainable development: the Norra Djurgårdenstaden project provides continuation of Hammarby Sjöstad with regard to reducing the environmental impact.

In relation to environmental issues, the Royal Seaport sets itself three main goals: to become fossil fuel free by 2030; to reduce CO_2 emissions by about a third before 2020, bringing them to below 1.5 tons per inhabitant (in 2008, the average emissions per inhabitant were 4.5 tons); and to prepare itself for climate change, including increased rainfall.

In relation to emissions control, a specific model (Hammarby Model) was prepared to manage the ecological cycle and, in particular, the cycles of energy, waste, and water.

Also for the Hagastaden area (approximately 96 ha), the creation of a new mixed neighborhood of apartments (5,000 new housing units), workplaces (50,000 new jobs), cultural attractions, green areas, and leading organizations in the field of global research and highly specialized medical treatments are planned, amounting to a total investment of around 60 million Swedish kronas. The presence of the Stockholm Resilience Centre of research is of considerable importance. Set up in 2007, it arose from a joint initiative between Stockholm University and the Beijer International Institute of Ecological Economics of the Royal Swedish Academy of Sciences, funded by the Foundation for Strategic Environmental Research (Mistra).

From its outset, the goal was to create a world-leading cross-disciplinary research center to conduct a study of complex socio-ecological systems, and generate new intuitions, papers, and tools for the development of management and governance practices.

Greater knowledge of how to strengthen the resilience of society and nature is becoming increasingly important in addressing the strain caused by climate change and by other environmental impacts.

In recent years, the concept of resilience is more and more the focus of attention as a guide for adopting strategies to address sudden changes, which could increase in frequency and intensity, and to avoid

Gamla Stan

continuing to respond to them in a disorganized manner.
In the Stockholm Resilience Centre approach, resilience is defined as the long-term ability of a system to face changes and continue to develop.
The thematic research group on urban socio-ecological systems analyses urban resilience and sustainability, considering humanity, social systems, ecosystems and their services, and biodiversity as interacting and interdependent, and aims to create a knowledge base and better understand what challenges cities are called to face.

The City, Jakobsbergsgatan

Station T-Centralen

Hammarby Sjöstad

Hammarby Sjöstad

NOT CONVENTIONAL MAPS

Hammarby Sjöstad

Norra Djurgårdenstaden

Hammarby Sjöstad

RE-CYCLE ITALY

Lyon re-nown

The starting point of strategies to strengthen the city of Lyon as a European metropolis of innovation and scientific research (which has attracted investments, the localization of new businesses, and new residents) can be found in the commitment of Grand Lyon (an inter-municipal association corresponding to the metropolitan city). In the 1990s, Grand Lyon prepared the "Lyon 2010" Strategic Plan, structured into 5 lines: transformation of the city into a technical-scientific hub; extension and improvement of the urban transport system and of regional, national, and international connections; development of residential attractiveness; enhancement of touristic potential and international accommodation; and development of an environmental policy.

The plan for the Confluence area is exemplary of this process of development, reconversion, and internationalization of the city, being one of the most ambitious nodes of the urban planning program involving the whole metropolitan area of Lyon. The Confluence area corresponds to the south part of the peninsula, where the Saône and Rhône rivers merge. The tip of the peninsula was uninhabited until 1700, when the awe-inspiring transformation and urbanization of the area began, devoting a strip of land of around 200 hectares exclusively to industrial areas.

The peninsula was isolated from the rest of the city because of the barriers formed by the railway and motorway, and because of the functions that had found a home there.

The area's vocation in logistics reached its peak in the 1960s and 1970s, thanks to the construction of the A7 motorway, the Perrache interchange, and the presence of the wholesale market.

Following the gradual decline of heavy industry, the area started to lose various functions and in the 1990s, reflections on the future of this part of the peninsula began. The large urban renewal program denominated "Lyon Confluence" aims to regenerate the central area of the peninsula, on which, starting from the conversion of abandoned industries, various new functions are localized: residential, tertiary, port, commercial, service, and public attractiveness.

One of the most ambitious nodes of the urban planning programme of the metropolis, the project intends to generate a new urban centrality in the area — characterized by a strategic position and by the presence of numerous abandoned industrial areas — offering a model of a multipurpose city open to social diversity, and developing an autonomous creative community capable of fuelling the existing productive fabric and generating new economies.

The Confluence area was defined by the Plan Local d'Urbanisme (PLU) as a Zone d'Aménagement Concerté (ZAC) for the creation of a regeneration project, being capable of translating itself into a specific negotiated and designed urban planning desire, defining an implementation perimeter, within which the competent authority ensures land control and has tools to steer construction through public and private promoters. In 2003, the Grand Lyon assembly approved the first phase of the Confluence project (ZAC 1) and entrusted the construction of public amenities to a SEM (Mixed Economy Company). The SEM plays also the role of project manager on behalf of Grand Lyon and is responsible for the whole operational and management process until the implementation phase.

The ZAC 1 designed a new district and reclaimed port buildings, creating: a central attractive space bearing an image of innovation and dynamism; 1,670 housing units; 95,000 m^2 of retail spaces, hotels and services; 130,000 m^2 for the service sector; and 30,000 m^2 for public amenities.

In 2010, the second phase of the Conf luence project began with the approval of ZAC 2. The project intends to pursue a mixed and balanced functional program and promote slow mobility, improving connections with the city by extending the tram line to Metro Line B and building new bridges. Specifically, the Marché district to the north will be allocated to offices, housing, trade, and public facilities; while to the south, the Le Champ project will provide a green area with walking and cycling trails and spaces for cultural and innovative activities. In short, the program envisages: 160,000 m^2 of housing; 12,000 m^2 of retail spaces, hotels and services; 160,000 m^2 for the service sector; 18,000 m^2 for public facilities; and 70,000 m^2 of towers. In addition to the ZAC 1 and ZAC 2 projects, the transformation of Conf luence will also include other urban regeneration interventions.

Along the Rives de Saône, the project provides for the extension of the Saône Park beyond the Kitchener Bridge. The park's creation is the backbone of the project and allows the peninsula to delineate a new relationship with the river landscape: the avenues along the river are transformed into a large urban park, perfectly integrated into the residential neighborhood.

The Sainte-Blandine district is the target of an eco-sustainable renewal program that aims to reconvert the existing buildings in accordance with the directives of the *Programme d'éco-rénovation*, in keeping with the *Plan Climat de la Métropole de Lyon*. The project also includes the implementation of the Perrache station and of the Pôle d'Echange Multimodal. Another important intervention for the city economy is the plan for the Part-Dieu district, the second-largest decision-making and service hub in France and reference district for the tertiary functions of Lyon, with approximately 1,600,000 m^2 of areas devoted to the service sector and over 50,000 jobs. The project intends to pursue development to become one of the European districts of reference for the management and planning of new industrial, energy, urban, and infrastructure systems, including the ICT and digital fields, which will contribute to strengthening its status internationally.

Confluence

Confluence, Euronews - Pavillon Vert

Confluence, Dark Point

Confluence, Pavillon del Douanes

Confluence, Pavillon del SAlins - Cube orange

Lyon Catholic University (ex Prison St. Paul)

Pont Raymond Barre

Quartier des États-Unis

NOT CONVENTIONAL MAPS

Confluence, Parc de Saône

Confluence, Place Nautique

Site archéologique gallo-romain

LabUrba 2015/2016

NOT CONVENTIONAL MAPS

4.4 RE-POSTCARDS

ANNALISA CONTATO

The following postcards are an extract of the Palermo Research Unit's contribution to the "Re-cycle Italy" National Interest Research Project at the international seminar "Recycling and Infrastructure Plan for the Territory. Selection, Maintenance, and New Models", organized by the Politecnico di Milano Research Unit on the 26th and 27th February 2015. The poster session of postcards from territories with infrastructure is based, as the call states, on the:
- "Selection of elements on which to base the recycling project, in order to steer resources towards cases that can still be put back into operation, in order to plan and manage the decline of some portions of territory or think about the treatment of incomplete and incongruous artifacts, potentially even with a view to their removal and demolition;
- "Maintenance" as a potential future for planning practices to correspond to the actual availability of economic resources, in order to operate with maximum effectiveness, within the context of territories with infrastructure, on what is already there, supporting the quality of soil, fabrics, and artifacts and their relationships with the reference settings;
- Definition of new models to anticipate unprecedented practices of building city and territorial infrastructure, weaving together the physical dimension and new technological and cultural perspectives (from logistics and smart contents to ICT) in a fresh way, overcoming the idea of infrastructure based on the paradigm and image of hardware and armature sustaining the processes of economic development and physical transformation of the city" (Politecnico di Milano Research Unit, call for postcards as part of the international seminar "Recycling and Infrastructure Planning for the Territory. Selection, Maintenance, and New Models", Politecnico di Milano, 26th and 27th February 2015).

The Palermo Research Unit's re-cyclical postcards explore the whole territorial Platform of Western Sicily, featuring some visits to Southern and Eastern Sicily, and submit places and planning conditions on which to base the birth of new life cycles.

The Great Cretto.
Epilog of an urban life cycle

In front of the ruins of the city of Gibellina, which was destroyed by an earthquake in 1968, Alberto Burri conceived of the Great Cretto, "The most important chapter of Italian art in the second half of the 20th century and among the most extraordinary artworks in the world" (Calvesi).
A shroud of white cement — dried out material binder forever sealing the fragments of a city pulverized by the earthquake, lying on the side of the hill where Gibellina once rose — retraces the old roads of the city, its form, its identity, and its history with arid and deceased cracks in the deep grooves of its surface, modelled like the wrinkles of a hand. The Great Cretto is a celebration of the death of a city — of the definitive end of its life cycle. Yet, in the name of who knows what flaunted sustainability goal, the administrators of this poetic patch of Sicilian hinterland have heinously permitted the installation of a wind farm.

by Angela Alessandra Badami

Inland territories and local resilience

The Monti Sicani area is a resilient system, capable of absorbing negative shocks caused by the marginalization process evident in its outlying location and poor infrastructure and virtual connectivity, to return to a position of equilibrium. This territory is a "new model" of a community that is reinventing its development by reactivating identity-forming capital. The agricultural landscape, historical and archaeological heritage, and energy sources open unprecedented scenarios to various quality of life models focused on the relationship between the territory and the local community, and the fusion of ancient traditions and new technologies. Active territorial coalitions are open to forms of development that aspire to the recapitalization of the territory through the reclamation of rural value, the search for environmental quality, the construction of short production and consumption networks, quality living, and tourism.

di **Marilena Orlando**

Custonaci: the pearly quarry side

Custonaci, north-western coast of the province of Trapani: the precious materials extracted from these mountains cross the Mediterranean to reach the rich and budding markets of the Far and Middle East.
They leave nothing on the territory's landscape, except for quarry residue and hyper-trophic infrastructure. The new development model does not change the focus on the precious material extraction, but it does change the approach to the way territories experience the presence of mining. The processing waste and sawmills have created new territorial conditions but not a new landscape.
The recycling logic for a new development model of the area is based on the up-cycling of scrap materials, but also on a cradle-to-cradle treatment, in which each extracted block is a resource for the territory's future.

di Daniele Ronsivalle

Paternò, Plain of Catania: (un)useful urbanized spaces

To support agricultural production, the Plain of Catania today features an infrastructure system that is much larger than it really needs to be.

Thousands of cubic meters of warehouses, distribution centers, and centers for the processing of citrus products that are no longer connected to the production systems. The logic underlying the new vision of territorial planning is linked to a dual retreat: the city, which reduces its urbanization limits due to the reduced population, and the countryside, which reduces its agricultural production spaces.

The residual "non-city" and "non-country" space is the subject of negotiation to create public service spaces and public utilities for the citizens where, until a short time ago, there were the civic uses of local communities.

di Daniele Ronsivalle

Poggioreale Vecchia: new life in the red zone

The red zone of Poggioreale, which has remained as such since the 1968 Belìce earthquake, is a prime example of the selection of a place in which to take advantage of the characteristics it has accidentally acquired.

Today, recycling Poggioreale Vecchia means entrusting the management of the red zone to the Fire Department, which is concretely developing training activities for both dog lovers and for the teams ensuring the safety of structures in danger of collapse. The logic adopted by the Municipal Administration of Poggioreale, therefore, is the strategic sub-cycle: nearly fifty years after the earthquake, it's impossible to conceive of rebuilding the site in the face of the very large population reduction of the whole Valle del Belìce. Using the ruin for its intrinsic ruin characteristics has thus become the winning strategy.

di Daniele Ronsivalle

Poggioreale Nuova: future views of territories past

The settlement of Poggioreale Nuova arose from a huge post-earthquake reconstruction operation that has changed the face of the Belìce valley: Poggioreale, together with Gibellina and Salaparuta, have been moved and rebuilt elsewhere, far from their roots. Beyond the social, economic, and cultural effects that have developed over time, today we see a static condition due to the absence of positive demographic trends.

The center of Poggioreale Nuova can accommodate 10,000 inhabitants but only has about 1,500; its instability is causing the abandonment of large parts of the urban territory and the commendable planning of the urban fabric of the new town is no longer recognizable. Producing maintenance actions coordinated with careful de-urbanization and reduction actions is one of the possible paths towards rebalancing the urban system in relation to the agricultural system context.

Meanwhile, Poggioreale stands by to watch.

di Daniele Ronsivalle

Palermo South Coast

The South Coast of Palermo is a territory whose fragile physical and social identity manifests itself in a haphazard series of public housing settlements, terraced buildings, discontinued or abandoned production areas, voids, and fragments of landscape untidily coexisting beyond the Oreto River, generating an overall image of marginality and degradation.

For too long, the city has shown an attitude of disinterest and abandonment towards the South Coast, using the beach as a dumping ground for the accumulation of backfill, the result of the area's urbanization processes.

Today, the seafront beyond the Oreto River holds valuable potential in prefiguring possible new transformation scenarios and in proposing exemplary themes for the city, such as restoring its relationship with the sea and a "fresh look southwards".

di Barbara Lino

Palermo South Coast: property seized from the mafia

The San Paolo Palace Hotel in Palermo is one of the assets confiscated from organized crime. The property towers above the surrounding built fabric and is located in a coastal area of the city of Palermo called Sant'Erasmo.

According to official data published by the National Association of Seized and Confiscated Assets, Italy has 11,238 confiscated properties and 1,780 companies confiscated from organized crime, amounting to an economic value of 30 billion euros. 17.31% of these assets are located in the city of Palermo alone and consist of 1,945 properties and 234 companies (2012 data), amounting to a value of 333 million euros. The magnitude of the phenomenon suggests the opportunity to overcome the current logic of "precise" and "isolated" custody, anticipating a strategic, systemic, and integrated approach to reactivate production cycles and facilitate the social infrastructure of the territory.

di Michele Anzalone

Re-cycling Bandita

Situated in the south-eastern part of the city of Palermo, the little port of Bandita is the ancient dock of the seaside village of the same name. It is located in one of the stretches of coast most affected by physical and, above all, cultural degradation. A coastal strip improperly used as a dumping ground to the point of compromising bathing, today it is also strongly disadvantaged by the loss of fishing activities as a result of the continuous siltation of the port. It suffers above all, however, from a loss of identity. Morphologically and strategically, the little port forms a connection between the various urban identities surrounding it: the territory at its rear, characterized by strong economic and social hardship; the coastal strip to the north-east; and the so-called "mamelon" to the south-east, which is an artificial hill overlooking the sea, created from backfill, and the subject of uncompleted urban regeneration attempts.

di Annalisa Contato

Palermo.
Re-thinking the urban seaside

The state-owned area of the South Coast of the city of Palermo is devoid of specific functions and, despite its morphological characteristics being favorable to coastal use, the conditions of neglect and water and land pollution discourage use of the sea for bathing, sport, and recreational purposes.

By acknowledging resiliencies that can reactivate the "coastal cycle" in this part of the city, it can be proposed as a new model in which to test different development modes through the paradigm of Urban Acupuncture, intervening foremost on several nerve centers to reactivate the entire nervous system of the coast. The seasonal alternation of coastal functions could become a strong point on which to program different ways of using and experiencing the urban beach, and no longer a factor to motivate the state of abandonment that is perpetuated at the beginning of every winter season.

di Annalisa Contato

A road between the sea and the city

The reactivation of the metabolic system of the South Coast of the city of Palermo is related to the coastal use of the urban beach. This inevitably passes through a new definition of the Via Mesina Marine roadway, which over the years, has lost its urban role as a coastal route connecting the city with the fishing villages to the south, becoming the preferential access route to the Port of Palermo. This critical issue, together with the beach's loss of bathing quality, has thrown the local trade system, which is tied to seasonal use of the sea, into crisis. The interventions required to reactivate the "coastal cycle" pass through the redefinition and reactivation of three disrupted and/or dormant cycles: gray (redefinition of traffic type and speed), blue (reactivation of the sea-related ecosystem), and brown (reactivation of local trade and activities related to seaside tourism).

di Carmelo Galati Tardanico

La foce dell'Oreto e la città. Riciclo e resilienza

Today, the Oreto River mouth is a canal system and the city ignores its presence. A potential intervention on the river would need to act on the quality of the landscape and public spaces, working on its resilience — that is, lowering the level of hydraulic risk connected to floods by means of integrated actions to protect the territory and make the ground permeable, in accordance with the time and energy cycles entailed by a delicate system, such as a river mouth in an urban setting.

A key action for this future project on the Oreto River is the re-naturalization of the riverbed. During floods, detention basins could contain the river water within a defined area, producing different riverscapes that change with the rhythm of the water. Increased ground permeability, combined with specific collection and distribution systems, could also allow for the reuse of rainwater. Within this new concept of a river park, shared gardens will shape a new relationship between housing and the river.

di Jessica Smeralda Oliva

The intelligent city: outlooks (starting from the citizens)

Reflections/City. The contemporary city presents a framework that is not always neat: historical pre-existing elements, public housing neighborhoods, multi-storey buildings, and signs of nature beyond infrastructural components intensely populate the contemporary urban territory. The addition of certain materials — infrastructure for mobility in the image — often occurs in a traumatic manner: the tramway passes oblivious to the city built around it and, above all, to its citizens.

Outlooks/Smart-City Users. Using ICT to manage services and infrastructure, the intelligent city approach provides new opportunities with which to reinterpret the city space, starting from turning its inhabitants into modern city users: freed of traditional conditions, it builds a different, more democratic, participatory, social, and inclusive city that is reactive to the transformations and changes underway.

di Raffaella Riva Sanseverino

Agrigenthome, recycling of an invasive station

The construction (1933) of the railroad branch from Girgenti Bassa station to the terminal station was undertaken at the expense of a monastery, part of the ancient walls, five towers from the Norman period and, above all, triggered the process of "colonization" of the hill that led to the famous landslide (1967).

The station of approximately 2,500 m² — much too large for the city at the time (28,677, 1931 Census) — has two floors. The first, on the square, symbolically indicates access to the nineteenth-century avenue and is now completely abandoned. The second, subdued by the slope of the hill and with a separate road entrance, has had a rebirth since 2013 thanks to the granting of custody to a private company for part of the lower buildings (about 300 m²) adjacent to the arrival of the line, which, abandoned for decades, were once devoted to offices and a dormitory for railway workers. This assignment to Aparthotel responds to a certain ferment of cultural, social, and touristic "rebirth" of the historic center that is strongly felt and may be a prototype to be implemented.

di Valeria Scavone

5

RE-FORMING ROME

5.1 **ROMA 20-25. NEW LIFE CYCLES FOR THE METROPOLIS**
Maurizio Carta

5.2 **IMPACT REGENERATIVE DESIGN: PARADIGMS, STRATEGIES, AND MAPPING**
ENABLING TECHNOLOGIES FOR THE CITY-LABORATORY
IN THE METROPOLITAN CITY OF REGGIO CALABRIA
Consuelo Nava

5.3 **THE RESEARCH "MACRO"**

5.4 **ROME AGRI-FAB CITY**
A PRODUCTIVE LANDSCAPE FOR
A SELF-SUFFICIENT METROPOLIS
Manuel Gausa Navarro, Silvia Brandi, Marco Ingrassia

5.5 **RE-FORMING ROME**
THE AGRI/FAB METROPOLIS
Maurizio Carta

5.6 **OPEN SOURCE&SHARED URBAN DESIGN PLATFORM**
Barbara Lino

5.7 **CITYFORMING ROME: IDEAS AND PROJECTS**
Angelica Agnello and Mariateresa Caeti, Madalina Culcasi,
Francesca Montagna, Milena Lauretta

5.8 **RE-FORMING ROME EXHIBITION: A PEDAGOGICAL MACHINE**
Annalisa Contato and Jessica Smeralda Oliva

5.1

ROMA 20-25.
NEW LIFE CYCLES
FOR THE
METROPOLIS

MAURIZIO CARTA

The initiative "ROMA 20-25. New Life Cycles for the Metropolis", which invoked twenty-five schools of architecture in Italian and international universities to interpret the present urban situation in Rome and imagine its future through an international design workshop and exhibition, involved the University of Palermo through the Research Unit of the National Interest Research Project "RE-CYCLE Italy. New Life Cycles for Architecture and Infrastructure of Cities and Landscape", of which I am the Head of Research. The project "ROMA 20-25. New Life Cycles for the Metropolis" was supported by the Department of Urban Transformation of the Municipality of Rome and MAXXI, the National Museum of 21st Century Arts.

A new map of the metropolitan city, identified as the large area of social and economic life of Rome today, extending 50 km per side, was overlaid by a grid of 25 squares and each university was entrusted with a portion of the territory to interpret and plan, a Macro with 10 km sides, within which to place a small tile of 1 km^2, on which to test a fully developed planning proposal.

The project area entrusted to the University of Palermo was Macro no. 12, crossed from east to west by the Tiber River and by an important infrastructure network. The area comprises the Eur district, an area of architectural and urban planning prestige, various settlement fabrics, districts of uniform public housing, such as the Corviale building, suburbs like Trullo and Magliana, agricultural areas, and nature reserves. The first site inspection phase provided a structural interpretation of the area, from which a fragmented identity emerged — a disconnected set of "islands", "island-communities", and environmental enclaves, whose fragmentation is accentuated by the infrastructure boundaries. From a large-scale perspective, the area is crossed by centre-outskirt flows, intersecting the motorway and railway corridor to and from the airport, a multimodal infrastructure corridor that generates potential accessibility and separation at the same time. The GRA ring road establishes a very clear-cut caesura between in and out — the city inside and the city outside (of the ring road). In its current state, the Tiber also forms a separation.

Four prevalent identities, or four cities, can be recognized: the Ager Romanus, the outer villages, the city of large transformation, and the resilience reserves.

The Ager Romanus area extends mostly in the northwest sector, where, between the A91 motorway and the Tiber, we find over 1,500 hectares of irrigated arable land, which is part of the State Nature Reserve of the Roman Coastline.

The outer villages include the suburbs of Vitinia, Casal Bernocchi, and Spinaceto, settlements which arose mainly in the 1950s-1970s, and the nature reserves Decima Malafede and Tenuta di Castelporziano.

The city of large transformation

includes the Eur district, the new Eur-Castellaccio center, and the racecourse area, where the building of a new stadium is planned.

The city of resilience reserves is in both geographical and ideal contrast with the city of large transformation, being characterized by public housing centers and settlements, such as the Corviale building, Magliana, and Trullo. Beginning from an interpretation of the resources and identities of the area, with an approach that interprets creativity as a proactive and enabling factor, the Palermo work group, in partnership and perspective sharing with the IAAC of Barcelona, adopted the Agri/FabCity model to transform the area into a city of new production, in accordance with the principles of a circular economy, in which the citizens are not just consumers, but increasingly producers for self-consumption.

It is particularly in the districts of stigmatized marginality that a city can start over, knowing how to put its capital back into the game, integrating the social effect of a growing demand for sharing, with the economic effect increasingly oriented by circularity, and the technological effect guided by distributed intelligence: components which are now structural parts of building the city, becoming planning issues/instruments/laws for a new urban metabolism.

The Agri/Fab Metropolis project proposed a process-based and incremental approach to urban regeneration grounded on recycling (*Recycle-based CityForming*), which, through the phases of colonisation/consolidation/development, applies the paradigms of Creative Re-cyclical Urbanism to the ordinary city, meeting basic needs and designing new open and collaborative "socio-rhythms", rather than perpetrating an urban metabolism of separate islands, working towards a polycentric vision that provides an alternative to the large-center model.

From island fragmentation — of communities, infrastructure, functions —, by means of a Re-forming (re-cycle + cityforming) process, the project aims to define a new metabolic metropolitan archipelago, in which the blue-green and mobility infrastructure do not separate, but connect the city's centers.

In the process-based dynamic of Cityforming, big events, such as the building of the new stadium, the 2024 Olympics [cancelled by new administration], and the 2025 Jubilee, are seen as opportunities — activators of non-episodic urbanities, making a contribution to the reactivation and regeneration of the ordinary city.

The Re-forming process applies the paradigms and instruments of recyclical urbanism through creative, intelligent, and sustainable planning devices to respond to demands that emerge from the territory and to generate physical, social, and economic resilience.

The project has been elaborated using several keywords/issues, intended as topics for the project, to be considered in an integrated and interdependent vision: living (new housing and new aggregation spaces); moving (high and low speed); producing (urban agriculture, self-consumption, and manufacturing); consuming (different consumption patterns and new business venues); generating (self-sufficient energy districts and solar communities); and creating (reactivating the spatial and social urban capital).

IMPACT REGENERATIVE DESIGN: PARADIGMS, STRATEGIES, AND MAPPING

ENABLING TECHNOLOGIES FOR THE CITY-LABORATORY IN THE METROPOLITAN CITY OF REGGIO CALABRIA

CONSUELO NAVA

The trajectory

"Regenerative cities" are those which, more than others, avoiding any possible hierarchical urban dimension, trust in the ability of transformations as effects of urban acupuncture and their power to emanate other values and vital energy.

"Vulnerable Urbanism", as defined by Ellin (2003), no longer considers the user to be a product of transformations, but a collaborator in sustainable planning based on "a context that regenerates and is reborn". In the circular urban metabolism (flows of materials, energy, water, vegetation, and land as resources and ecosystem services) and in recycling activities (*repair and reclaim*), this trajectory finds its most lively productive dimension on the architecture and on the territories; it becomes the feasible direction in planning the innovation and sustainability of transformations and in open and self-informed processes of "transitioning communities"[1].

Defining regenerative design scenarios at all scales means establishing meanings and meaningful values of a new condition of knowledge, in which territories and cities become the physical and relational space of "sustainable innovative actions", and in which "a new enabling technologies service" ensures that devices are compatible with the continuous transformations and no longer pertain to a certain time, or to a given timeframe. The "resilience condition", which all physical and relational spaces must answer to, should be measured against "the social time", which, surpassing the meaning of the short, medium and long-term scenario projection, typical of wellknown sustainability theories, is found each time in the action and reaction measured and adjusted by the smart ecosystems of regenerative cities; they themselves trigger conditions of balance and response to transformations with a cradle to cradle life cycle, typical of recycling and circular economy processes.

The theory and reference paradigms

The trajectory drawn out moves according to the structure of the most radical innovation and towards the idea that we need to build a new narrative of "humanized" and "intelligent" urban ecosystems in a newfound relationship between "plural process and knowledge city". In this direction, it is important to delineate the new sustainability paradigms on the issues of "diverse contexts", and "advanced hybrid knowledge" that can be built through experiences that are not merely a convention of the production of research and innovation, but rather, as new "productive networks of information", the latter supported by the architecture of the network between the nodes that produce, feed, and maintain it.

Also in this formulation of "new paradigms", technologies play an absolutely functional role, adopted as a reference and availability of implementation instruments (devices and methods), in their "collective intelligence", thus called upon to convert

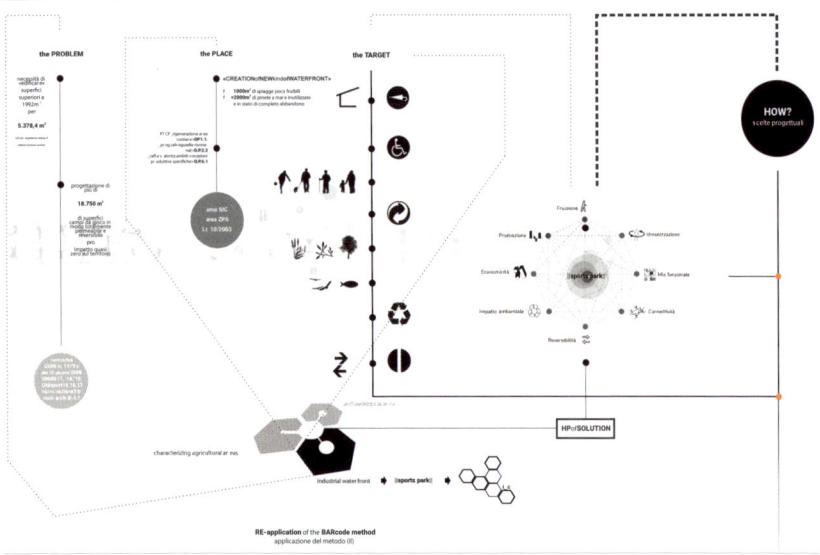

Meta-project process scheme on pre-master plan sustainable scenarios.
(Graphics by Federica Laura Ciccone, thesis project 2015, "Territory research, method and project for the sustainable development of the coastal area of Palmi, self-information and sustainable scenarios detected using the barcode method process").

each "regenerative" process into "plural intelligence".

1. Diverse contexts.
A new ecological narrative is possible when the levels of innovation in their plural formation depend on "diverse contexts", on which transformation actions are taken. In this sense, the humanization of networks advocated by De Biase (2015) and their efficacy compared to intelligent platforms of information or service management, even in territorial contexts, triggers a level of proactive participation capable of supporting transformations and functions and monitoring their impacts. The service-user relationship, seen for example in urban metabolism scenarios, supports technologies and devices in the phases of compensation or surplus of demand. It is that which has commonly led to innovation in the energy districts through the smart-grid system, a resilient and self-sufficient energy network, in which the level of "interoperability" of the networks themselves is ensured by the human accountability system, by means of which users participate in the management and are always informed of the meaning of the productive nodes and whether these carry out

a function of generation, storage, or distribution of energy. This energy exchange scenario, however, affects the transformation of environmental systems and landscapes and upholds their rules and ability to produce future visions, to talk about the transformations, uses, and maintenance of the systems themselves[2].

2. Advanced hybrid knowledge.
A new knowledge project oriented towards "circular models, against the waste of resources", as described in the proposal of Lacy *et alii* (2016), becomes the key to the success of each action that measures itself against economic and social sustainability. A transformed approach to the obsolescence of innovated technologies measures this trend and steers the acceleration towards more conscious development. In the age of networks and of the intelligence of urban and social systems, the term "quality" is compared with the term "quantity", in a new global scenario that proposes very cogent instruments and actions at a local level. The recycling and ecological repair of the sensitive systems of regenerative cities involve levels of knowledge and exchange (sharing) in which economies of the resources and the intelligence of the community (smart communities) are also implemented. Consider, for example, sustainable urban regeneration models, with technologies for the use and management of land as catalysts and producers of new air quality due to the storage of CO2. What is created with de-sealing and the transformation into productive rooftops, in fact, becomes a new scenario condition for networking new devices for the management of water, energy, waste, biomass, and human activities. It also fulfils the condition of controlling the impacts of transformations on the resilient planning of territories and cities in climate adaptation plans, as much through "urban *run-off*" tactics and techniques, as with tactics of "recycling and reuse of the public spaces in cities", by means of temporary projects, according to the strategies of *placemaking*, for the regenerative hybrid city[3].

3. Productive networks of information.
It is possible to measure the efficacy of the network, which is transformed from intelligent into collective and plural, in systems where the exchange is continuous and also hybrid (*flowing knowledge*), but also where it surpasses the traditional and conventional conditions of the relations and production of innovation, and is compared with the efficacy of the nodes of a new network of "knowledge city", as advocated by Manzini (2015)[4]. It is an innovative and innovated model, capable of producing new systems and maps that facilitate access to and availability of data, flows, information, and references to scenarios on which to build future visions of change. In this sense, the network, in its open digital systems, finds the characteristics of self-information, for the contribution that each user-producer can provide

to the network itself at any moment of interaction. It follows that in the human smart city model, the learning ecocity theories of Linch also become collaborative practices of "learning by making" and the cities and territories transfer the model of perception of the quality of life, in the complexity of the states of urban and territorial performance. Equally, smart planning tools or the use of "enabling technologies" depend on the capacity of the communities to interact and communicate in a network; in the physical spaces of exchange and actions (*city making*), participating in the building of information devices, open-data, and maps of sensitive scenarios on sustainable visions.

Impact Regenerative Design using enabling technologies
The need to formulate sustainable strategies and adopt enabling technologies to control transformations of the built environment by implementing impact regenerative design models more coherently defines the nature of the term "environmental impact" with its meaning strictly connected to "the social impact". The pressure states of the impacts in a regenerative system can be operated by natural agents, but are certainly subject to biophysical changes and to (re)actions of human factors, which can also originate from outside of the triggered processes (deadweight).
A positive dimension of the circular and regenerative metabolism produces the effect of a city that can "boost" its performance and "reduce"
the irreversible nature of its impacts. This condition is particularly favored in the resilience condition, however, if as Carta (2016) says, the "dividend" of the augmented city can count on the contribution of recycling processes and paradigms[5].
In the case of "regenerative urban systems", these must respond with resilience to any possible changing impact condition, so the dual environmental- social value is certainly supported by the effects produced by their transformations on the urban metabolism and by the need to measure them and bring them towards successful performance in terms of innovation. The extent of the impact and the extent of the change become the combined measures governed with enabling technologies, towards the sustainable scenarios of the human smart city, as a social and active dimension of the knowledge city.
The paradigmatic difference between regenerated and regenerative system, is not only marked by the role that any process operates in an action of transformation and change but represents the ability of the system to "trigger" or "graft" change transformations. The regenerated systems are the subject of change through the "compatible" use of enabling technologies, whose applied devices and tools play the role of implementing a recycling action on the compromised requirements and of enabling others, innovating a new or recovered process, "triggering" new qualities for the system itself. In this condition, in the case of cities or human settlements, sustainability

thus becomes the target, on which to test new levels of value for the project with high environmental and social performance, in the short-medium term. The regenerative systems have the ability to produce change actions through the "resilient" use of enabling technologies, for which the devices themselves become "catalysts" of new tools acting on all the highly proactive processes they can "trigger". In this other condition, in the case of cities and human settlements, sustainability becomes the strategic program to be entrusted with new levels of value and sense for projects with high environmental and social performance, in the medium- long term.

A system capable of expressing regeneration, thus of being regenerative, must have absorbed and must be adapted to regeneration actions; not all regenerated systems, however, are necessarily enabled to be regenerative. Their expressive capacity is verified through the qualities of the project, which finds actions, devices, and performance in a logical and meta- project process, in its pre-master plan development even before its drawing one.

The measure of the impact of regenerative systems oriented to sustainable and social innovation for transformation actions in knowledge cities intercept and trigger incoming (*in*) and outgoing (*output*) process aspects (*process design*) and product aspects (*product design*), regarding:
- the ecosystems of resources;
- producible scenarios;
- the practicality of the networks.

These three reference domains feed one another and manage values connected to the available data, detected performances, reactivated resources, the operation of devices, the configuration of different geographic models, and the variable and flexible layouts of the territories and contexts (co-territories).

The measure of the change, oriented to innovation in the control of environmental and social impacts, can make use of the "dividend" mentioned in the paragraph introduction, precisely because it is generated by the dichotomy of potential combinations of paradigms and actions of that regenerative city that shows its intelligence in its ability to become a "laboratory" of innovation and experimentation, sustainability and recycling, discontinuance and reconfiguration, flexibility and connections. All qualities which, seemingly opposite, mark the possible coexistence of values "combined" to restore meanings and configurations to increasingly adaptive and inclusive transformation actions, just as Gausa (2016) says, in commenting the representative paradigms of the theories put forward by Nava (2016)[6].

Strategies and mapping for the "Human Smart City"

In identifying the strategies oriented to generating visions for the *human smart city*, the system of support for more coherent decisions certainly appears to be "the process of design-driven innovation", which is able to learn from the most significant (enabling) technologies to manage the relations useful to the internal and external knowledge network, as referred to by Verganti (2009) in his theories[7].

The purpose of measuring the impact and transferring its information to specialized maps with a high degree of collaborative content responds to three specific questions about the process, providing expert support for deciding, learning, and informing communities and territories. The technologies transfer the technical-cognitive value of method and model to the graphic information of the maps in their specific definitions. Thus, mapping becomes fundamental for regenerative systems: - to decide upon the trajectory that a program or project must adopt, to anticipate possible and sustainable scenarios, to provide the input information that will make the proposed interventions feasible; - to decide whether to make a project "open", with the integration of other possible scenarios or visions; - to learn whether to export and "scale up" a pilot project;
- to learn how to adapt a program or successful project to other contexts;
- to notify users about information and services identified with the built scenarios, on the configured trajectories;
- to inform about the levels of sustainability and innovation of the project, applicable with the enabling technologies and the devices compatible with the prefigured scenarios;
- to inform the potential beneficiaries and communities of the positive effects of the transformation, whose objective is change, within the established time and with the reasons to support the assessment of impacts on the reference contexts.

Experiments with the City_Laboratory of the metropolitan city of Reggio Calabria. Impact Map

The "city-laboratory" theme, as an investigation within the Re-cycle Italy research project, is an important opportunity to contribute to "rewriting the intentions" that weld several approaches and contributions from the "cross-disciplinary nature" of the theoretical positions and of the most applied experiences, on the issues of transforming cities, their current state, and their ability to seize environmental and social challenges, with a view to preserving the future by activating new life cycles. A condition characterized simultaneously by the dimensions of crisis on the one hand and innovation radicalism on the other, for a future with strong oppositional variations, but whose utopia appears to push itself without limits and too many rules to represent and give new meaning to contemporary reality (Nava, 2015).

The cultural and physical scenario in which we find practices connected to urban and architectural recycling, as a strategy answering to the changed economic and social conditions of communities and to the environmental urgencies regarding the management of resources, becomes precisely that of a city-laboratory, in which a new intelligence of the city and its communities is based firstly on the ability to use advanced technology, information, actions, and decisions with the same logic in an "open" process. Therefore, to entrust the achievement of a new beauty of cities to architectural and landscape planning, also through the second life of abandoned spaces, the recycling of materials and flows of data and energy, and services. For a new sustainable and responsible urban metabolism, capable of including the communities and their actions, imagining a new way of narrating the cities of the future in the events of the present. Of a new way of using artificial intelligence for collective intelligence, from advanced technologies to enabling technologies.

In accordance with this approach, the technologies enabling the processes of transformation and new life of territories and cities will be able to be broken down in their ecological dimension. Social time and transformations become the reference contexts of the real dimension, while the domain of these more adaptive technologies becomes the project and the possible aspiration[8].

The maps presented for the city-laboratory actions on metropolitan Reggio Calabria (Nava, 2016), through *city making* by the Pensando Meridiano association (see the "regenerativedesign_ impactmap", edited by G. Mangano), offer different levels of reading, measuring and localizing projects.

Detecting the impacts of social innovation and the "performance dimension" of the triggered products, processes and services carries out an equation on the results (outcomes), which are essential to the efficacy of "change" processes, towards which each regenerative project must tend in human smart city models.

Thus, in an intermediate survey time of three years of activity, the mapping is fed with the definition and interpretation of the resources that introduce many levels of pro-activity and information in a collaborative style: the players involved in the processes, the sharing community, the management of products and services created and innovated to carry out projects, the economic impact and the sharing economy, as well as the references to the environmental impact controlled in a sustainable way, in crossing the territories of the city-laboratory to achieve actions and dissemination.

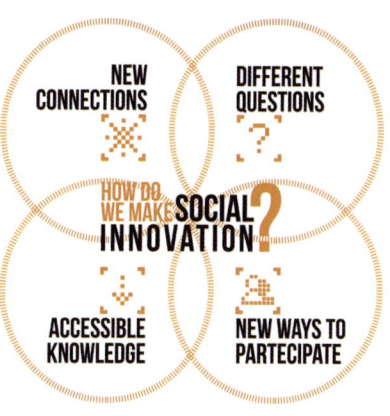

The themes of social innovation delineated in the ReAction City project.

Re-action city Women.
Construction site of the social innovation event: images of preparatory activities.

(Photos: Alessia Rita Palermiti and Danilo Emo. www.pensandomeridiano.com).

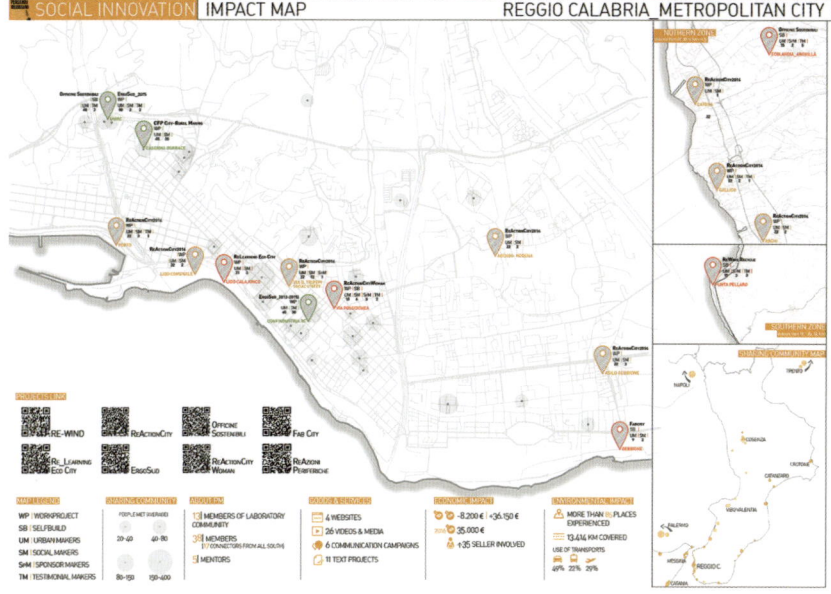

Regenerativedesign_impactmap to measure the impacts on the tactics of projects by the Pensando Meridiano association 2013-2016.
(Graphics by Giuseppe Mangano. www.pensandomeridiano.com).

Bibliography

Carta, M. (2016), "Augmented City is where the ideas have sex: urbanism as connection", in Nava, C., eds., *The Laboratory City. Sustainable recycle and key enabling technologies.* Roma: Aracne Int.le.
De Biase, L. (2015), *Homo pluralis. Essere umani nell'era tecnologica.* Torino: Codice, p. 191. Ellin, N. (2003), "A Vulnerable Urbanism", in Spellman, C., Re-envisioning Landscape/Architecture. Barcelona: Actar.
Gausa, M. (2016), "Leb Key", in Nava, C., eds., *The Laboratory City. Sustainable recycle and key enabling technologies.* Roma: Aracne Int.le.
Lacy, P., Rutqvist, J., Lamonica, B. (2016), *Circular Economy. Dallo spreco al valore.* Milano: Egea.

Marini, S. (2013), "Post Produzioni o del problema della scelta", in Marini, S., Santangelo, V., *Recycland.* Roma: Aracne, pp. 16-17.
Manzini, E. (2015), *Design, Everybody Designs. An Introduction to design for social innovation.* Cambridge (MA): MIT press.
Nava, C., a cura di (2016), *The Laboratory City. Sustainable recycle and key enabling technologies.* Roma: Aracne Int.le.
Nava, C. (2015), "Future 1/1.The Laboratory- City: Recycle and Repair, in Marini S., *Future_Utopia.* Venezia: Bruno, Carte Blanche.
Verganti, R. (2009), *Design Drive Innovation. Cambiare le regole della competizione innovando radicalmente il significato dei prodotti e dei servizi.* Milano: Rizzoli, pp.58-59.

1. "A vulnerable urbanism allows things to happen, things that may be unforeseen. Gilles Deleuze and Felix Guattari might describe this process as liberating the natural flows of desire from the repressive and hierarchical modern city. This approach might also be regarded as a form of "urban acupuncture" that liberates chi, or the life force. Applied to existing built environments, as well as new development, these interventions may have a tentacular (wiscombe) or domino effect by catalyzing other transformations. A vulnerable urbanism highlights the role of users since the process of building continues within habitation and appropriation. Users become collaborators rather than products, suggesting that education for environmental design be context-based and self-reflective rather than object-centered" (Ellin, 2003, pp. 224-225).
2. «(..) In the ecological narrative, development is all the more interesting, in a qualitative and quantitative sense, the more the contexts are equipped with diversity, connections, and energy. The metaphor works, above all, if a holistic approach is applied to the interlacing of new low-cost technologies and cultural changes. [...] From this point of view, collective intelligence evolves in the idea of plural intelligence, which does not flatten the individuals on the homogenizing structure of the platform, but calls them constantly to the multiplicity of dimensions of the human person and of life" (De Biase, 2015, 207- 208).
3. «[...] New technologies have put enterprises into a condition to accelerate progress towards a circular economy. [...] Today, the confluence of digital, engineering, and hybrid technologies is generating a new wave of circular enterprises that seem inevitably destined to grow in the wake of technological evolution. Still today, however, despite being so promising, the technologies themselves do not give enterprises what they need to excel in the circular business models they choose to apply. They must be combined with a range of new cross-cutting abilities, essential so that new ways of working develop and become operational [...]" (Lacy, Rutqvist, Lamonica, 2016).
4. "[...] Where and how is the required design knowledge produced? Where and how will it be produced in the future, given that the demand for it will inevitably grow in the transition toward sustainability? The traditional answer falls on the existence of (and need to develop) public and private research centers. However, in my view, this answer is incomplete, and more importantly, it leads us to think that the design research we are talking about can be limited to a few research professionals. In a connected world, this is no longer so. In a connected world, designing networks also tends to become design research networks, producing constructive enquiry at their nodes" (Manzini, 2015, 71-72).
5. "An augmented city is recycling-based and calls for a paradigm shift for metamorphosis cities that not only re-duce, re-use, re-cycle their tangible and intangible resources, but design a new circular metabolism by including the planned recycling among the components of the project. Thus it is resilient, that means accepting the task for adaptive, circular and self-sufficient cities for winning the climate change challenge, producing and distributing effectively the "resilience dividend" (Rodin, 2014): an instrument of urban ecological equalization in the economy of the transition to decarbonised development» (Carta, 2016, 15-16).
6. «[...] Many of them, as can be appreciated in the titles of the central texts that accompany them, seem to suggest other possible dual conjugations, apparently dichotomic but combined, however, quite naturally: Recycling and Innovation (Recycling waste landscapes: experimental projects for Reggio Calabria Metropolitan City); Demolition and Form (Demolition activity as a form of resilience in the metropolitan context); Metropolization and Humanization (Metropolitan policies and landscapes recycle: an opportunity to re-humanize city in times of crisis); Quality and Anarchy (Four qualities of an anarchic landscape. Learning from Reggio Calabria); Flexibility

and Connection (Cultivating connections. Flexible agriculture to link landscape and community); Thought and action, Replacement vs Reuse [...]" (Gausa, 2016, 19-20).
7. «[...] It is a pro-active process that involves the creation of a new and unique proposal that requires the internal capacity to absorb external knowledge more effectively than its competitors, to find combinations not yet identified, to generate unique visions through internal experiments [...]It is based more on participation than observation. It implies changing the dominant cultural paradigms and generating new meanings [...]; it is based on the ability to build and sustain an external and internal network of relations rather than to follow a specific method or sequence of steps" (Verganti, 2009, 141).
8. "According to this approach, the technologies enabling the processes of transformation and new life of territories and cities will be able to break down in their ecological dimension. Social time and transformations become the reference contexts of the real dimension, while the domain of these more adaptive technologies becomes the project and the possible aspiration" (Nava, 2016, 37-41; author's translation).

THE RESEARCH "MACRO"

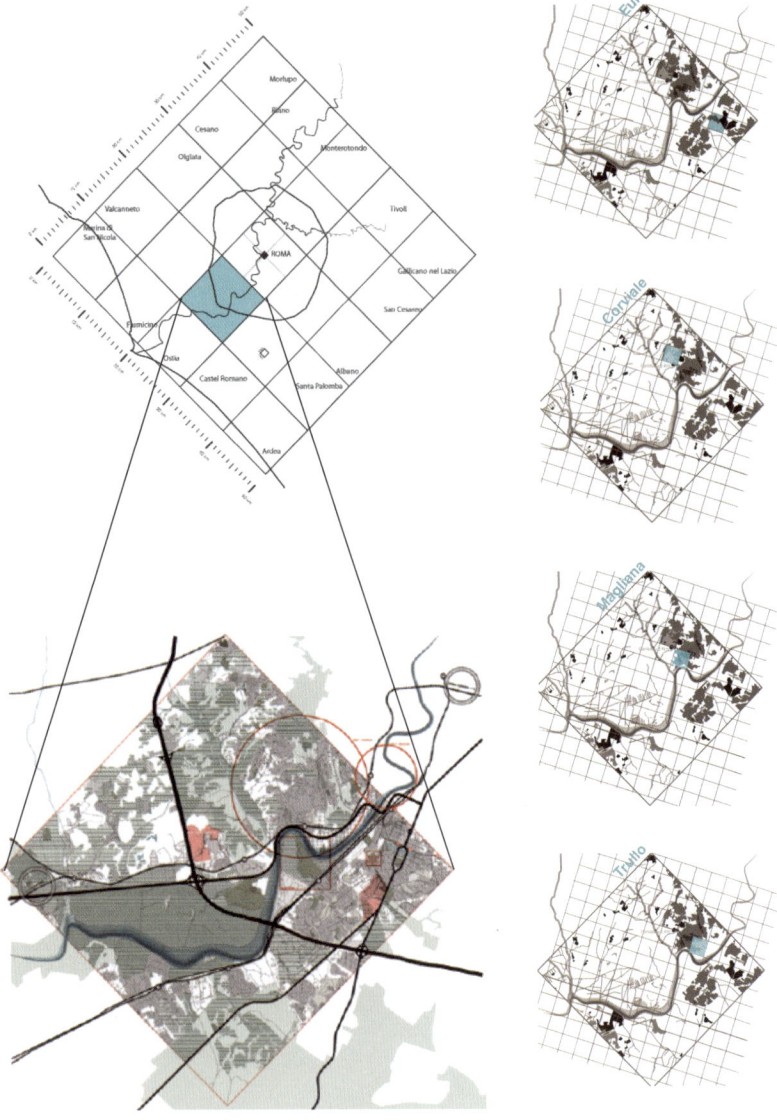

Macro 12 and the districts in the project area.

RE-CYCLICAL URBANISM

Metropolitan Metabolism.
On a large scale, the area is traversed by the GRA ring road and by center-outskirts flows, intersecting the highway and railway corridors to the airport, which, while generating potential accessibility, actually produces separation. The Tiber also forms a separation rather than blue connecting infrastructure.
Different layers of planning materials can be recognized in the Macro, requiring a new connective metabolism.

Social activity as urban design tool.
The social effects of a growing demand for economic sharing oriented to circularity and technological sharing led by distributed intelligence are the structural components of the city project, becoming planning issues/instruments/rules for a new urban metabolism.

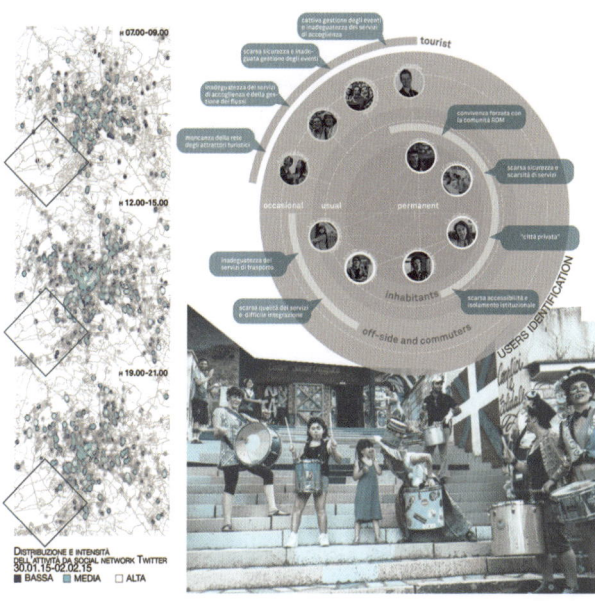

RE-FORMING ROME

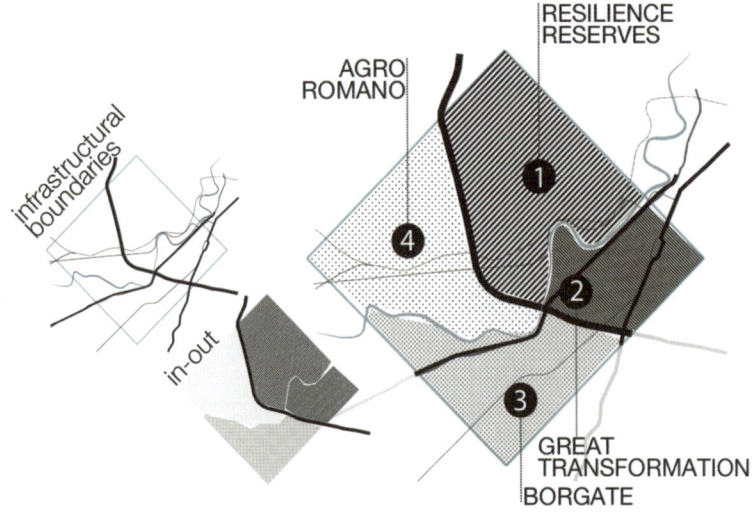

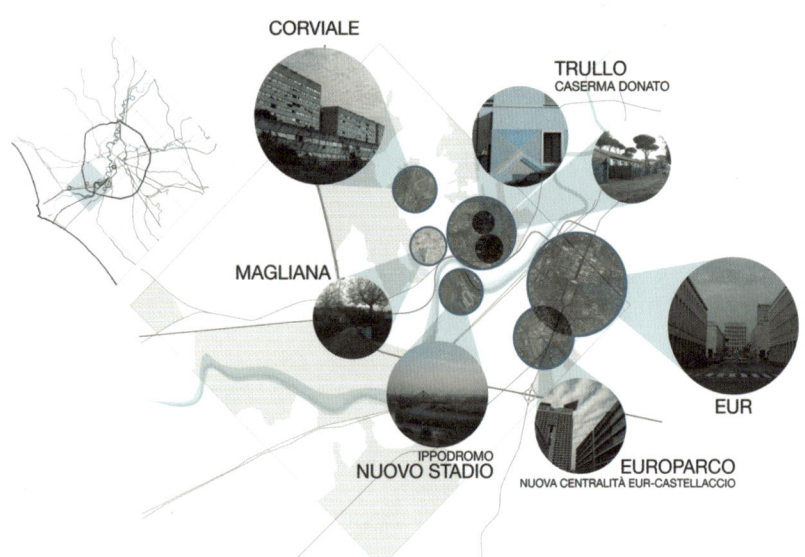

Rur-Urban Metropolitan Archipelago. The area is characterized by a fragmented identity, a disjointed set of "islands" and "island communities", environmental enclaves, whose fragmentation is exacerbated by the infrastructural boundaries.

RE-CYCLICAL URBANISM

The constant presence of the Tiber.
An identity-bearing feature that crosses the whole Macro from east to west, the Tiber River currently forms a caesura and does not express its landscape and ecological potential, both due to the presence of the railway network that limits accessibility to it and due to the absence of a system of use and crossing. This, in fact, produces urban, functional, and social separation in the Macro.

The GRA Ring Road
An infrastructural corridor of considerable importance at a metropolitan level, it represents potential accessibility for the project Macro but also a physical component of separation, generating urban fragmentation, separating instead of connecting, and moving away instead of drawing nearer.

The Magliana district.
Dense in sites of historical-archaeological interest, it extends between the GRA ring road, the Tiber and beyond the Magliana trench, which crosses the Tenuta dei Massimi reserve. Different areas belong to the Magliana district: the Parco dei Medici, where the Business Center is found, along with other offices of important national and international companies, around which hotels and luxury services have sprung up; the Muratella area, characterized by the presence of the former Alitalia central office, which is currently undergoing transformation; the Tenuta Somaini; the Borgata Magliana, that is, the area around the Magliana station and Colle del Sole, whose urbanization dates back to the early 1900s and is made up primarily of residential settlements; finally, the area of Idrovore della Magliana, a productive industrial area located on the right bank of the Tiber river and today partially discontinued.

The Corviale public housing building.
The Corviale, a uniform public housing building complex designed in the 1970s by Mario Fiorentino for around 8,500 inhabitants, is a 1 km building-district, a "snake" landscape that has been adopted by the work group as a unit of measurement for the area and as a generator of the grid that delimits the 1 km^2 sub-squares (or tiles).
30 years from its creation, the model that guided the planning of the district has never reached its initial goals, which envisaged the creation of common areas and services — such as shops, offices and commercial venues — in addition to housing, on the so-called "free floor", still illegally occupied by over 400 people for housing purposes. In spite of often being described as a symbol of social hardship, untapped potential can be recognized in it, not just because of the structure of the building, but above all, for the cohesion of its inhabitants.

The Trullo district.
Created in 1939 by initiative of the Autonomous Fascist Institute of Public Housing as a residential settlement to accommodate displaced persons and then returnees, the village of Trullo forms the original core around which numerous other residential buildings sprang up after the war without altering its original structure and recognisability.
Over the past year, Trullo has been subjected to the action of a group of volunteers and self-organized inhabitants, the "Anonymous Painters", who use color and street art as a vehicle to give the district a new image and build a sense of community, as a resilience tactic. The Monte Cucco hill, which is relevant to the landscape, is also found in the Trullo area, along with the Donato military base, an abandoned area of around 16 hectares holding untapped potential.

The EUR area.
A prestigious architectural and urban planning complex, designed and built in the 1930s under the direction of Marcello Piacentini for the World Expo of Rome of 1942 (which never took place), it was completed towards the end of the 1950s for the XVII Olympiad. Today, the EUR is a residential area, characterized, above all, by important public offices (such as the Ministry of the Environment and the Central State Archive), private offices, and museums (such as the Museum of Roman Civilization and the National Museum of the Early Middle Ages) and is also the site of the Palazzo dello Sport, designed by Nervi and Piacentini.
The area to the south of the district was the subject of recent transformations with the construction of the new EUR-Castellaccio center, which houses offices of public importance, shopping centers, and residences.

ROME AGRI_FAB CITY
A PRODUCTIVE LANDSCAPE FOR A SELF-SUFFICIENT METROPOLIS

MANUEL GAUSA NAVARRO
SILVIA BRANDI
MARCO INGRASSIA

In 2015, the IAAC participated in the Rome 20-25 research project, where 25 Italian and international universities proposed visions and urban paradigms for the metropolitan area of Rome.

The research project assigned a 10x10 km area to each participating university by overlaying a 50x50 km orthogonal grid on the city map. This abstract subdivision provocatively ignored any city-landscape, center-periphery or historic-contemporary dichotomies and, for the first time, represented Rome in its territorial dimension and fragmented composition.

While the new century has brought forth a new, more interconnected, heterogeneous and cosmopolitan scenario of technological and social transformations, the systemic crisis of our economic, settlement and ecological model has configured a new idea of progress — no longer the "imposition of a new universal order", but the "(dis)positive and informational re-activation" of reality itself — capable of answering to the issues of climate change, scarcity of resources, and environmental degradation. Entry into the urban age has highlighted the need to return to urban innovation through shared research and conceptual challenges in various fields and cultural and scientific contexts. In the "Rome 2025" workshop, this multi-player and multi-disciplinary vision found a field and action to prefigure new paradigms for Mediterranean and European metropolises.

This is the target with which the Institute for Advanced Architecture of Catalonia has applied its multi- scale, informational, and technological vision to the metropolitan area of Rome.

Investigations on the assigned area cannot overlook a holistic vision, capable of analyzing territorial-scale dynamics and relations that exist between it and the other parts of the urban ecosystem. Despite this, the identification of geometrically defined areas can outline an interesting methodological approach in transforming the area into a case study, a comparative tool, and field of exploration of proposals for the metropolis. No longer a city of administrative municipal borders, but a "(never) interrupted Rome" of continuous and uncontrollable growth, a metropolitan organism with a territorial dimension and tentacle shape: a "multi-city"[1] of linear systems that have grown through processes of densification and extension, along the *Consolari* radial road system.

The tissues of the various linear cities (Roma Casilina, Roma Tuscolana, Roma Ostiense, and so on) open up to configure an extended and discontinuous urban organism, crossed by landscape systems — the ancient Ager Romanus, the system of gorges, the forest areas, wetlands, and the river systems — that penetrate the city to its archaeological center. While in the 20th century the compact, mono-nodal Rome of the postwar period (that we define as Rome 1.0) has evolved towards

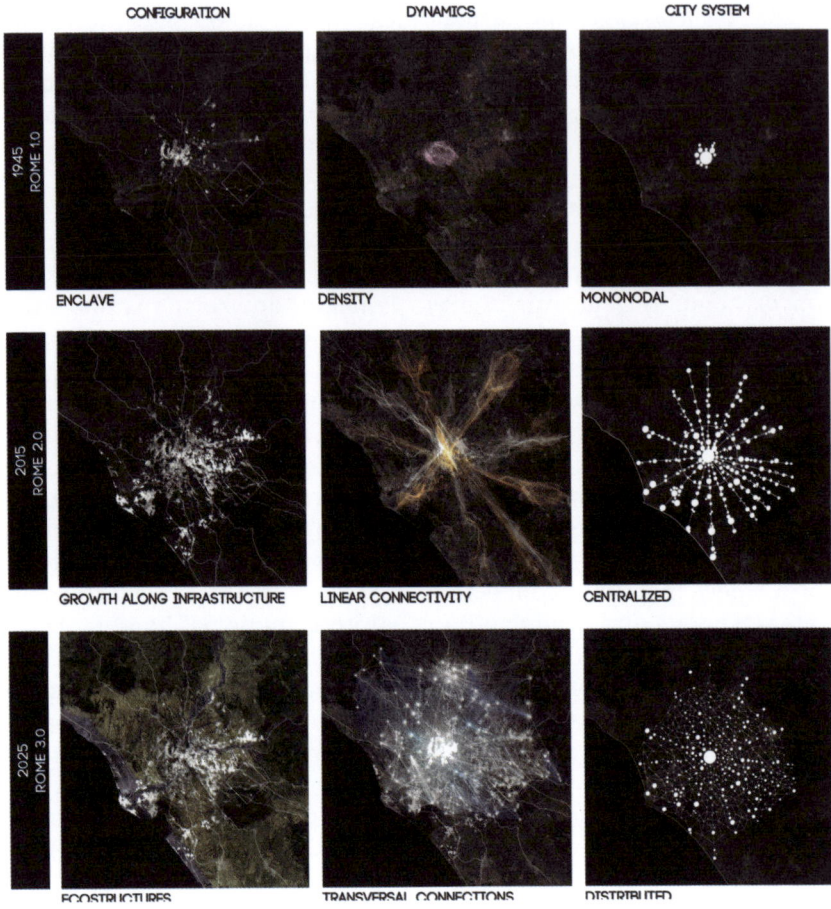

Physical configurations, metropolitan dynamics, and systemic representation, for an interpretation of Rome in three phases.
Rome 1.0 – compact city and territorial enclave, with mobility flows and dynamics concentrated in a mono-nodal system – evolved in the 20th century in Rome 2.0, a linear multi-city, a centralized system innervated by center-periphery connections along the radial infrastructure. In 2025 we can define Rome 3.0 as an Agri-Fab city, a territorial metropolis structured by productive landscape systems and transversal connections in a distributed system.

a centralized multipolar system (Rome 2.0), structured by center-periphery connections along the radial infrastructure system, the 21st century can see the transformation of the metropolis into a distributed and resilient system[2]: Roma 3.0 as an Agri-Fab city, a self-sufficient, interconnected, and creative city[3], structured by a "productive landscape"[4] as a new territorial framework and urban protocol. The current urban perspective allows us to reflect on the discontinuous, complex, and interlaced dimension of a new kind of relational geography: a networked "geo-urbanity" associated with a necessary vision of the territory as an articulate and open mesh, called upon to combine intensive movements and extensive developments. It is passing from an "extra-urban" territory to an "intra-urban" one. From a territory-surface to a territory- mesh.

From a passive territory to an active territory:
- by strengthening and reactivating the existing urban structures;
- by articulating the different infrastructural (and programming) networks;
- by coordinating the various landscape "patterns" into new models of integrated planning.

Today, we might interpret infrastructure as landscapes and landscapes as infrastructure; or rather, the "infra- structures" as "eco-structures" and the "eco-structures" as "intra" and "infra-structures". An overall approach associated with the new challenges of open space, public space, and "interactive" space (social, environmental and cultural) and with the active redevelopment of existing heritage. The territorial city can thus be proposed as a "non-linear" structure of situations, processes and sequential programs, related to heterogeneous physical and virtual networks, structured in turn by a combinatory and evolutionary logic capable of promoting exchanges, interrelations and crosscutting, but also of providing a possible "interlaced freedom" in events and movements. If Rome 2.0 is structured by "(*Consolari*) infrast ructure" and by "node-structures (urban nodes)", Rome 3.0 can find a new resilient and efficient configuration of "eco" and "info-structures".

Today we can overcome opposing visions of the landscape — an idealized, pastoral place subject to contemplation, or territory available for the growth of the future city — to converge into a concept of "Productive Landscape" as a multipurpose system, capable of producing energy (through new self-sufficient systems on a territorial scale), food (strengthening the agricultural characteristics of the territory), objects (through the potential of a diffused network of FabLabs), and relations (reactivating the local communities and economies). If production represents an identity- forming tool that testifies to ancestral activities and historical relations with the territory, rediscovering this value in production can empower local communities and redefine the urban space, no longer as a place of consumption, but as a relational space.

It is with this view that, through a process involving the students of the Master in Advanced Architecture 2014/2015 from 20 different countries — with the collaboration of the FabLabBarcelona and the Green Fab Lab, IAAC elaborated a two-step polyphonic proposal, based on an open and multi-scale logic, not aimed at simply defining planning forms, but at identifying processes, strategies, and economies. An urban protocol structured by an innovative methodology, capable of interpreting the territory through the collection and visualization of real-time data and of proposing devices, technologies and spatial strategies for a relational and informational urban ecosystem.

Today, if large-scale urban regeneration projects are anachronistic and made impossible by the lack of resources and credible public players, apparently avant-garde projects reveal their concreteness in defining processes where technological innovation offers accessible tools, capable of identifying the main players in local communities to change the spatial, economic urban context. The first phase of this work was focused on the territorial scale and developed by the "Encrypted Rome" seminar, in which 7 groups of students analyzed the assigned 10x10 km area. The students proposed visions of speculative models of agrarian growth, using an experimental methodology that employed the tools of IT programming to define aprioristic parametric models that, when applied to the territory, highlight the unexpected potential for territorial and relational development.

Open-source processing software was used to define a script responding to site-specific analysis: with the input of data from the territory, the software generates different data-responsive visions, applying automated models of organization for a distributed system. The result is a territory supported by the existing or proposed nodes interconnected by continuous meshes that represent their physical and virtual interactions.

The proposal for the area identifies new connections — transversal to the radial infrastructures of the city — through landscape and slow mobility systems, which relink existing urban centers and generate relations on a local and metropolitan scale, reconnecting the "linear cities" that pass through the area. A network of new collective and productive spaces is thus defined, together with the re-signification of existing "nodes" scattered over the territory (farmhouses, historic buildings, sports facilities, and factories).

In the second phase of work, the proposals were made concrete at a landscape scale. The "Rome Agri-Fab City" workshop explored the new "eco-structural" connection between the villages of Colonna and Montecompatri. Each group of students explored a 1x1 km area — part of a strip of 5 Macros — where six projects proposed strategies and processes for the definition of a self-sufficient and interconnected habitat. Territorial networks where production once again permeates the collective space, reactivates nodes of the sprawled city, and structures functional relations through multiple devices and projects: a mobility infrastructure to inhabit the landscape where algae produce energy and purify the air; a complex of water storage systems that capture groundwater like sponges and transform it into hydrogen to fuel agricultural machinery; aeronautical balloons that harvest atmospheric humidity to irrigate fields and the dispersed energy of highway vibrations to power public lighting; a network of fablabs capable of closing the production cycle between physical resources, human resources and production scraps; infrastructure serving public spaces that use pyrolysis to transform urban and agricultural waste into energy. These are the visions of IAAC for Rome 2025: a polycentric, interconnected, productive and self-sufficient city based on local economies in a global network.

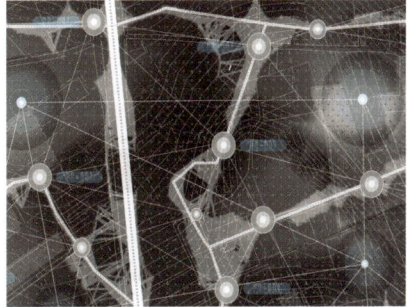

"Rome Agri/Fab City" workshop– "Rural Oxymoron" project.
A system of digitally fabricated productive devices to boost the productive potential of the area and structure a territorial network: aerostatic balloons that harvest humidity from the air to irrigate fields and the dispersed energy of highway vibrations to power public lighting.

"Rome Agri/Fab City" workshop – "ProdActive Landscape" project.
Organic waste from the agricultural and residential area is transformed into biogas and fertilizer through a pyrolysis system. Integrated into a parametric architecture device, node of a system of public spaces in strategic areas such as the urban center, agricultural areas, sprawled area, and unused lots.

Curators: Manuel Gausa Navarro, Silvia Brandi, Marco Ingrassia.
"Encrypted Rome" seminar
Lecturers: Pablo Ros.
"Rome Agri-Fab City" workshop.
Lecturers: Manuel Gausa Navarro, Silvia Brandi, Marco Ingrassia, Mathilde Marengo, Jonathan Minchin, Lina Monaco, Carmelo Zappulla.
Graphics: IAAC - Federica Ciccone.
Videos: IAAC - Carmen AguilarWedge, Cristian Rizzuti, EceTankal.
3D modelling and fabrication: IAAC / Fab Lab Barcelona - Rodrigo Aguirre, Anna Popova.
Photos: Matteo Canestraro.
"Encrypted Rome" seminar
Students: (group 1) Mehmet Yilmaz Akdogan, Asya Guney, Neel Kaul, Juan Diego Ramirez Leon; (group 2) Jayant Khanuja, Ran Shabtay; (group 3) Pia Grobner, Tamara Ivanovic, Shashank Shahabadi, Maulidianti Wulansari; (group 4) Farah Alayeli, Prawit Kittinchanthira, Marina Lazareva, Luisa Roth; (group 5) Ayaan Barodawala, Luisangello Coarite Asencio, Jinyang Han; (group 6) Kunaljit Chadha, Salvador Martinez, Fatimath Sujna Shakir; (group 7) Saad Saheen Delanthabettu Kanyana, Taiesha Edwards, Denis Li.
"Rome Agri-Fab City" workshop students: (group A) Josep Alcover Llubia, Matteo Silverio, Ji Won Jun; (group B) Pia Grobner, Panagiota Sarantinoudi, Maulidianti Wulansari; (group C) Sara Casciano, Francesco Maria Massetti, Alessia Vendetta; (group D) Ksenia Dyusembaeva, Edgar Navarrete Sanchez, Juan Diego Ramirez Leòn; (group E) Mattia Benatti, Federica Ciccone, Irene Meta; (group F) Denis Li, BorislavShalev.

1. Gausa, M., *"Hiperterritorios–multiciudades–geourbanidades"*, en Gausa, M., Guallart, V., Müller, W., *HyperCatalunya, Territorios de Investigación*. Barcelona: Generalitat de Catalunya, 2003.
2. Baran, P., *On distributed Communication Networks*. USA: IEEE Transactions of the Professional Technical Group on Communications Systems, vol. CS-12, n.1, 1964. Paul Baran, among the inventors of ARPANET, the prodrome of the Internet, defines "mesh distribution systems" — those structured by peripheral connections independent of the center, less vulnerable, flexible systems preferable to "star centralized" systems, with center-peripheral connections.
3. Guallart, V., *La Ciudad autosuficiente. Habitar en la sociedad de la información*. Barcelona: RBA libros, 2012.
4. Viljoen, A., Howe, J., *Continuous Productive Urban Landscapes, Designing Urban Agriculture for Sustainable Cities*. Burlington (MA): Architectural Press, 2005.

RE_FORMING ROME.
THE AGRI/FAB METROPOLIS

MAURIZIO CARTA

Macro no. 12 gathers important centres (EUR and the health district), contains traces of the identity-forming palimpsest (Magliana, Trullo, and the Corviale), and possesses tiles of the landscape mosaic (the Tiber and nature reserves). These are experienced as disconnected urban islands without any functional or territorial relationship, each with its own "idiorhythm", to use Roland Barthes's term. The result is a divided identity, or disconnected set of island communities, whose fragmentation is accentuated by the infrastructural boundaries.

On a large scale, the area is crossed by flows between the center and outskirts, intersecting the highway and railway corridors to the airport, which, while generating potential accessibility, actually produces separation. The GRA ring road establishes a clear-cut caesura between the city inside and outside of it and its congestion erodes territorial values for many kilometers. The Tiber also forms a separation rather than blue connecting infrastructure. Four cities can thus be recognized in the Macro: the Ager Romanus, in productive decline; the outer suburbs, in search of a new metropolitan identity; the cities of large incomplete transformation; and the valuable resilience reserves contained in the inner villages and suspended outside of the contemporary world.

The Re-Forming Rome project is thus proposed as an action to reshape the physical, social, and productive space. If focuses on the suburbs inside the ring road and aims to recreate a rur/urban archipelago, in which even the landscape connections and infrastructural armatures serve as components of the area's new metabolism. A circular metabolism based on an alternative settlement to that of central Rome, fuelled by the agricultural resources and manufacturing tied to it, to reactivate the Trullo district — which is already the subject of urban proto-creativity — and the former *Caserma Donato* (Donato Barracks) as a cell of the Agri/Fab Metropolis that supplements the urban agriculture opportunities with new digital manufacturing and energy communities to propose a new place/way of living/working in the post-metropolis.

The planning device used is the Cityforming© Protocol, developed by the Creative City Lab of UNIPA. This device is required to reverse the traditional masterplan project — which is ineffective in this area — with a more powerful masterprogramming process articulated over a decade. Cityforming © is an urban regeneration protocol capable of reactivating the metabolism of a crisis area in subsequent stages, starting from its latent regenerative components. It activates multiple cycles with increasing intensity to create a new urban ecosystem that is sustainable over time. Strategic Cityforming works in incremental and adaptive phases to produce partial results, which then become the generative basis of the subsequent phase. By progressing through the phases of "colonisation", "consolidation", and "development", it produces the

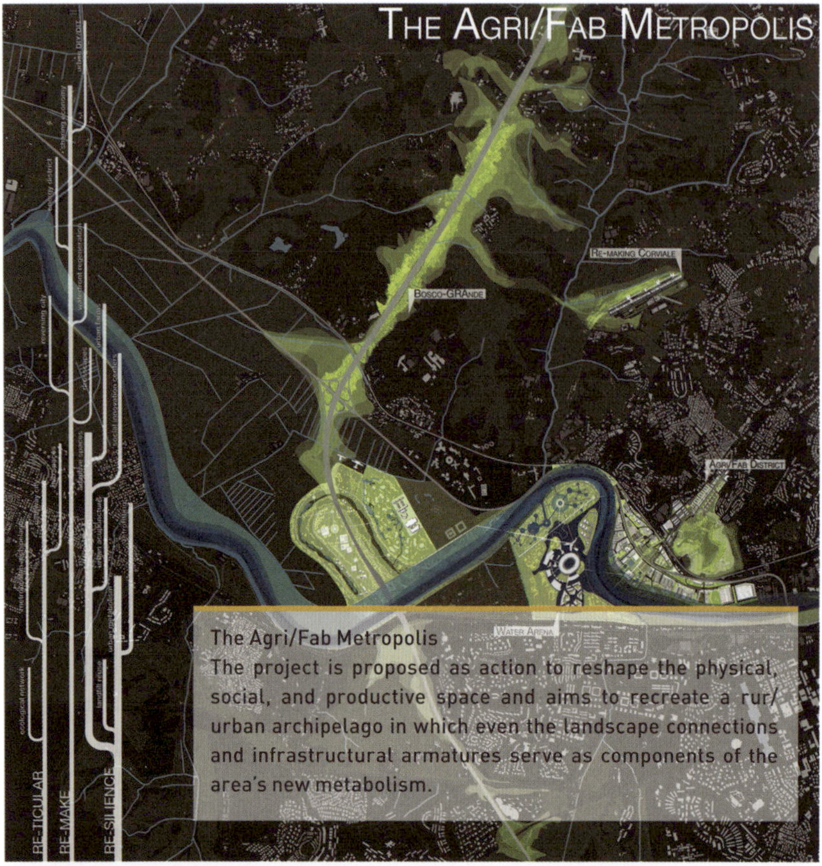

The Agri/Fab Metropolis

The Agri/Fab Metropolis
The project is proposed as action to reshape the physical, social, and productive space and aims to recreate a rur/urban archipelago in which even the landscape connections and infrastructural armatures serve as components of the area's new metabolism.

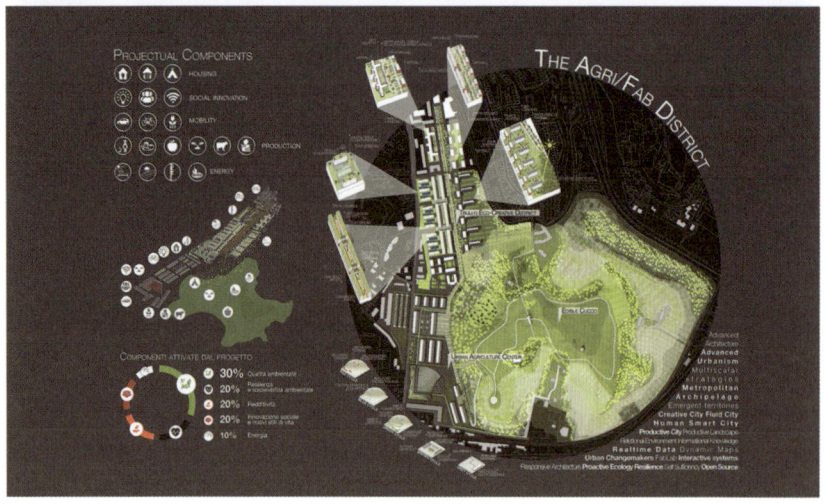

RE-CYCLICAL URBANISM

necessary "urban oxygen" for the formation of an ecosystem adequate to generate a new urban metabolism to reanimate inactive cycles, reconnect disrupted ones, or activate new ones more suited to the new identity of the places.

The first phase is "colonisation", with a low transformational intensity and high tactical energy. It involves the integration of several regenerative devices in the courtyards of Trullo and the localization of places to reactivate the agricultural, energy, and water cycles. In the colonisation phase, the Donato Barracks is opened to temporary reappropriation functions, also housing several initial activities tied to the urban/rural manufacturing district of Trullo and Monte Cucco. The heart of the Trullo neighborhood, where its social, artistic, and economic activities intertwine, is the linear plaza which, revamped by artists, is transformed into a "social platform" connecting the whole neighborhood, from San Raffaele Church to the former Donato Barracks, via the market, workshops, theater, and school. The Agri/Fab project thus amounts to an ecological, non-erosive densifier, which provides for hydroponic cultivation, community composting, solar and micro wind power, rainwater collection, and phytoremediation. The ecological network insinuates the courtyards — new spaces for sociality and shared production — and homes with rooftop gardens and green facades. The courtyards are enriched with new workshops designed as "parasitic" architecture for local artists and craftspeople. The edible park "Edible Cucco" feeds the neighborhood and provides raw material for local start-ups in the agricultural sector. The subsequent phase is "consolidation", which entrenches the new urban and rural functions through the cooperation of the local community in the completion of planning actions, using the parametric devices proposed in the project (re-naturalization, water recycling, densification without consumption of land, energy districts, and makers communities), and with the transformation of the Barracks into a new ecological and micro-manufacturing district tied to urban agriculture and to the new settlement forms of the makers and farmers.

The warehouses of the former Donato Barracks are fertile ground for the settlement of an ecological energy system that interacts with the edible park; an agro-food business incubator and national-level permaculture center. The former Barracks and Monte Cucco are enriched, moreover, by fixed and temporary housing and by new ways of living, such as Eco B&Bs and Agricamping.

Finally, the "development" phase will operate at a stage in which sufficient evolutionary mass and energy have been created to fuel the overall reconversion/ reconnection projects. The whole Macro is structured by a new Fluid Metabolism that connects the urban islands in a fluid archipelago: the northern area, in direct contact with the Tiber, is interpreted as a water gate, with the reclamation of areas to create a green promenade

Recycle-based Cityforming

RE-FORMING ROME

working on the ordinary city, satisfying basic needs, drawing new open "socio-rhythms"

and the repurposing of existing property to be used as observatory-homes; the wetland of Spinaceto will be dedicated to camping/glamping activities of reduced environmental impact, while the reclamation of ponds is destined to organic aquaculture. The regeneration of the water will occur by means of phytoremediation, supported by aquaponic farming. Finally, reshaping of the flood plain will allow a redefinition of the Olympic Park envisaged as Water Arena, in which water flooding becomes project material. The temporary housing was intended for the athletes during the Olympic period and pilgrims during the Jubilee, to then become temporary housing for standard use for the nomadic people who cross Rome [the Olympic Games candidature of Rome was cancelled by the current administration after the Rome 20-25 competition].

The *Bosco GRAnde* (Ring Road Forest) envisages the transformation of the GRA ring road into a linear forest, or ecological backbone, whose purpose will be to improve the quality of the area, reduce emissions of CO_2, $PM10$, and heavy metals — high percentages of which are currently found. This linear forest also connects the huge vegetation system that already exists within the Macro. Finally, the project envisages transforming the Magliana area into a self-sufficient Eco-energy District, reconverting the neighborhood's industrial area into a renewable energy district of reuse and recycling for the production of clean energy (biogas, solar power, and garden rooftops), building an ecological island for the storage and logistics of recyclable waste, strengthening the productive function of the area, and introducing a technological-scientific research center.

RE-CYCLICAL URBANISM

Towards the Agri/Fab Metropolis

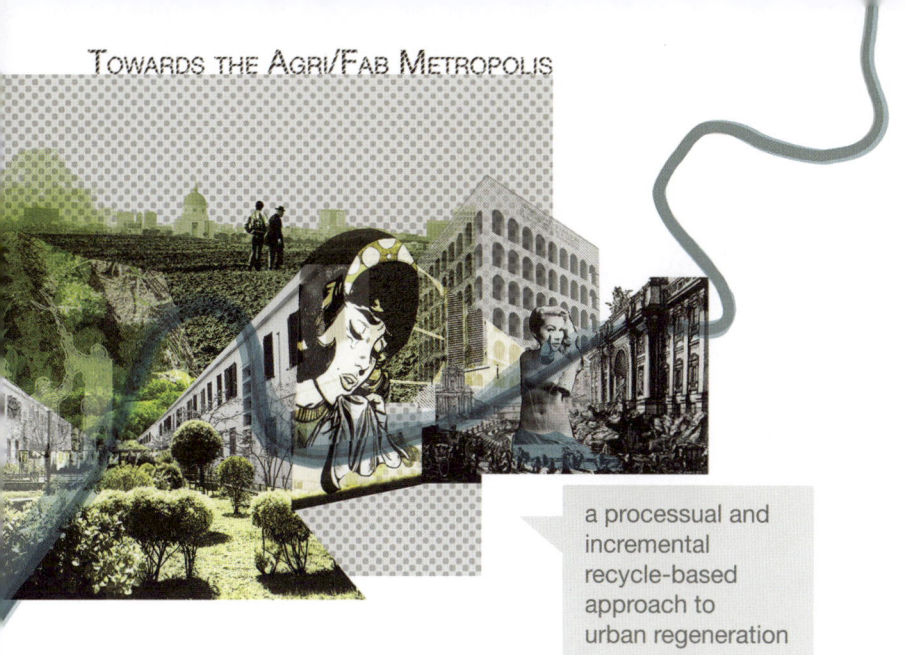

a processual and incremental recycle-based approach to urban regeneration

The Cityforming approach is not limited to implementing a predefined vision for extracts of time, a vision that is the result of a preliminary process presuming enormous economic resources for its complete implementation or requiring the activation of high land or real estate revenue in order to carry out its works.

Rather, Cityforming generates a program of actions that are put together and defined as a function of partial results, based on the consolidation of new urban roles of the area and on the values and expectations generated by new inhabitants, new services and forms of collaboration, taxation opportunities, and new urban economies generated in the first two phases, which are capable of triggering the third.

Cityforming works constantly within the dimensions of the project and process and activates actions within a predicted scenario whose effects make up their specification and definition, consolidating the trend scenario or contributing to forming a new programmatic scenario. Re-forming Rome, therefore, generates physical, social, and economic resilience, rejecting segregating idiorhythms and designing new open, collaborative, and generative "sociorhythms", rather than perpetuating an urban metabolism interrupted by the cycles of the different separate islands (the real "interrupted Rome").

Re-forming Rome is thus a manifesto/project of a polycentric, hyper-cyclical vision alternative to the now obsolete model of large gravitational centers, which are the daughters of an ineffectual vision in the era of the post-metropolitan, polycentric, and reticular metamorphosis.

OPEN SOURCE & SHARED URBAN DESIGN PLATFORM

BARBARA LINO

The contribution of the University of Palermo Research Unit, "Re-forming Rome. Towards the Agri/Fab- City 20-25", was an opportunity to test a collaborative urbanism work methodology.

Through a call directed to students and new graduates of the University of Palermo and of other Italian and foreign universities, participants were selected for a planning workshop, in which the Palermo Research Unit formulated its visions for the future of Rome. The mentors, tutors, students, and young architects who took part in the workshop came from Paris, Barcelona, Reggio Calabria, Venice, and Palermo, giving rise to an atmosphere of confrontation and dynamic and creative experimentation that combined more traditional work methods with those provided by the use of new technologies.

In a sort of collaborative platform, the mentors and tutors1 worked with the participants using an open-source approach: opportunities for encounter, experimentation and exchange of materials, ideas, and planning solutions and inspections were opportunities for joint work, together with virtual meetings, conference calls, and web streaming. The workshop generated a small "intelligent" planning community that tested a collaborative approach allowing the convergence of ideas, insights, and proposals within the Agri/FabCity project for Rome 20-25. The general methodology proposed by the "Rome 2025" project, which subdivided the whole municipal territory into even squares (Macros), provided a sort of territorial morpho-typological "probing".

Each Research Unit worked within an assigned 10x10 km Macro, addressing the local conditions as exemplary of a more general condition of urban livability.

The various inspections carried out in the Macro assigned to the Palermo Research Unit, Macro 12, through a sprawling mosaic of situations, provided a city image featuring multiple suburban conditions, recognizable in a disjointed archipelago of functional islands and identity-forming centers — the outcome of the superimposition and layering of planned and "spontaneous" transformations. Almost like a stratified sample, Macro 12 revealed the fragmentary nature of a city, today made up of heterogeneous expanding centers located near nodes or large infrastructure, and which has spread over the territory through merging and welding with the villages, the Ager Romanus and the new poles organized around the large structures of mass consumption and directionality.

In Macro 12 and its fragments, we can recognize the results of specific actions and general actions and public policies regarding infrastructure and services (suffice it to recall the idea of the urban and metropolitan centralities of the General Strategic Plan of Rome) and the effect of transformation action by multiple players that orient and are subjected to the forces of the urban change process. Large real estate companies have transformed the areas near EUR, where today, due to the housing crisis, we can find a large portion of unsold property. Public players, on the other hand, have sponsored large transformations, such as those of the Corviale district — a 1 km public housing building that proposed a compact high-density settlement model, today stigma of a negative peripheral condition — and, much earlier, of other more measured social housing interventions, as in the case of the Trullo district.

During one of the inspections carried out in the project area, the discovery of the Trullo district was instrumental for the genesis of the general vision of the Macro.

To our eyes, as researchers and planners, the image arose of a district in which, due to a movement of citizens promoting street art activities, micro-transformations are occurring that are radically changing the image and livability of the district. Observation of the practices of using common spaces, courtyards, and facades, and of the methods of transforming the living spaces revealed a transformative vivacity of the settled communities, which was also considered one of the main components of the general project vision. Although micro-transformations, to close observers these transformative tensions resulting from a spontaneous dynamism of the local communities could represent, if accompanied by more structured actions, sparks of transformation capable of triggering a more general process of change. In this regard, the adjacent abandoned public property, the Donato military base, was considered a powerful resilience reserve to be connected to the district and to the whole Macro, to accommodate mixed functions, capable of triggering changes both at a local scale and in a broader perspective. Finally, the general project idea proposed in the workshop formulates a systemic vision capable of integrating the various scales (local and not) and the forces of transformation in play within a common regenerative drive. The *Agri/FabCity* vision, to which the project aspires, is that of a city that deeply revises its way of living, working and moving in the outskirts, uniting the contemporary agricultural dimension with the dimension of artisan production, proposing a settlement model that unhinges the current closed idio-rhythms of the settled communities and the consolidated home/work/free time dynamics, and offers an alternative archipelago model, in which the element that is placed between the "islands" is transformed from a disconnecting factor into an element of integration and osmosis.

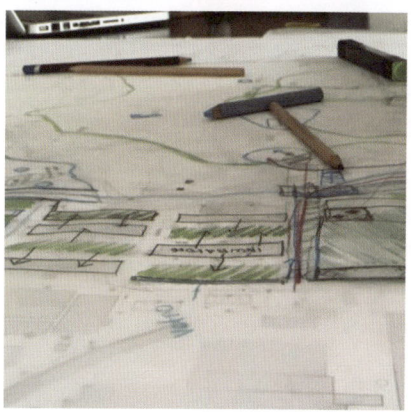 

Curators: Maurizio Carta (coordinator), Angela Alessandra Badami, Consuelo Nava. Re-forming Rome. Towards the Agri/FabCity 20-25 workshop.
Tutorship: Barbara Lino (coordinator), Annalisa Contato, Carmelo Galati Tardanico, Marco Ingrassia, Jessica Smeralda Oliva, Marilena Orlando, Daniele Ronsivalle

"Re-forming Rome. Towards the Agri/Fab- City 20-25" workshop:
Group 1: Angelica Agnello (tutor jr), Mariateresa Caeti (tutor jr), Bianca Andaloro, Cristina Arcuri, Alessia Argento, Ugo Brancato, Claudia Cannatella, Elisabetta Caruso, Giulia De Francisci, Laura La Mendola, Maria Chiara Lo Bianco, Martina Lo Re, Benedetto Mazzullo, Francesco Taddeo.
Group 2: Madalina Culcasi (tutor jr), Davide Gianluca Abbate, Maria Luana Caiola, Maria Antonietta Calì, Roberto Durante, Giancarlo Gallitano, Barbara Gubernale.
Group 3: Francesca Montagna (tutor jr), Federico Calcara, Cosimo Camarda, Floriana D'Amaro, Marianna Lombardo, Gloria Pavone.
Group 4: Milena Lauretta (tutor jr), Floriana Gentile, Roberta Lena, Delia Roxana Negrusa, Antonio Salvaggio, MadalinaSasa, Luca Torrisi.

CITYFORMING ROME: IDEAS AND PROJECTS

ANGELICA AGNELLO

MARIATERESA CAETI

MADALINA CULCASI

FRANCESCA MONTAGNA

MILENA LAURETTA

The Agri/Fab District
by Angelica Agnello and Mariateresa Caeti

Work group: Angelica Agnello (tutor jr), Mariateresa Caeti (tutor jr), Bianca Andaloro, Cristina Arcuri, Alessia Argento, Ugo Brancato, Claudia Cannatella, Elisabetta Caruso, Giulia De Francisci, Laura La Mendola, Maria Chiara Lo Bianco, Martina Lo Re, Benedetto Mazzullo, Francesco Taddeo.

The colonisation process, recently initiated by the artists of Trullo, has set in motion the restaoration of a strong identity which, starting from the courtyards, influences the whole project area and what's happening there. Monte Cucco nearby and the warehouses of the former Donato military base are fertile ground for the settlement of an ecological and energy system based on the interaction of an edible park, an agro-food business incubator, and a permaculture center that could become a national-level attraction. Oriented in this sense are aquaponic and hydroponic cultivation experiments, community composting, photovoltaic and micro wind energy production, rainwater collection to irrigate shared gardens, phytoremediation systems and the linear park along the nearby motorway. The ecological network insinuates the courtyards, which are reconfigured as spaces for sociality and shared production, and homes with rooftop gardens and green facades. The whole district benef its from the economic and environmental sustainability of the transformations: tax deductions of 65% for green roofs, self-production, correction of micro-climate, improvement of the energy performances and, naturally, of vital environmental quality.

The edible park, in addition to fuelling the ecological network of the district, favors the settlement and development of zero km markets and supplies the raw material for local start-ups that use protective flowers and medicinal herbs.

If the productive aspect of these transformations is fundamental, it is essential to understand how it works through the social participation of the inhabitants thanks to educational farms, farmhouse nurseries and pre-schools for children, shared condominium gardens, and organic waste collection for composting.

Between tradition and innovation, the courtyards maintain an important role in the life of the district and are enriched with playgrounds, cycl ing tracks, new workshops designed as "parasitic" architecture for the local artists and artisans, and phytoremediation tanks. The heart of the district, where its social, artistic, and economic activities intertwine, is the linear piazza which, revamped by Trullo artists, is transformed into a social platform connecting the whole neighborhood, from San Raffaele Church to the former Donato military base. The former military base and Monte Cucco are enriched, moreover, by fixed and temporary housing and by new ways of living: Eco B&Bs and Agricamping.

CITYFORMING PROTOCOL

The Agri/Fab Metropolis. The project is proposed as action to reshape the physical, social, and productive space and aims to recreate a rur/urban archipelago, in which even the landscape connections and infrastructural frameworks serve as components of the new metabolism of the area.

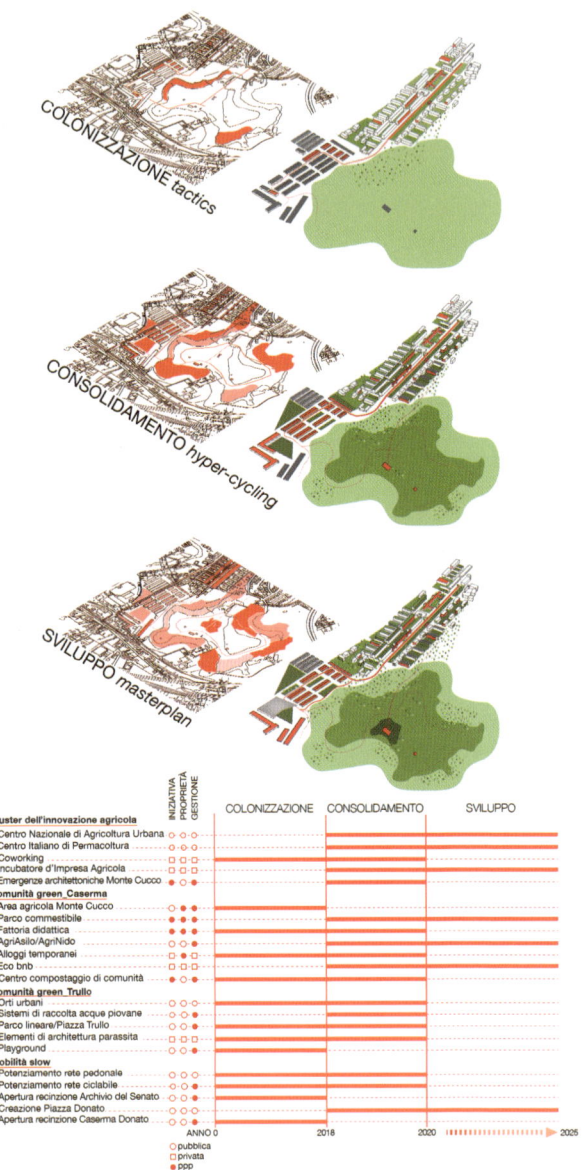

PROJECT TARGETS

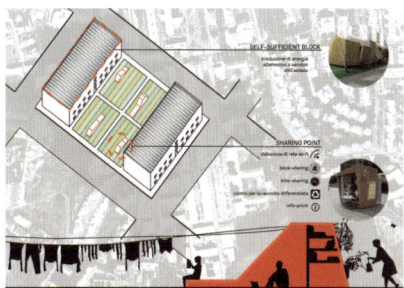

Ecological network. The Donato military base as a biodiversity center.

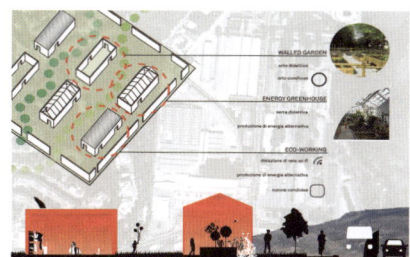

Adaptive spaces. The open block as a sharing space.

VISIONS

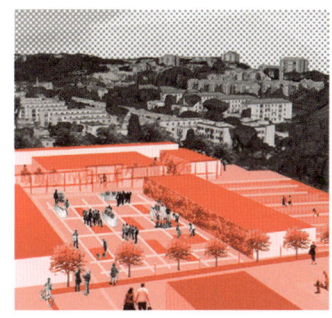

Urban Agricolture Center & Edible Cucco

COMPONENTS RE-LOADED

30% Environmental quality

20% Resilience and Environmental sustainability

20% Profit

20% Social innovation and new lifestyles

10% Energy

RE-FORMING ROME

Magliana Eco-Energy District
by Madalina Culcasi

Work group: Madalina Culcasi (tutor jr), Davide Gianluca Abbate, Maria Luana Caiola, Maria Antonietta Calì, Roberto Durante, Giancarlo Gallitano, Barbara Gubernale.

The project contributes to achieving the general goal of activating new urban cycles capable of making the islands/districts of the area work as a veritable metropolitan archipelago, envisaging the construction of an eco-energy district that is able to transform the area into a self-sufficient energy district, reconverting the industrial area of the Magliana district into an energy eco-district of reuse and recycling for the production of clean energy from renewable sources, but also economy and culture.

The project provides for: the production of clean energy (biogas and solar), energy savings (rooftop garden) and re-naturalization, the construction of an ecological island that favours the storage and logistics of recyclable waste, interventions for the strengthening of the productive function of the area, and the introduction of a technological-scientific and artistic research center.

Through the processing of river algae (which abound due to the eutrophication process underway), agricultural waste from urban and extra-urban horticulture, pruning plant and forest waste (particularly that of the linear forest along the GRA ring road), animal waste from the educational farms in the area, but also industrial waste, urban sewage and solid waste, biofuels and electrical and thermal energy can be obtained to power both the energy requirements of 65,000 residents of the districts/islands, and that of the production, agricultural and industrial sector, also favouring sustainable mobility. Thanks to the re-naturalization of the industrial area paving and the construction of green roofs on warehouses, we can obtain a considerable reduction in energy consumption and an improvement in air quality, as well as a reduction in the typically high temperatures of urbanized areas.

During the colonisation phase, the project envisages the start of the first actions needed to achieve the energy autonomy of the district; this will be fully satisfied in the consolidation phase, initiating the conservation of the resources needed for the third phase; in the last project phase, the development phase, the conserved resources can be invested (thanks to the reduction of energy consumption and the elimination of energy dependence from the national network) in the urban transformation of the area through indirectly productive interventions on the system of natural and cultural heritage, and on the infrastructure supporting fast and slow mobility.

PROJECT CONCEPT

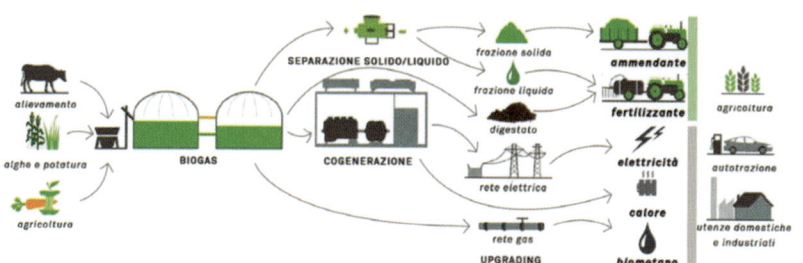

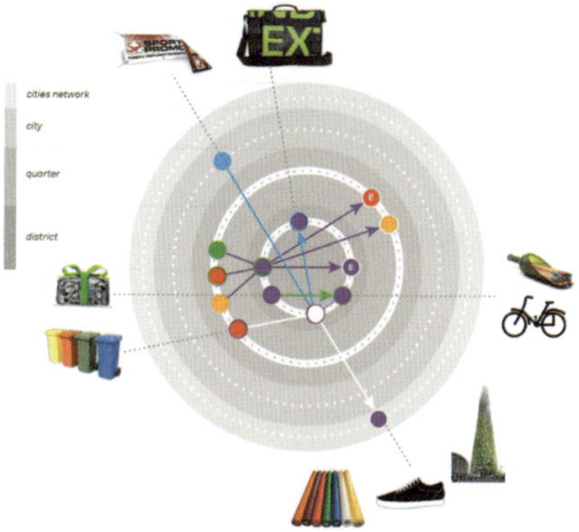

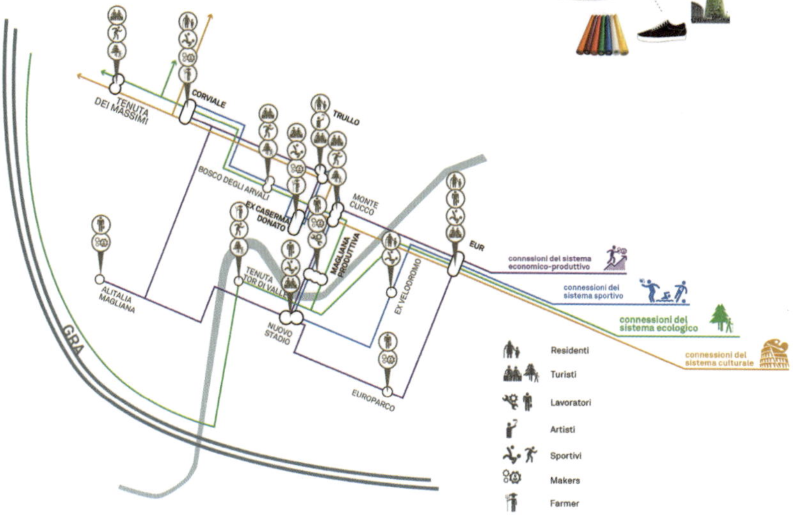

RE-FORMING ROME

CITYFORMING PROTOCOL

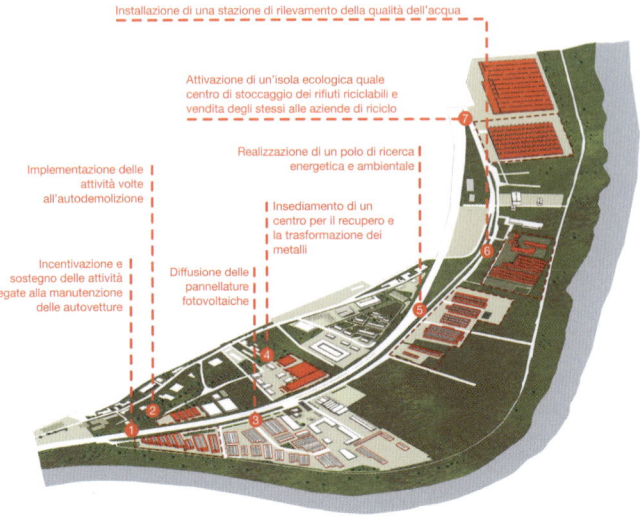

Colonisation

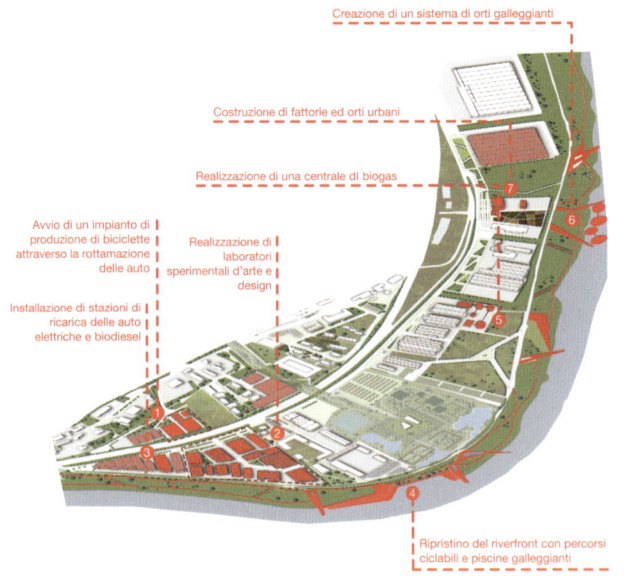

Consolidation

RE-CYCLICAL URBANISM

CITYFORMING PROTOCOL

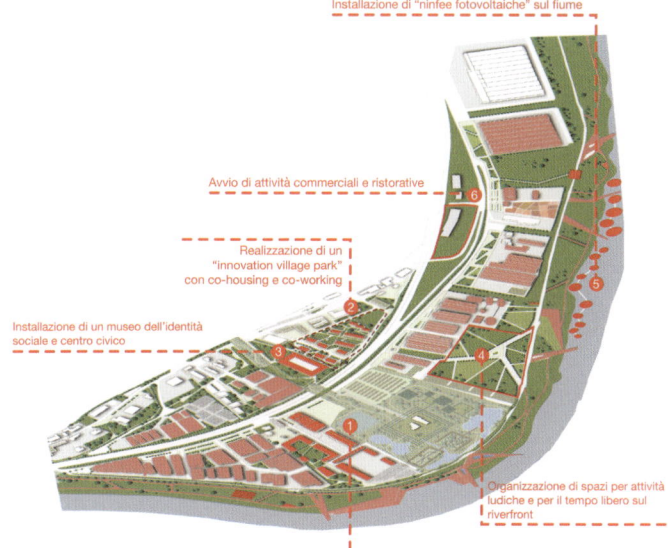

Installazione di "ninfee fotovoltaiche" sul fiume

Avvio di attività commerciali e ristorative

Realizzazione di un "innovation village park" con co-housing e co-working

Installazione di un museo dell'identità sociale e centro civico

Organizzazione di spazi per attività ludiche e per il tempo libero sul riverfront

Development

VISIONS

PROJECT DEVICES

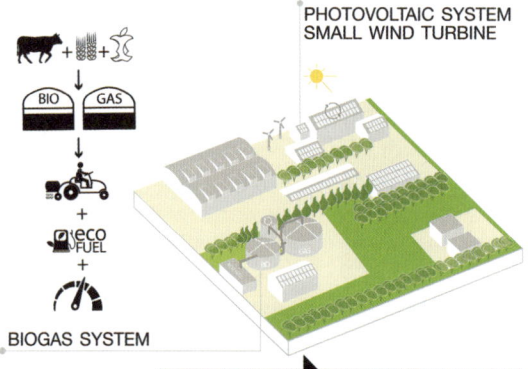

PHOTOVOLTAIC SYSTEM
SMALL WIND TURBINE

BIOGAS SYSTEM

SELF-SUFFICIENT ENERGY DISTRICT

RE-LOADED COMPONENTS

- **30%** Resilience and Environmental sustainability
- **30%** Energy
- **20%** Profit
- **10%** Environmental quality
- **10%** Social innovation and new lifestyles

RE-CYCLICAL URBANISM

Water system
by Francesca Montagna

Work group: Francesca Montagna (tutor jr), Federico Calcara, Cosimo Camarda, Floriana D'Amaro, Marianna Lombardo, Gloria Pavone.

The process of mending the urban islands envisages an articulation of the Macro into three main areas: the area to the north in direct contact with the Tiber and the EUR area, which has been interpreted as a water-gate; the central area, attributable to the Tiber-Fossa della Magliana system, involves interventions related to open urbanism and leisure; the last area, the dead cove of Spinaceto, develops interventions aimed at energy production and sustainable development.

The project involves the restoration of the existing pedestrian overpasses, the opening of new bicycle and pedestrian overpasses along the whole river system (floating and/or garden bridges), the reclamation of areas to build a green walkway, the repurposing of existing properties to be allocated to observatory houses, artistic repainting and lighting projects and/or iconic Pop-Up Urbanism/DIY interventions.

Spinaceto Cove. The Spinaceto wetland (of high environmental quality) will be devoted to camping/glamping activities with a low environmental impact, while the reclamation of the small lakes could be allocated to organic aquaculture activities. The regeneration of the water will occur by means of phytoremediation, supported by processes of aquaponic agriculture. Water dist r ict. Energy-saving devices envisage the creation of domestic systems of drainage, reuse and collection of water, which will then be encoded as a Micro District of water, in which rainwater will be fed to canals, catchment basins and pumping systems at a district and/or block scale. Urban horticulture will also be integrated with the water collection system (gravel beds for the accumulation of clean water for irrigation, rainwater collection ponds, and irrigation canals).

Water Arena. The reconfiguration of the river bank will permit a suitable location for the new Olympic Park and the multi-purpose center for sports/cultural activities, where temporary residences will be allocated to the athletes during the Olympic Games and to pilgrims during the Jubilee.

Rain garden. The partial interring of the infrastructure corridor near Magliana Vecchia, and the creation of a rain garden, with systems of rainwater collection and recycling tanks, partly reused for irrigation and partly fed back into the river, serving to strengthen the connection between the two river banks.

PROJECT CONCEPT

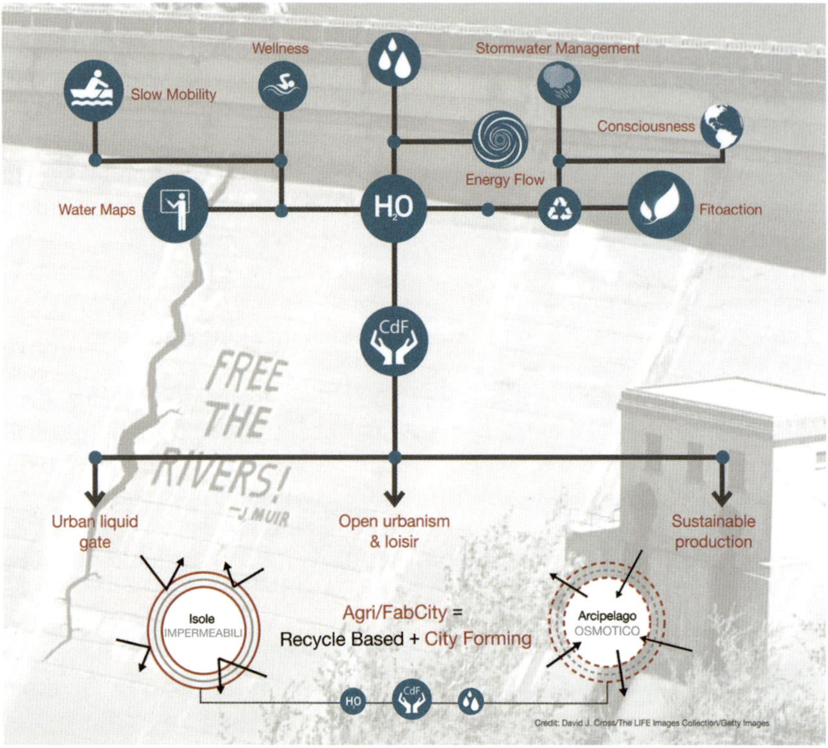

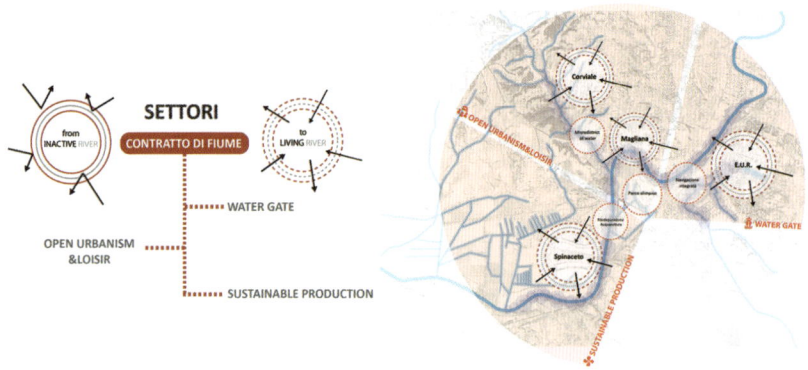

RE-CYCLICAL URBANISM

CITYFORMING PROTOCOL

ATTRAVERSAMENTI FLUVIALI

1) Ripristino sovrappassi pedonali esistenti e riapertura delle zone di accesso al fiume in prossimità del viadotto Morandi

2) Rifunzionalizzazione degli immobili esistenti da desitinare a CASE-OSSERVATORIO: punti di contatto con la popolazione, sede di performance, jam session, attività di network ed incubatore di idee sul possibile futuro del fiume

3) Progetto artistico di riverniciatura ed illuminazione dei sovrappassi ed interventi iconici di Pop-Up Urbanism/DIY (graffiti, guerriglia knitting, gardening ecc.) basati sul coinvolgimento degli artisti del Trullo e della popolazione residente

SISTEMA CICLOPEDONALE E NAVIGAZIONE INTEGRATA

4) Ricucitura dei tracciati esistenti e censimento/manutenzione dei sovrappassi e sottopassi esistenti

5) Recupero e messa a sistema degli approdi fluviali esistenti (prima gestione in affido al circolo Eur canottaggio)

AREE AD ALTA QUALITA' PAESISTICO/AMBIENTALE

6) Ansa morta di Spinaceto: attività di camping/glamping a ridotto impatto ambientale e recupero dei punti d'osservazione fauna selvatica

7) Uso dei laghetti naturali della zona umida di Spinaceto per attività di acquacoltura biologica

8) Approccio di riscoperta ed incremento della fruizione collettiva dei canali secondari tramite attività di condivisione e messa in rete di "water maps"(open urbanism, social street, uso della risorsa idrica per autoproduzione)

9) Istituzione di un comitato promotore (a scala locale) in adesione al processo già in atto di definizione del CdF Tevere Roma

10) Riuso delle aree perifluviali del Demanio Idrico e del Comune di Roma da dedicare a zone solarium e/o attività acquatiche

Colonisation

ATTRAVERSAMENTI FLUVIALI

1) Realizzazione di nuovi sovrappassi ciclopedonali lungo l'intero sistema fluviale (ponti galleggianti e/o garden bridges)

2) Bonifica delle aree interessate da precedente rifunzionalizzazione e definizione di una prima promenade verde d'ambito perifluviale

SISTEMA CICLOPEDONALE E NAVIGAZIONE INTEGRATA

3) Estensione della rete ciclopedonale tramite la realizzazione di nuovi tracciati lungo le vie d'acqua

4) Definizione di nuovi approdi fluviali e codificazione di una rete di navigazione integrata al sistema terrestre di mobilità slow (punti di bike sharing/segway a gestione pubblica)

AREE AD ALTA QUALITA' PAESISTICO/AMBIENTALE

5) Rigenerazione delle acque tramite sistemi di fitodepurazione affiancata a processi di agricoltura acquaponica

6) Realizzazione di primi sistemi domestici di drenaggio, riuso ed accumulo delle acque (serbatoi di raccolta delle acque piovane/tetti verdi/piccoli sistemi filtranti, ecc.)

7) Recupero del Casale Gautieri da destinare a sede dell'ente parco fluviale Tevere sud: luogo da identificare come centro nevralgico delle attività legate alla gestione del costituendo Contratto di Fiume

8) Inserimento di micro turbine idroelettriche per la produzione di energia pulita

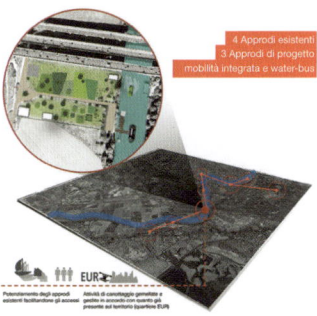

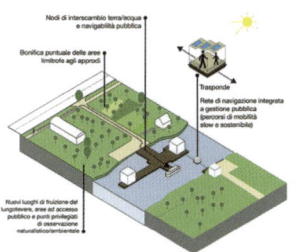

Consolidation

CITYFORMING PROTOCOL

ATTRAVERSAMENTI FLUVIALI

1) Interramento parziale del corridoio infrastrutturale in prossimità del nuovo Parco Olimpico per rafforzare la connessione fra le due sponde fluviali

2) Ripristino dell'intero sistema di vegetazione ripariale e di greto della zona umida (conforme alle fasce fluviali d'esondazione "AA" del P.A.I.)

SISTEMA CICLOPEDONALE E NAVIGAZIONE INTEGRATA

3) Realizzazione, in prossimità del Ponte della Magliana e Torrino GRA, di nuovi interventi per la navigabilità (soglia di fondo/conca di navigazione, nuova darsena).
Fonte: Studio Fattibilità VAMS Fiume Tevere (2010)

AREE AD ALTA QUALITA' PAESISTICO/AMBIENTALE

4) Codificazione, a scala di quartiere, di MicroDistrict of water in cui le acque meteoriche sono guidate all'interno di canali che portano a bacini di raccolta a loro volta collegati a sistemi di pompaggio per usi domestici ed irrigazione. (Water square/ Rain gardens)

5) Istituzione del Parco Fluviale Tevere Sud come intervento d'innalzamento dei livelli di fruibilità del fiume.
Fonte: Piano Strategico Roma Capitale

6) Costruzione del nuovo Parco Olimpico e del centro polifunzionale per attività sportive/culturali e riconfigurazione della sponda fluviale

7) Istituzione dell'ecoIndustrialPark come nuova area dello sviluppo sostenibile (Isola ecologica, aree di compostaggio, distretto energetico autosuffuciente)

[**FITO POWER**
Acquacoltura biologica associata a produzione energetica sostenibile a supporto delle aree turistico-sportive limitrofe]

[**HYDROPOWER**
Acqua come risorsa energetica: da potenziale a cinetica. Inserimento di turbine lungo alcuni tratti del letto fluviale per la produzione di energia pulita]

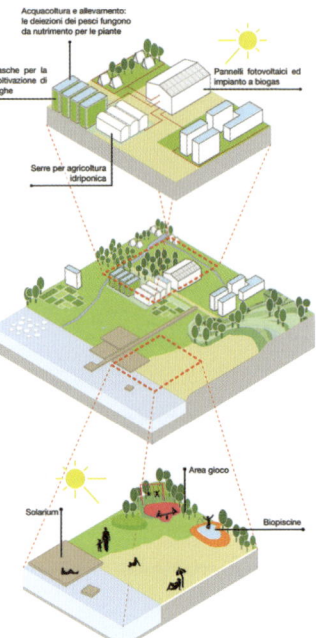

Development

VISION

RE-CYCLICAL URBANISM

PROJECT DEVICES

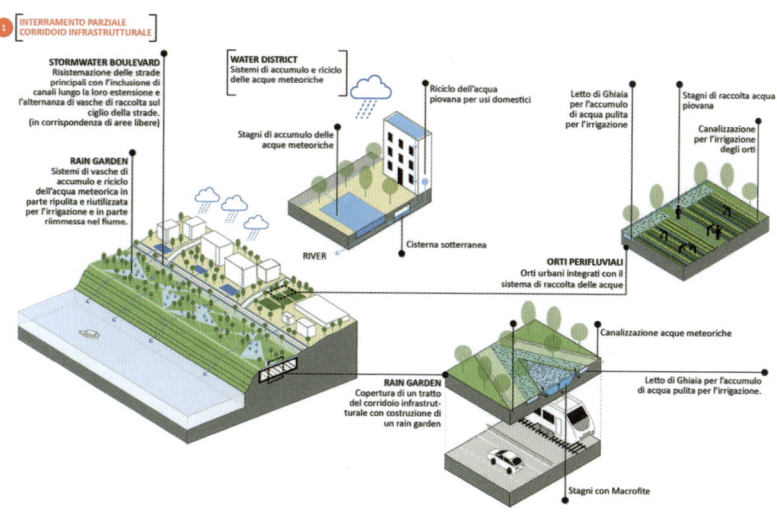

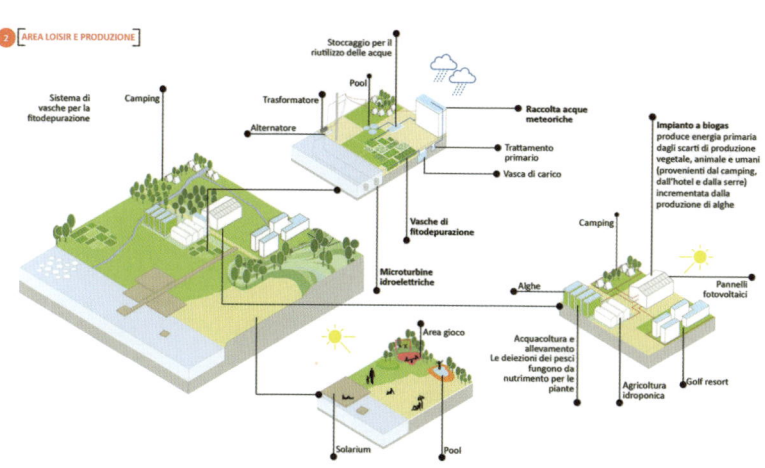

PROJECT DEVICES

3 [APPRODO TIPO]

[CORVIALE WATER SISTEM]

4 [STADIO OLIMPICO WATER SISTEM]

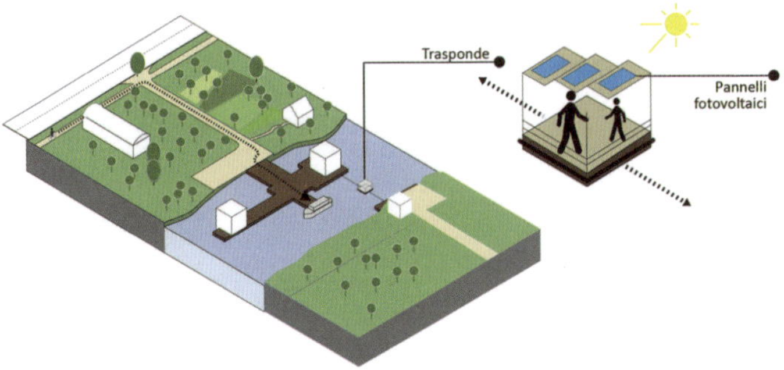

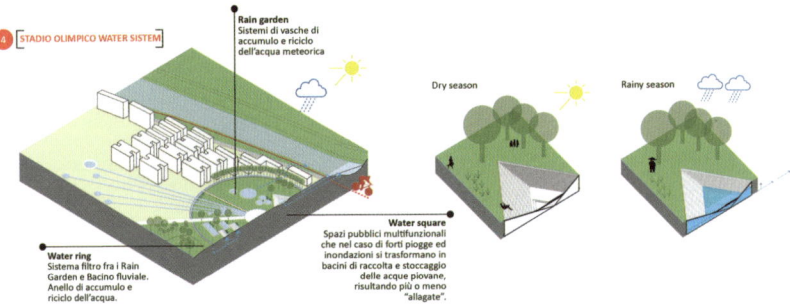

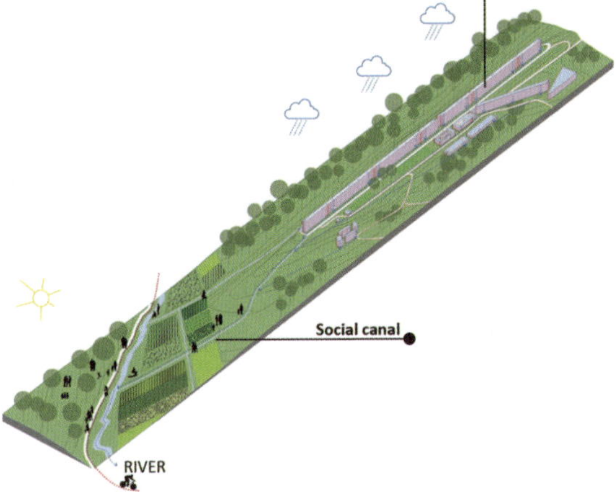

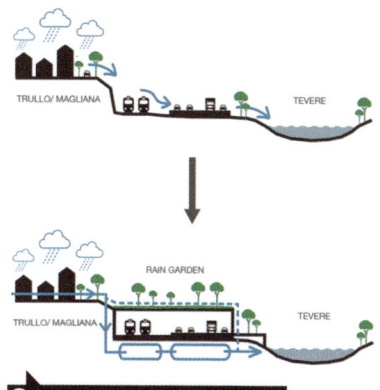

Stormwater Detention

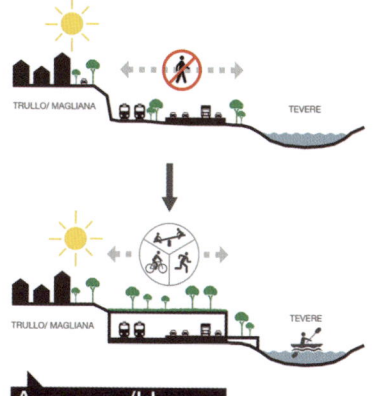

Activities/Users

Rain garden.
The project involves the creation of a rain garden by means of the partial interring of a section of the infrastructure corridor separating the areas of Magliana and Trullo from the Tiber River. The integrated system of filtering, collection, and recycling of rainwater, partly reused for irrigation and partly fed back to the river, forms a new public space that will generate multiple benefits from an environmental and ecological, but also social point of view, through the introduction of new leisure activities and thus the attraction of new users, strengthening, moreover, the connection between the two river banks.

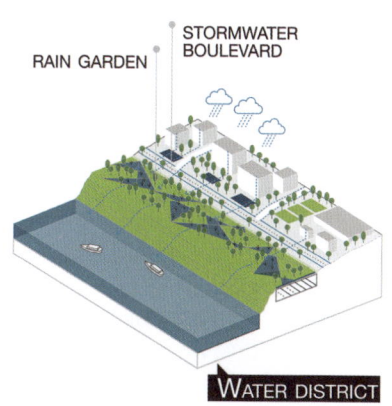

RE-LOADED COMPONENTS

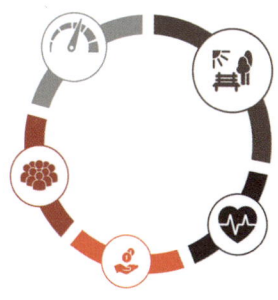

25% Environmental quality

23% Energy

19% Social innovation and new lifestyles

18% Resilience and Environmental sustainability

15% Profit

Bosco GRAnde
by Milena Lauretta

Work group: Milena Lauretta (tutor jr), Floriana Gentile, Roberta Lena, Delia Roxana Negrusa, Antonio Salvaggio, Madalina Sasa, Luca Torrisi.

The project envisages the transformation of the GRA ring road into a linear forest through a green system, an Ecological Backbone, whose purpose, first of all, is to improve air quality, reduce the high percentage of emissions of CO_2, $PM10$, and heavy metals. This linear forest also aims to become a connector of the huge green system that already exists within the Macro, that is, Tenuta dei Massimi and Valle dei Casali. These two reserves are veritable pockets of resilience, spaced out by plentiful patches of the Ager Romanus, which make the whole area even more fragmented. The project also envisages the creation of infiltration basins that allow the rainwater to be channelled and used for the purpose of irrigation, the use of catalytic antismog paving for pedestrian and cycling trails and noise barriers, the creation of meta-natural places and useful and educational pathways, and totally green walkways for the purpose of invading the existing infrastructure with the green system. The actions will be planned over time through the incremental and procedural Cityforming protocol approach in its three phases: Colonisation, Consolidation, and Development. In the project specifications, the creation of the woodland strips, meta-natural places, and the creation of useful and educational pathways will fall under the colonisation phase, whose completion will take a period of about three years; the subsequent phase of consolidation involves the activation of the albergo diffuso (widespread hotel) function inside the Tenuta dei Massimi reserve, the creation of infiltration basins and grassy channels equipped with biofilters and the standardization of the system of peri-urban horticulture; finally, the development phase will consist of the completion of routes along and across the GRA ring road through the building of totally green walkways. The goal of the development phase is also to invade the infrastructure with a green system and replace the fast mobility, used today, with a system of slow & green mobility.
The Bosco GRAnde will thus become a new city "gateway", a crossing element, rather than the closing/disruptive feature it is today. It will, therefore, be an ecological connector, a re-activator of the pockets of resilience present in the territory, but also an urban and social connector, which mends the fragmented islands in the territory and transforms them into a metropolitan archipelago.

PROJECT CONCEPT

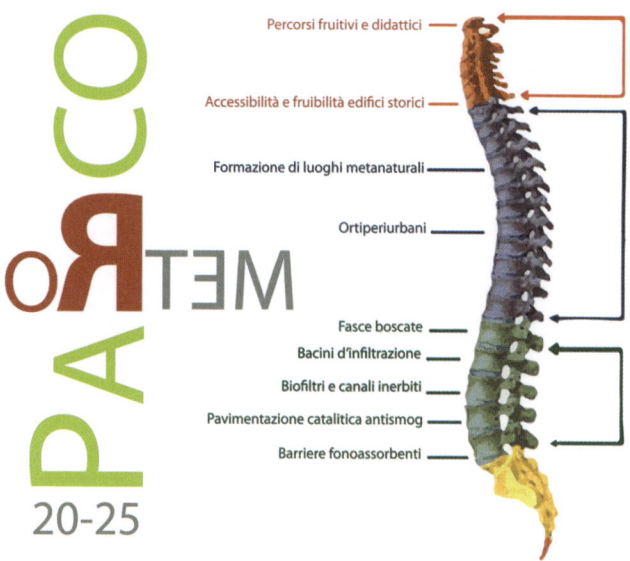

PARCO METRO 20-25

- Percorsi fruitivi e didattici
- Accessibilità e fruibilità edifici storici
- Formazione di luoghi metanaturali
- Ortiperiurbani
- Fasce boscate
- Bacini d'infiltrazione
- Biofiltri e canali inerbiti
- Pavimentazione catalitica antismog
- Barriere fonoassorbenti

FASCIA BOSCATA

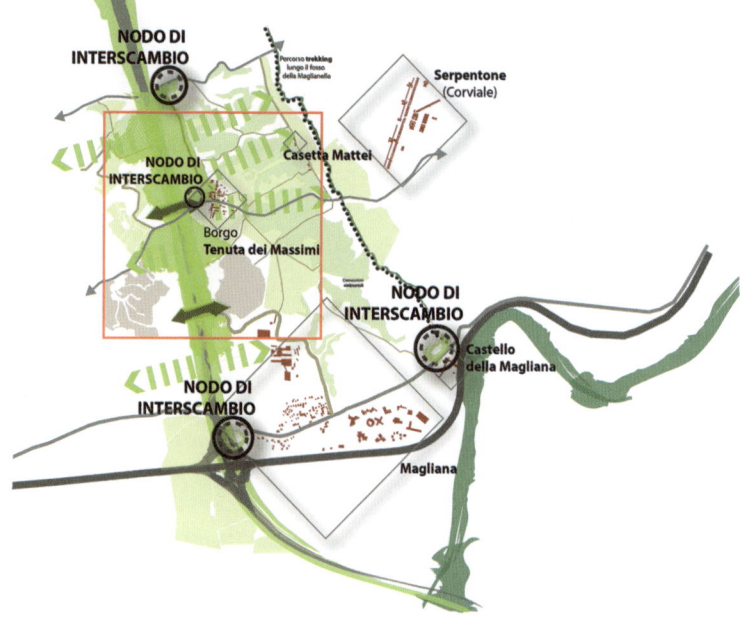

RE-FORMING ROME

CITYFORMING PROTOCOL

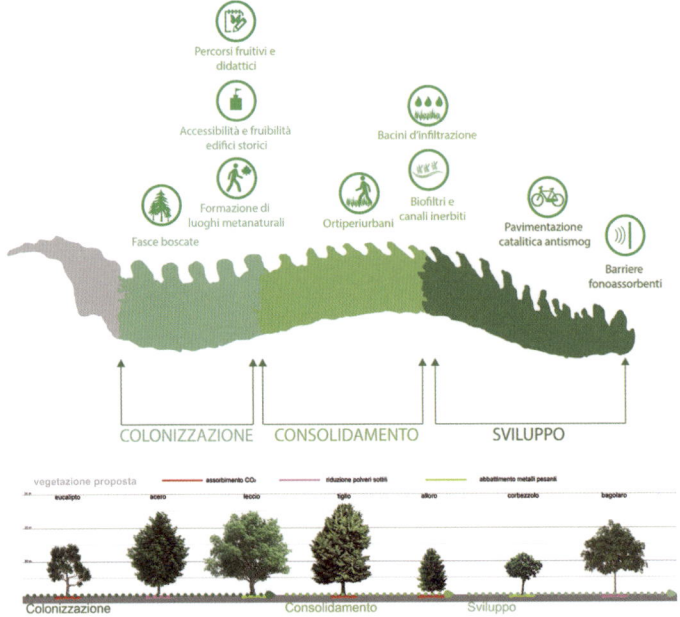

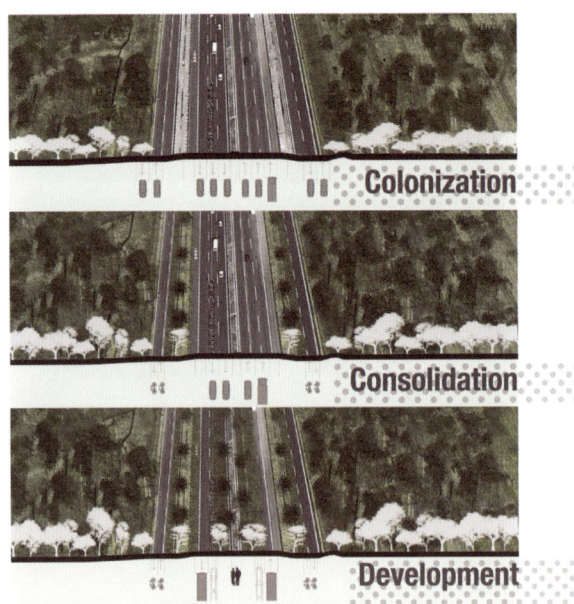

RE-CYCLICAL URBANISM

PROJECT DEVICES

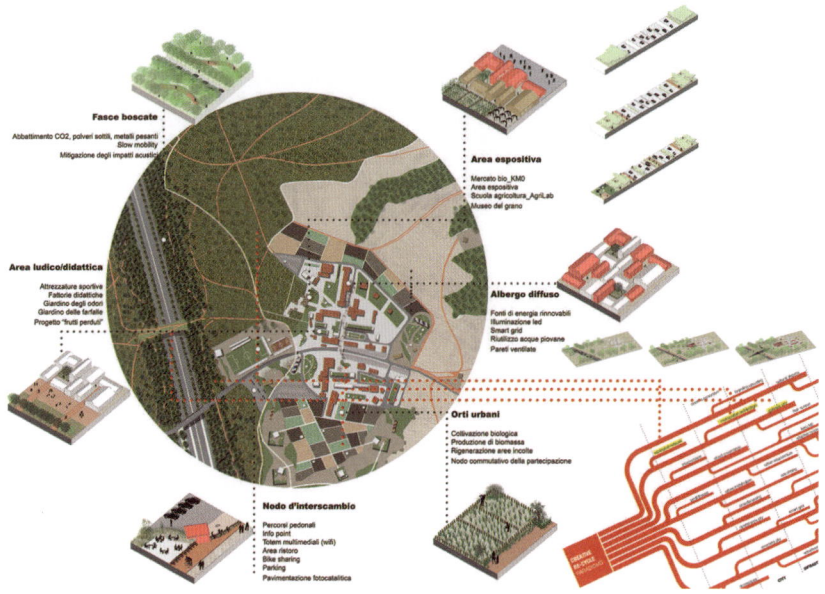

RE-LOADED COMPONENTS

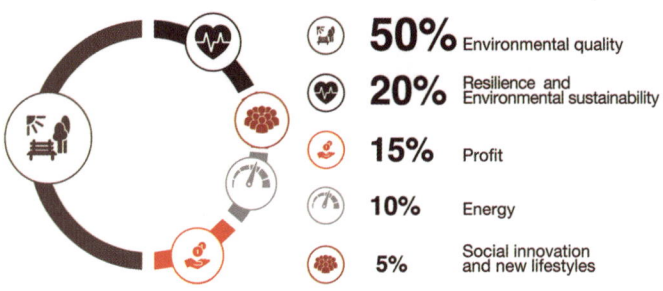

50% Environmental quality

20% Resilience and Environmental sustainability

15% Profit

10% Energy

5% Social innovation and new lifestyles

RE-FORMING ROME

RE-FORMING ROME EXHIBITION: A PEDAGOGICAL MACHINE

ANNALISA CONTATO
JESSICA SMERALDA OLIVA

The exhibition "Rome 20-25. New Life Cycles for the Metropolis", which opened on 18th December 2015 in the Claudia Gian Ferrari room of the MAXXI Museum in Rome, was a valuable opportunity for discussion with the other 24 international universities that took part in the project. For a month, the exhibition was also an opportunity to show the public the results of the Rome 20-25 project, a month in which visitors could observe the 25 projects proposed for Rome, consult on the future of the city and on their potential as players in the process, while appreciating the wealth of different visions, thoughts, approaches, and languages that each school brought with it and expressed in its own exhibition space.

Through the exhibition, the University of Palermo wanted to revive the methodological, experimental, and planning process and results in a multi-dimensional narrative.

The spatial configuration selected, the pavilion, urged visitors to cross the exhibition space, experience it from the inside, as though entering a different reality, where the Macro of Rome comes to life and the temporary inhabitant can explore it and discover its wealth, imagining a future sparked by active participation; it urged them to enter the process of urban-sensory testing. The visitor was thus involved in an immersive storytelling experience through texts, drawings, images, videos, and materials to watch, browse, listen to, and touch.

It was a "pedagogical machine" that encouraged and invited the audience to establish sensory relationships between it and them, to take part in an unconventional lesson, and to learn creative recycling by being an integral part of it, becoming key players in the process.

Inside the pavilion, in fact, the feet came in contact with the trunk of the *Creative Recycling Urbanism*[1] tree and the visitors, grafted to it and crossed by its generating and creative sap, became new potential branches, bearers of the fruits of innovation, rooted in the paradigms that bring new urban tactics to life.

Submerging its roots in the territory of Rome and drawing nourishment and character, the *Creative Recycling Urbanism* tree opened out its paradigm branches within the space, producing reflections, analysis and, therefore, visions and projects for an Agri/FabMetropolis, in which the physical, relational and productive spaces are "re-formed" for a new metabolism. If, on the one hand, a wall summarized the vision for Macro no. 12, then focusing on the project of the Donato military base - Monte Cucco - Trullo district, on the opposite side, a branching game narrated the conceptual meanings, process, creative wealth, and variety of planning tactics that characterized the experience of the Rome 20- 25 workshop and were summarized in the exhibition.

The fragmentary identity of the islands in the area is transformed by the project into an environment in which diversity is opportunity and distinctive features are emphasized, in a new interconnected rur/urban metropolitan archipelago, where the space between the islands is no longer an urban void that simply needs to be crossed, but a place loaded with identity, dense in functions and specializations.

A structuring life force in the process of formation of the archipelago is the human and social capital of the area, its inhabitants, active communities, and occasional, temporary users or the commuters that cross it and experience it. There are three paradigm branches that the project taps into the most and which were, therefore, more clearly developed and articulated in the exhibition setup. For each of these branches, one or more urban design outputs were illustrated with the aid of graphics, photomontage, diagrams, devices, and browsable books, which emerged and disrupted the pavilion space with their three-dimensionality, inviting interaction.

The exhibition developed: the RE-TICULAR paradigm, on whose branch the vision of the Macro as an archipelago unfolded, examining the theme of the ecological network through the Bosco-GRAnde project; the gravitational and branched RE-SILIENCE paradigm, where social innovation, urban metabolism, and adaptive spaces were found, elaborated in the *Water System* project and the new circular metabolism activated by the *Agri/FabDistrict* (*urban farms*) project; and the REMAKE paradigm, which referred to the civic activism of urban DIY/DIT and to the ability of the new makers of an energy district of reuse and recycling for the production of clean energy and technological research, analysed in the Magliana *Eco-energy District project*. Furthermore, the aim was to provide a material dimension within the exhibition space.

Six transparent cubes containing some of the physical materials of the project protruded from the branches: the colour characterized and represented the creative eco-system; vegetation is the fundamental material of ecological networks; water is the element *par excellence* of adaptive spaces; the seeds house and protect the vital potential of urban farms; with a view to circularity, compost represents reuse of organic waste for productive and energy purposes within the energy districts; scrap materials can assume new life in the work of new urban artisans practicing urban DIY/DIT.

Finally, a video told the story of the journey taken by the University of Palermo group in this part of Rome, showing the creative process, revealing the faces, bringing people back into the installation and to the center of the experience.

The exhibition space also contained an accessible mini-library[2], through which to analyze the issues proposed by the project.

The exhibition could thus be read as a large hypertext, from which to draw in order to explore the world of Creative Recycling Urbanism, which found in the experience of the Rome 20-25 Workshop a concrete place, time, and space for experimentation.

1. For a deepening on Re-cycle Urban Paradigms see the essay by Carta, page 6.
2. The issues addressed in the project can be studied, as well as in this volume, even in the following texts: Carta, M., *Reimagining Urbanism. Creative, Smart and Green Cities for the Changing Times*. Barcelona-Trento: ListLab, 2014; Carta, M., Lino, B., a cura di, *Urban Hyper-Metabolism*. Roma: Aracne Int. le, 2015; Lino, B., *Periferie in trasfor-azione. Riflessioni dai "margini" delle città*. Firenze: Alinea, 2013.

Rome 20-25. New Life Cycles for the Metropolis (18.12.2015-17.01.2016, MAXXI, Rome). Details of the multi-dimensional narrative pedagogical machine that the Palermo Research Unit set up in order to share an urban-sensory experiment with visitors to the exhibition.

RE-FORMING ROME

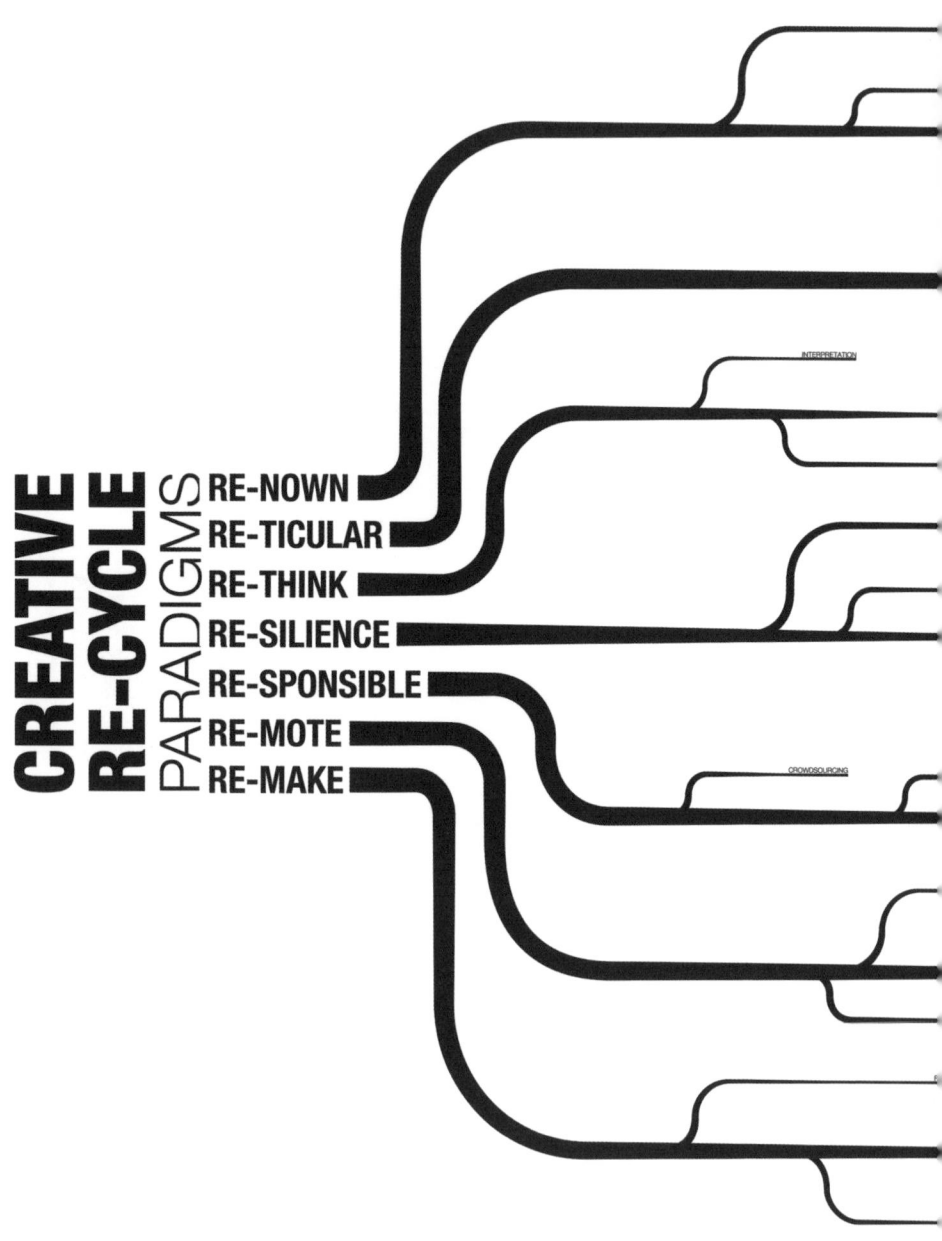

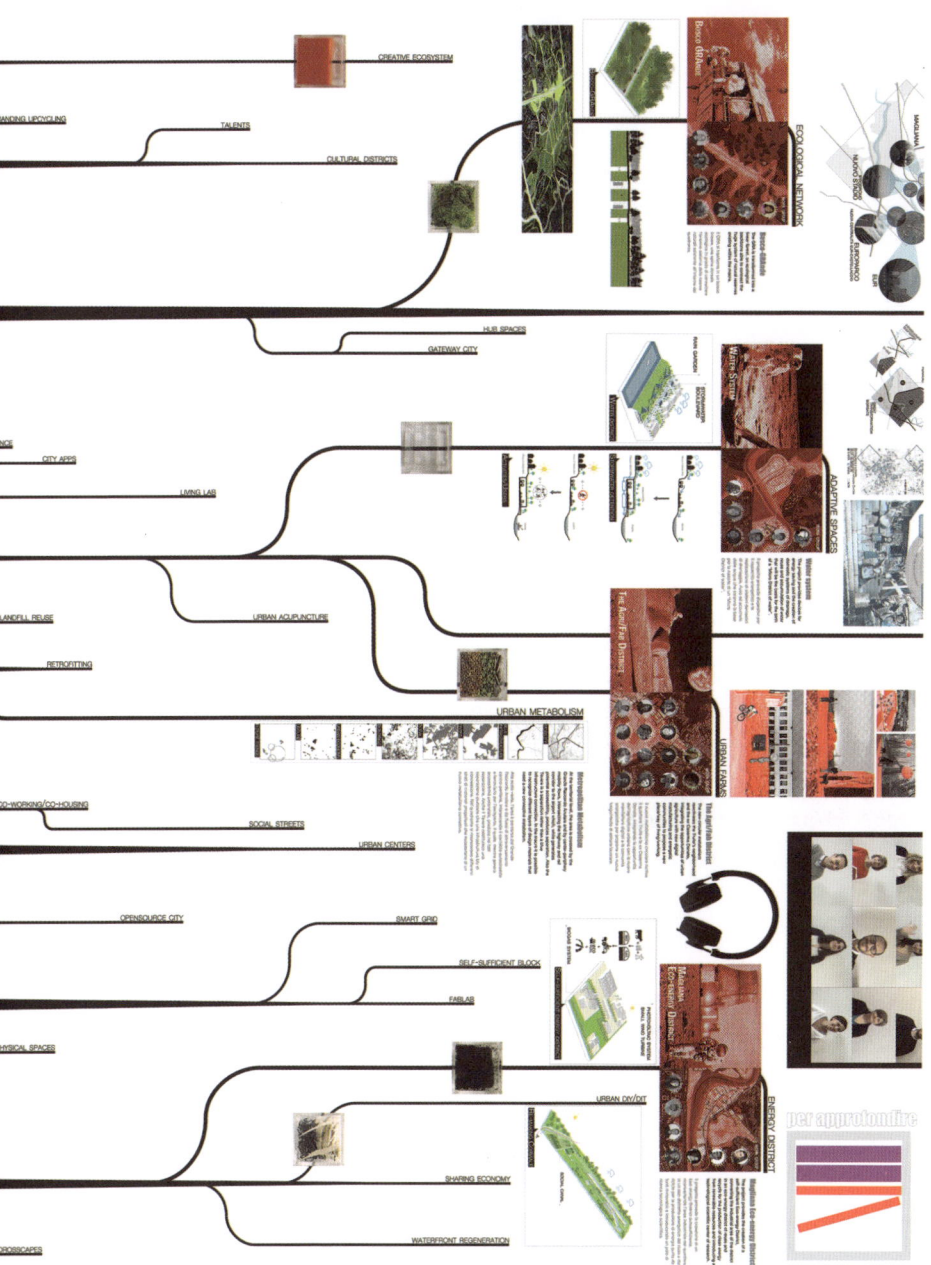

RE-FORMING ROME

Published by
LISt Lab
info@listlab.eu
listlab.eu

Production
GreenTrenDesign Factory
Piazza Manifattura, 1
38068 Rovereto (TN) - Italy
T: +39 0464 443427
info@greentrendesign.it

Editors
Maurizio Carta
Barbara Lino
Daniele Ronsivalle

Editorial director
Pino Scaglione

Editorial Assistant
Gioia Marana

Translation
Johanna Worton

Art Director & Graphic Design
Blacklist Creative Studio, Barcelona
blacklist-creative.com

ISBN 9788899854188
Printed and bound in the European Union
2017

All rights reserved
© of the edition LISt Lab
© of the texts the authors
© of the images the authors

Promotion and distribution
Messaggerie Libri, Spa, Milano,
Numero verde 800.804.900
assistenza.ordini@meli.it

International promotion and distribution
ACC - London

The Scientific Committee of the issues List
Eve Blau (Harvard GSD), Maurizio Carta (University of Palermo), Eva Castro (Architectural Association London) Alberto Clementi (University of Chieti), Alberto Cecchetto (University of Venezia), Stefano De Martino (University of Innsbruck), Corrado Diamantini (University of Trento), Antonio De Rossi (University of Torino), Franco Farinelli (University of Bologna), Carlo Gasparrini (University of Napoli), Manuel Gausa (University of Genova), Giovanni Maciocco (University of Sassari/Alghero), Antonio Paris (University of Roma), Mosè Ricci (University of Trento), Roger Riewe (University of Graz), Pino Scaglione (University of Trento).

LISt Lab is an editorial workshop, based in Europe, that works on contemporary issues. LISt Lab not only publishes, but also researches, proposes, promotes, produces, creates networks.

LISt Lab is a green company committed to respect the environment. Paper, ink, glues and all processings come from short supply chains and aim at limiting pollution. The print run of books and magazines is based on consumption patterns, thus preventing waste of paper and surpluses. LISt Lab aims at the responsibility of the authors and markets, towards the knowledge of a new publishing culture based on resource management.

This book contains the results of research conducted by the Research Unit of the University of Palermo (coord. Prof. Maurizio Carta) within the PRIN 2010-2011 "Re-cycle Italy. New life cycles for the architectures and infrastructures of cities and landscape".

Book Series BABEL THEORY

BABEL